MAXIMIZING EFFECTIVENESS IN DYNAMIC PSYCHOTHERAPY

The best therapists embody the changes they attempt to facilitate in their patients. In other words, they practice what they preach and are an authentic and engaged, as well as highly skilled, presence. *Maximizing Effectiveness in Dynamic Psychotherapy* demonstrates how and why therapists can and must develop the specific skills and personal qualities required to produce consistently effective results. The six factors now associated with brain change and positive outcome in psychotherapy are front and center in this volume. Each factor is elucidated and illustrated with detailed, verbatim case transcripts. In addition, intensive short-term dynamic psychotherapy, a method of treatment that incorporates all these key factors, is introduced to the reader.

Therapists of every stripe will learn to develop and integrate the clinical skills presented in this book to improve their interventions, enhance effectiveness and, ultimately, help more patients in a deeper and more lasting fashion.

Patricia Coughlin (Della Selva), PhD, is a clinical psychologist with more than thirty years of experience as a psychodynamic therapist, international teacher/ trainer, and author. She has been a clinical professor of psychiatry at Northwestern University School of Medicine, Albany Medical College, and Jefferson Medical College. Currently, she conducts a private psychotherapy practice in Albany, New York, and she is a visiting scholar at the University of New Mexico School of Medicine. Her book *Intensive Short-Term Dynamic Psychotherapy* is considered a classic in the field.

D1606651

MAXIMIZING EFFECTIVENESS IN DYNAMIC PSYCHOTHERAPY

PATRICIA COUGHLIN

Routledge
Taylor & Francis Group

NEW YORK AND LONDON

First published 2017
by Routledge
711 Third Avenue, New York, NY 10017

and by Routledge
2 Park Square, Milton Park, Abingdon, Oxon, OX14 4RN

Routledge is an imprint of the Taylor & Francis Group, an informa business

Library of Congress Cataloging-in-Publication Data
Names: Della Selva, Patricia Coughlin, 1954– author.
Title: Maximizing effectiveness in dynamic psychotherapy / Patricia
    Coughlin.
Description: New York, NY : Routledge, 2016. | Includes bibliographical
    references and index.
Identifiers: LCCN 2015050555 | ISBN 9781138824966 (hardback :
    alk. paper) | ISBN 9781138824973 (pbk. : alk. paper) |
    ISBN 9781315740249 (ebook)
Subjects: LCSH: Psychodynamic psychotherapy.
Classification: LCC RC489.P72 D45 2016 | DDC 616.89/14—dc23
LC record available at http://lccn.loc.gov/2015050555

ISBN: 978-1-138-82496-6 (hbk)
ISBN: 978-1-138-82497-3 (pbk)
ISBN: 978-1-315-74024-9 (ebk)

Typeset in Minion
by Apex CoVantage, LLC

Printed and bound in Great Britain by
TJ International Ltd, Padstow, Cornwall

To my patients and trainees, who have contributed more to my life than they'll ever know.

Contents

Acknowledgments

It is a genuine privilege to be a partner in the transformation of patients' lives, from suffering and constriction, to aliveness and authenticity. The remarkable courage and generosity of those who have allowed their treatments to be videotaped, shared, and studied in an effort to help others is both touching and inspiring. I am a far better person and therapist for having known you all.

I am profoundly grateful to Drs. Habib Davanloo and David Malan for their courageous and steadfast determination to discover new and effective means for reaching ambitious therapeutic results in a rapid and consistent fashion. Their contributions to the field have been immense. It is my hope that this book will aid in the dissemination of this vital information to a broad audience of therapists who are eager to learn more productive and efficient ways to help their patients.

My trainees have taught me much, and I learn from each and every one of them. Special thanks to Torben Palmer Hansen and Mark Vail, who spent countless hours editing and subtitling my videotapes for training purposes, and to Angela Cooper for reading several of these chapters along the way, and Lucas Jones, who edited the volume with great care. To Tor Wennerberg, enormous thanks for the countless invigorating and illuminating discussions about every aspect of theory and technique—not to mention life itself!

My colleagues have been remarkable resources and, in many cases, have become valued friends. My work and my life have been deeply affected by you all. In particular, Allan Abbass, Bjorn Elwin, Jon Frederickson, Diana Fosha, Allen Kalpin, Jeff Katzman, Laura Mott, Kristin Osborn, and David Wolff have been models of compassion, devotion, and dedication to excellence in our field. Their inspiration and support have been invaluable.

To all my dear friends and comrades in arms, especially Elaine Appellof, Diane Byster, Susan Fisher, Karen Hastings, Bonnie Miller, Sandy Rainbow, Diana Shulman, Lise Suino, Andrew Ursino, Kathy Thiel, and Jody Whitehouse. I can't imagine my life without you.

Finally, I owe an enormous debt of gratitude to Bruce Ecker, who introduced me to Anna Moore at Routledge. And, last but not least, to Zoey Peresman, for her kind, constructive, and incisive feedback on this manuscript. The book is far better for her contribution to it.

Chapter One
Maximizing Effectiveness in Dynamic Psychotherapy

Introduction

Therapist: Why don't you start by telling me what brings you and what kind of help you are looking for?

Patient: I don't know. I think I have to decide. This is the problem—and I do have a close friend I talk to about this. I may be—uh—I have sat—uh—all my life and because of anxiety—she feels—and I asked her because she knows me since graduate school—a lack of self-esteem, anxiety, inability to make a decision. I just sit and I really haven't gotten any . . . I think it's too late to get where I want to get at 69, so I go through a little anger about this nastiness about being an old maid.

This 69-year-old woman had seen countless therapists over many decades without receiving any benefits. Her opening statement was both incoherent and dismissive in tone, suggesting a highly disorganized attachment style; while her nonverbal communication consisted of rather bizarre and distorted facial expressions. She was apparently driving her primary care physician to distraction with repeated calls for appointments to address vague and varied physical complaints. Overall, she personifies the kind of complex and difficult patient therapists often see, but too rarely help.

How can we refine our skills and develop our full capacity as healers, so that we can have a better chance of helping such patients? This book will attempt to answer this question. I will introduce the reader to six factors associated with brain change in adults, along with the specific techniques of demonstrated efficacy associated with these factors: (1) focus and repetition, (2) creating and maintaining a collaborative alliance, (3) inducing moderate levels of anxiety,

(4) facilitating multiple levels of emotional activation, (5) creating "profound moments of meeting," and (6) developing a coherent life narrative. In order to accomplish these goals, specific skills designed to help patients relinquish the defenses that interfere with optimal emotional activation and active collaboration with the therapist are required. No matter how effective our methods and techniques, they will be rendered useless if patients remain uninvolved in the process.

In the present volume, each of these factors will be elucidated and illustrated with detailed and verbatim transcripts of actual therapy sessions. This first chapter presents an overview of the manuscript and includes an outline of what is to come. The second chapter will specify a method of assessment designed to determine the underlying cause of the patient's symptoms and disturbances, as well as her capacity to engage in treatment. Then, in the third chapter, we will focus on anxiety and its regulation, such that the patient's optimal level of anxiety can be maintained. The fourth chapter will focus on the defenses and resistance that, unless removed, form barriers to therapeutic engagement. Activating, regulating, and integrating complex emotions will be the focus of the fifth chapter. The creation and maintenance of a strong conscious and unconscious alliance will be addressed in the sixth chapter. In chapter seven, we will focus on the need to create an atmosphere of intimacy and emotional closeness in the treatment relationship. In order to develop the type of intimacy required to promote "profound moments of meeting," resistances to closeness must be removed. Specified ways to accomplish these goals will be included. Finally, in chapter eight, the process of working through toward integration and consolidation of change will be highlighted.

Intensive Short-Term Dynamic Psychotherapy: An Integrated Approach

In addition to introducing each of these therapeutic factors in separate chapters, the reader will be introduced to a method of treatment that incorporates all of these specific factors—Intensive Short-Term Dynamic Psychotherapy (ISTDP; Davanloo, 1990, 2000). This complex and elegant method of treatment has been designed to assess and treat a wide range of patients. While often associated with the notion of a breakthrough of intense emotion, ISTDP is actually a multifaceted treatment model that is both structured and flexible, allowing the clinician to adapt the method to the needs and capacities of a wide range of patients (Abbass, 2015; Coughlin Della Selva, 1996/2004; Frederickson, 2013; Malan & Coughlin Della Selva, 2006).

ISTDP is based on psychoanalytic theory and a thorough understanding of the implicit, unconscious processes that are responsible for most of our patient's symptoms and suffering (Ecker, Ticic, & Hulley, 2012; Schore, 2012). This treatment model provides a systematic method for reliably revealing the unconscious origin of the patient's repetitive difficulties, as well as assessing, moment by moment, the patient's capacity to engage in the therapeutic process. By providing a clear approach to dynamic assessment, using the patient's responses to each intervention as both a diagnostic tool and guide to further intervention.

With psychoanalytic theory as his foundation, Davanloo (1990) took a scientific approach to the assessment and treatment of patients, testing out his hypotheses along the way. In long-term therapy and analysis, the clinical data are so voluminous that testing out hypotheses about specific mechanisms of change is nearly impossible. By accelerating and condensing the process, and videotaping all his psychotherapy sessions for review with colleagues and patients, Davanloo was able to ascertain which interventions were most effective, and with whom. If something worked in one case, he would systematically employ it in the next 10, and study the results. In this rather scientific manner, he continued to hone his skills and refine his methods.

Davanloo (1990) has asserted that dynamic psychotherapy can be not merely effective but uniquely effective. He suggested that therapeutic results are obtained by specific rather than nonspecific factors, namely the patients' true feelings about the present and the past. While the method as a whole incorporates all six factors associated with brain change, I want to suggest that this is not an all or nothing proposition. The more of these specific skills the clinician can master and employ, the more effective her therapies should become.

Of particular interest are the results suggesting that ISTDP is effective where most therapies are not, with cases of: (1) treatment resistant depression (Abbass, Hancock, Henderson, & Kisely, 2006; Driessen et al., 2010); (2) panic disorder (Wiborg & Dahl, 1996); (3) personality disorders (Abbass, Joffres, & Ogrodniczuk, 2008; Thomas et al., 2000; Town, Abbass, & Hardy, 2011; Winston et al., 1994); (4) somatic disorders (Abbass, Kisely, & Kroenke, 2009; Abbass, Lovas, & Purdy, 2008; Koelen et al., 2014; Schubiner & Betzhold, 2012); (5) conversion; and (6) medically unexplained symptoms (Abbass et al., 2010). In addition to traditional outpatient settings, this method is now being successfully adapted for use in the Emergency Room (Abbass, Campbell, & Tarzwell, 2009; Abbass et al., 2010), family medicine clinics (Abbass, 2015), and inpatient settings (Solbaken & Abbass, 2013). Pilot studies are exploring the viability of applying this method in a group setting (Hsu et al., 2010), as well as with children and adolescents (Abbass, Rabung, Leichsenring, Refseth, & Midgley, 2013).

Integration

In addition to integrating all six specific factors associated with brain change into his method of treatment, Davanloo also focused on the therapist's emotional availability and responsiveness, as well as his stand for growth and against anything destructive. Recent research supports this kind of synthesis of common and specific factors. In fact, the moderate use of specific factors, along with the common factors of empathy, safety, and curiosity, seem to yield the best results (McCarthy, Keefe, & Barber, 2015; Wampold, 2015). As previously noted (Orlinsky & Ronnestad, 2005; Weinberger, 1995), most therapists seem to use too few specific interventions designed to address specific problems. However, research suggests that too heavy a use of specific factors is also associated with relatively poor outcomes (McCarthy, Keefe, & Barber, 2015). Once again, therapists who integrate specific dynamic interventions with more "common" experiential interventions tend to achieve the best outcome (Barber, Muran, McCarthy, & Keefe, 2013; McCarthy, Keefe, & Barber, 2015). This evidence speaks to the kind of integration and flexibility that will be illustrated in the clinical examples to follow.

State of the Art

While psychotherapy works and works well (effect sizes between 0.68–1.51) for those who engage and stick with the process (Lambert & Ogles, 2004; Shedler, 2010; Smith, Glass, & Miller, 1980; Wampold, 2001, 2007, 2013), dropout rates, defined as terminating treatment before any benefit is realized, remain in the 40–50% range (Wierzbicki & Pekarik, 1993). In addition, a review of the outcome of 550 patients (Lambert & Ogles, 2004) revealed that 8% got worse as the result of treatment. Even when therapy appears to be immediately effective, using pre- and post-therapy measures, analysis of follow-up data also reveal relapse rates between 35% and 70% (Wiborg & Dahl, 1996). Since we are failing to engage and help almost half of the patients who come to us for psychotherapeutic assistance, and those who initially respond often relapse, we must develop more successful interventions in order to help more patients.

While most therapies are consistently effective with patients who are bright, psychologically minded, motivated, and relatively healthy, they are not nearly as productive in treating patients with long histories of multiple disorders, or those who have physical and somatic complaints, personality disorders, or treatment resistant conditions. Developing the skills required to apply specific interventions of proven power and precision should improve outcomes, contribute to the well-being of our patients, and improve the morale of dedicated therapists, who typically achieve erratic and disappointing results in the treatment of complex cases.

Research (Orlinsky & Ronnestad, 2005) suggests that most therapists are highly involved in, and committed to, their work with patients, deriving a great deal of professional and personal satisfaction from their role. While the majority of therapists report a well-developed ability to establish rapport with patients, often using a highly refined intuitive capacity to reach this end, 76% report lacking both skill and confidence in three crucial areas: (1) the ability to motivate patients to become actively involved in the therapeutic process,

(2) understanding the moment-to-moment process of therapy, and (3) knowing how and when to employ specific techniques to address specific problems and goals (Orlinsky & Ronnestad, 2005). Fewer than 47% of therapists, many of whom were highly educated and quite experienced, reported a sense of mastery as a clinician. It is my belief that this lack of mastery and competence contributes to the poor outcomes reported in the literature, as well as "burn out" in practitioners. However, it has been my experience that once therapists learn to intervene in such a way that consistently produces deep and lasting change, clinicians become reinvigorated and enthusiastic about their work.

In many ways, the 11,000 therapists included in Orlinsky and Ronnestad's study (2005) reflect the state of the art in our field. We have created sophisticated theories, and accumulated a wealth of empirical data on therapeutic process and outcome. At the same time, a lack of attention to the development of specific skills, and to the personal development of clinicians, has contributed to gaps in our knowledge. As a result, clinical outcomes have not improved in 50 years (Ecker, 2015).

Compounding the professional problems already cited, there is increasing polarization in our field. Currently, some factions focus almost exclusively on "empirically validated treatments," while others assert that the method doesn't matter and the therapist alone is the only critical variable involved (Duncan, 2010). My reading of the literature, and experience as both a therapist and teacher/supervisor for more than 30 years, has led me to conclude that consistent success as a psychotherapist is the result of both *who we are* and *what we do*. Supporting this viewpoint, Wampold (2007, 2013, 2015) has emphasized that "a coordinated and synchronized interaction of technique and relationship factors" is involved in the achievement of consistently positive therapeutic outcome. Further support for this hypothesis will be presented throughout the current volume.

Developing Competence

In order to be consistently effective over time and across patients, we must hone skills and develop techniques that flow from, and are internally consistent with, our theoretical understanding of human development (normal and pathological), and the process of change. These interventions must also be supported by research. The master clinician is knowledgeable and skilled in all three areas (theory, research, and technique). Practitioners who develop such metacognitive skills seem to get better results than their less developed colleagues (Wampold, 2010, 2015). I have referred to this cluster of integrated knowledge as the triangle of competence (Figure 1.1), in which theory, technique, and research are all related in a reciprocal fashion. Furthermore, the highly effective therapist is able to integrate this knowledge and skill with who she is as a person. With a solid theoretical basis for our work, highly refined specific skills and interventions, and the ongoing development of ourselves as human beings,

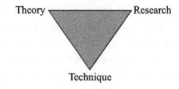

Figure 1.1 Triangle of Competence

we should be able to maximize our effectiveness and assist more of the patients who seek our help.

Expertise in psychotherapy involves a large knowledge base and deliberate practice, along with follow up and assessment, in order to evaluate performance and outcome. Research (Tracey, Wampold, Lichtenberg, & Goodyear, 2014) suggests that experts have (a) the ability to perceive large meaningful patterns; (b) greater information-processing speed and accuracy; (c) superior long- and short-term memory; (d) the ability to see and represent a problem at a deeper level than novices; (e) greater time spent understanding or analyzing problems; and (f) stronger self-monitoring skills. Deliberate practice of these factors should enhance expertise. If therapy sessions are videotaped and studied, and feedback from patients is obtained at termination and follow-up, competency should improve.

Much has been written about the art and science of psychotherapy (Hofmann & Weinberger, 2006; Schore, 2012; Soldz & McCullough, 2000). I would like to propose that we consider developing and refining our *craft*. Craftsmanship requires an integration of head and heart; art and science; technique and experimentation. Sennett (2008) has suggested that those who develop a high degree of mastery in their chosen craft work in a "liminal zone" between problem finding and problem solving. This requires an attitude of curiosity, active listening, and experimentation, rather than the implementation of rigid or formulaic responses. The notion of craftsmanship involves the creation of a culture of excellence. Implicit in this is an "aspiration for quality" that motivates the craftsman to improve and get better, rather than just get by (Sennett, 2008, p. 24). This aspiration involves learning by doing; trying and sometimes failing; growing through struggle and uncertainty; and, by engaging in intentional practice just beyond our current level of capacity, progressively improving our craft.

Skill in any craft requires hard work, persistence, and devotion to excellence for its own sake. True mastery, including that of psychotherapy, demands all of a person. Consequently, the latest research on the therapist variable will be included throughout the text. Since the therapist is the very vehicle of transmission for the treatment itself, his personal characteristics, as well the method he employs, have a direct and significant impact on outcome. Throughout this volume, verbatim transcripts from the author's own practice will be included to illustrate the concepts and processes being outlined, as well as revealing the personal style and flexibility required to treat a wide variety of patients.

Therapeutic Stance

In our field, we talk and write about *what* we do (Cognitive Behavior Therapy [CBT], EMDR, Emotion-Focused Couples Therapy, etc.) and *how* we do it (make interpretations, challenge pathological beliefs, etc.), but rarely articulate *why* we do it. However, questions such as, "What do you stand for?" and "What are you committed to in your work with patients and why?" are essential questions for all therapists to answer.

The "why" of practice involves our passion, our commitment, and our stance. When we operate from a clearly defined sense of why we do what we do, we can refine the clinical skills that are in alignment with our values and beliefs and, in so doing, improve treatment outcomes.

In his study of truly outstanding individuals and companies, Simon Sinek (2011) found that those who greatly outperform their competition do so not because their products are less expensive or even more effective, but because they are clear about *why* they do what they do. Sinek has asserted that consumers don't buy *what* you do, they buy *why* you do it. I would suggest that the same is true for psychotherapists. Being passionate, committed, and clear about *why* you do what you do, inspires confidence and enhances leadership, two important factors associated with the best performing therapists, teachers, and supervisors (Grawe, 2007; Wampold, 2011).

Simply put, our intentions matter. Whether we intend to treat a symptom or a person with a symptom, will dramatically affect both process and outcome. Furthermore, taking a stand for the health and capacity of the patient, and against unnecessary, self-inflicted suffering, can enhance outcome (Abbass, 2015; Davanloo, 1980, 1990; Duncan, 2010).

Cognitive Bias

The notion that a patient's emotional disturbances are the result of faulty thinking has little scientific evidence or support (Barlow, 2000). Consequently, restricting the therapist's focus to the patient's conscious thoughts has proven ineffective in many cases, as highlighted by a large study out of Sweden (Holmquist, Strom, & Foldemo, 2014). After spending huge sums of money to train CBT therapists, the data suggest the investment did not pay off. CBT had no therapeutic effect in cases of disabling anxiety and depression. Even more troubling was the finding that a significant number of patients who were symptomatic but functional at the start of therapy, became disabled after treatment. These patients were added to the already high number of Swedes on disability. Another quarter of the patients who received CBT dropped out prematurely, costing yet more money to the medical system. Perhaps as a result, the third wave of CBT has integrated these findings into an evolving method that includes an increased focus on emotional awareness and regulation (Barlow et al., 2011).

In contrast, treatment models such as Intensive Short-Term Dynamic Psychotherapy (ISTDP) have been explicitly designed to identify and resolve the underlying emotional problems causing symptomatic suffering. This treatment modality is based on a theory of the affective unconscious, and has accumulated a good deal of data supporting its cost and clinical effectiveness across a very wide spectrum of patients (Abbass, 2003, 2015; Abbass, Campbell, & Tarzwell, 2009; Shedler, 2010).

Costs Associated With a Medical/Pathology Model

It is essential that therapists of all stripes acquaint themselves with the latest research, in order to assess the efficacy of our interventions. Whether we view our patients as pathological, with disorders that they will have to manage all their lives, or as human beings who have the capacity to grow and heal, will directly affect both our interventions and therapeutic outcomes. For example, the notion that psychiatric symptoms are the result of faulty chemicals in the brain has been heavily promoted by pharmaceutical companies, but has no solid basis in scientific fact (Angell, 2011; Kirsch, 2008). Psychotropic medication alone (without the addition of psychotherapy) has relatively low rates of success, with effect sizes of approximately 0.3. Additionally, the largest population-based study on the effectiveness of antidepressants (Patten, 2004) revealed that those on medication experienced longer and more frequent depressive episodes than their unmedicated cohorts. The authors of two large meta-analyses (Kirsch, 2008; Kirsch & Sapirstein, 1998) concluded that 75% of the response to antidepressants could be attributed to the placebo effect. In contrast, effect sizes for CBT are approximately 0.68; 0.86 for dynamic psychotherapy; and 0.97 for ISTDP (Shedler, 2010). In addition, long-term follow-up data suggest that the therapeutic effects of ISTDP increases over time, once treatment has been terminated (Abbass, 2015; Abbass, Town, & Driessen, 2012; Shedler, 2010).

In contrast to the "drug effect," the impact of the relationship with the prescribing psychiatrist accounts for three times the variance of the medication itself (Ankarberg & Falkenstrom, 2008). The most effective psychiatrists obtained better results when prescribing a placebo than the least effective practitioners obtained when prescribing the active drug. Thus, the notion that biochemistry is more important than social and psychological factors in the treatment of emotional disorders seems to be without scientific support (Angell; 2011; McKay, Imel, & Wampold, 2006). This is not to suggest that medication can't be helpful, but the belief that medication alone is effective in the long run has little basis in fact. Instead, most research has demonstrated that, when required, a combination of medication and psychotherapy is far more effective than medication alone (Hollon, DeRubeis, & Evans, 1992; Hollon et al., 2014; Shedler, 2010).

This data, along with recent findings that psychotherapy changes the brain (Karlsson, 2011; Karlsson et al., 2010; Lehto, Tolmunen, & Joensnuu, 2008), suggest that enhanced training in specific therapeutic methods designed to facilitate both brain and behavior change would boost therapist effectiveness and improve patient care.

The Myth of Common Factors

The notion that all therapies are equally effective, due to the prevalence of common factors, is increasingly questioned. In 1995, Weinberger wrote an article on this very topic, entitled "Common Factors Are Not So Common." He conducted a meta-analysis that revealed five factors considered "common" across therapeutic models. These factors included: (1) the therapeutic relationship, (2) the revival of hope, (3) confronting problems, (4) developing a sense of mastery and competence, and (5) attributing success to one's own efforts. Even though these may appear to be "common factors," he discovered that most therapeutic modalities incorporated only one or two of these factors into their method. Weinberger (1995) wondered if the idea that common factors are responsible for the finding of "no difference" between models is actually the result of common *neglect* of potent therapeutic variables, rather than their common usage. More recently, Ecker (2015) suggested that the repeated finding of "no difference" between therapies is the result of all methods doing equally *badly*, instead of the notion they are all doing equally *well*.

An example of "common factors" being rather "uncommon" is the fact that many humanistic and supportive therapies focus almost exclusively on the therapeutic relationship as the curative factor, even though research suggests it is only responsible for about 11% of the variance (Horvath, Del Re, Fluckiger, & Symmonds, 2011; Martin, Garske, & Davis, 2000). A closer look at the data reveals that a solid working alliance is a *necessary but insufficient* variable for change. In contrast, Weinberger (1995) found that 40% of the variance was attributed to interventions designed to help patients confront what they have been avoiding. Despite these findings, there is a great deal of attention given to the development of the alliance, and very little on specific methods for helping patients confront the conflicts and difficulties they tend to avoid.

Reliance on data from randomized clinical trials (RCTs) contributes to the myth of common factors—that all therapies are effective, and there are no significant differences between them. The conviction that common factors, such as empathic listening, are responsible for the effectiveness of psychotherapy will be questioned here. I want to suggest that the conclusion that all therapies are equally effective may well be an artifact of the ways in which outcome research is typically conducted. For example, by averaging data, all the significant variation between treatments is lost. Rather than relying on averages to determine therapeutic effectiveness, we need to identify, study, and emulate the outliers—those therapies and therapists that achieve the most outstanding results. In order to do this, we must shift our emphasis to the study of what clinicians need to know—how to effect change within an individual over time as the result of specific intervention. Process research and N=1 studies will help us in this quest.

Therefore, instead of continuing to focus our attention on only one or two of these "common" factors, Weinberger (1995) advocated the development of an integrative model of therapy that incorporates all of these potent factors into a coherent system of intervention. Habib Davanloo (1978, 1990, 2000) has done just that. He developed a method composed of specific techniques designed to assess and regulate anxiety, as well as dismantling defense and resistance, so that patients can be helped to experience previously avoided emotions. In so doing, he developed a therapeutic procedure that effectively activates the unconscious emotional system, revealing the source of the patient's conflicts and suffering in a dramatic and unmistakable fashion.

Finally, recent research has suggested that the therapist is the most potent but neglected variable in psychotherapy research (Luborsky, McLellan, Diguer, Woody, & Seligman, 1997; Miller & Hubble, 2011; Norcross, 2002; Saxon & Barkham, 2012; Wampold, 2007, 2011). All psychotherapists are not alike. In fact, the top 20% tend to be more consistently effective than the other 80% combined (Miller & Hubble, 2011). This is especially so in the treatment of difficult and complex cases. Therefore, in addition to spelling out the most effective therapeutic strategies for producing deep and lasting change in our patients, the characteristics of the best therapists will also be examined throughout this volume.

The Person of the Therapist

In their classic text, Alexander and French (1946) wrote: "it is evident that greater, not less, knowledge of the manifold intricacies of human behavior is necessary before one can acquire skill in finding for each individual the most suitable and economical form of treatment" (p. iii). More recently (Duncan, 2010), it has been suggested that the best therapists possess a sophisticated set of interpersonal skills, combined with competence that has been attained through education, training, and experience. Those therapists who incorporate current research on best practices, and devote considerable time and effort to develop expertise and mastery in their craft, tend to get the best results (Wampold, 2010). There simply are no short cuts to excellence (Porras, Emery, & Thompson, 2007).

In addition to mastering specific skills to address a wide range of difficulties and complex clinical situations, attention to the development of the person of the therapist, now considered the most potent but neglected variable in psychotherapy research, is crucial (Crits-Christoph & Mintz, 1991; Luborsky,

McLellan, Diguer, Woody, & Seligman, 1997; Saxon & Barkham, 2012). Recent studies clearly reveal that some therapists are far more effective than most (Miller & Hubble, 2011; Miller, Hubble, & Duncan, 2007). These "super shrinks" (Ricks, 1974) are passionate and enthusiastic about their method; systematic but flexible in the application of this method; open to feedback; highly engaged and approachable; masters of interpersonal relating; confident yet humble; life-long learners; and committed to achieving outstanding results. The last factor is worth emphasizing. Dissatisfied with average results, master clinicians push themselves and their patients to achieve the best possible results (Gawande, 2004). While some therapists may be born with these innate capacities, others can be trained to develop them so that their effectiveness can be improved. Our own curiosity and passion about making a difference provides the fuel for the development of these complex skills. In turn, therapists are most likely to get enthusiastic and passionate about a method with proven results. Developing the skills to implement such a method should increase confidence and motivate us to pursue ambitious goals.

Over the past several decades, we have been neglecting the development of our trainees on a personal level, no longer requiring or even encouraging them to engage in their own therapies or other experiences designed to enhance self-awareness and growth (Garfield, 1997). This, despite the evidence to suggest that clinicians with no personal experience in their own therapy had the lowest rates of therapeutic progress and the highest rates of regression or stagnation in the therapies they conducted (Norcross & Orlinsky, 2005).

Even when presented with evidence regarding the most effective methods of psychotherapeutic intervention, most therapists fail to learn and incorporate them into their practice (Duncan, 2010; Miller, Hubble, & Duncan, 2007). Why is that? What is in the way of openness and flexibility on the part of so many therapists? It is not enough to teach therapeutic skills. To train therapists to use them effectively, teachers and supervisors must help them learn to deal directly with their own anxieties, defenses, and inner conflicts. Skill development alone, without attention to the person of the therapist, will not suffice for the development of clinical excellence. In order to enhance the effectiveness of training, teachers and supervisors must include the personal development of therapists in training, in addition to teaching theory and technique. Those therapists who practice what they preach, by attending to their own ongoing personal and professional development, embody the changes they attempt to facilitate in their patients. As such they are authentic, emotionally available, and highly engaged in their work—characteristics associated with the best outcomes (Wampold, 2011).

While much research remains to be done on effective ways to train therapists to achieve superior results, preliminary studies suggest it can be done (Abbass, 2004; Abbass, Kisely, Rasic, & Katzman, 2013; Katzman & Coughlin, 2013). Supervisors who develop a strong collaborative alliance with trainees, creating a trusting but challenging atmosphere, in which high expectations for clinical excellence prevail, tend to get superior results (Hess et al., 2008; Ladany & Bradley, 2010). These supervisors create diverse learning experiences for their students, provide direct and specific feedback, and incorporate the viewing of videotapes sessions, allowing for specific coaching and refinement of clinical interventions (Abbass & Town, 2013). It has been my experience that training therapists in this method of intensive, emotion-focused therapy increases efficacy and enhances mastery, while promoting therapist confidence, all of which bodes well for outcome.

In addition to the aforementioned factors, it is my strong belief that behaving with integrity, and practicing what we preach, are essential ingredients for achieving consistently excellent results. This includes a willingness to confront our own feelings, anxieties, and insecurities openly and directly, just as we ask our patients to do. The emotional availability and responsiveness of the therapist, as well as the specific skills he employs, are deemed equally important. Such an approach appears to be sorely needed in our field. Studies reveal high levels of deception in supervision, with a full 40% of therapists in training admitting they had omitted or distorted information they were uncomfortable sharing (Hess et al., 2008; Ladany & Bradley 2010). In addition to conscious distortion, therapists have unconscious motives that interfere with transparency. It goes without saying that trainees cannot report information they do not observe. Videotaped sessions provide the raw data for the therapist and supervisor to consider. Videotaped sessions reveal information and processes of which the supervisee was previously unaware.

I had a recent example of this in one of my own supervisory cases. My standard practice involves a review of the first five minutes of every session, before moving forward. While the therapist requested that we skip over the first minutes, I asked if we could examine it just the same. The videotape revealed that the patient started the session by making a comment about the therapist's tardiness. To her credit, the therapist asked the patient how she was feeling about being kept waiting. The patient responded by saying, "Oh, I am used to it—you are always 10 or 15 minutes late." While the trainee had not mentioned having difficulty maintaining the framework for therapy or managing her time, this difficulty was revealed on tape. The therapist then disclosed that she ends up running late by the end of the day because she does not know how to end sessions on time. Even though the therapist was embarrassed by her difficulty in structuring sessions, this was the very thing she needed help with. Without the videotape, this important information would have been lost.

Summary

Despite some of the dismal statistics on dropout rates and relapse, this is an exciting time in our field. Evidence from such diverse disciplines as neuroscience, developmental research, psychotherapy process and outcome research, and even ancient spiritual practices, are converging to provide a comprehensive understanding of both psychopathology and exceptional human functioning. Our understanding of the emotional and neurological underpinnings of both health and pathology can enhance our understanding of patients and guide therapeutic intervention (Grawe, 2007).

The current evidence suggests that there are more commonalities than differences underlying most psychiatric disorders. Specifically, disturbances in the areas of emotional awareness and regulation are involved in almost all psychiatric disturbances (Barlow, 2000; Barlow, 2010; Barlow, Allen, & Choate, 2004; Farchione, Fairholme, Ellard, Boisseau, & Barlow, 2012). This information provides the basis for the development of sophisticated, precise, and powerful interventions designed to enhance clinical effectiveness. With these interventions we can help patients move beyond symptom management and transform outmoded patterns of behavior. This is the kind of meaningful work most therapists want to do (Orlinsky & Ronnestad, 2005). However, most clinicians have simply not been provided the kind of training required to achieve enhanced results. Cognitive approaches have predominated training and practice for the past few decades, leaving clinicians ill prepared for the task of identifying and treating emotional disorders effectively, at their source. In fact, a study by Nyman, Nafziner, and Smith (2011) found that our standard training methods result in no appreciable improvement in the outcomes trainees are able to achieve. In contrast, training designed to develop emotionally focused skills tailored to the identification and regulation of emotion, particularly when accompanied by videotaped supervision, seems to yield far more impressive results (Abbass, 2004; Katzman & Coughlin, 2013).

The present volume is an attempt to fill in existing gaps in practice, by outlining specific interventions designed to "accelerate and condense" the therapeutic process (Coughlin Della Selva, 1996/2004), enhance therapist skill and competence, and improve outcomes. In addition, a focus on the personal development of the therapist will be included, so that the reader can learn to improve upon both what she knows and who she is. There will be an attempt to integrate all the best and most current information regarding effectiveness, rather than engaging in dichotomies that are neither helpful nor accurate. While "dichotomies provide convenient 'handles' which permit examination of otherwise unwieldy events," they often oversimplify complexity and lose sight of the totality of what we are studying (Butler & Strupp, 1986, p. 30). I hope that this volume will testify to the "complexity and subtlety of psychotherapeutic processes (that) cannot be reduced to a set of disembodied techniques" (Butler & Strupp, 1986, p. 33). Instead, my intention is to present an integrated view, in which specific and nonspecific factors are intertwined within the context of a caring and purposeful relationship between patient and therapist.

My hope is that this book will become a resource for novice and experienced therapists alike, outlining a method of assessing and treating a wide range of patients in a consistently effective manner. By helping therapists learn specific techniques designed to accelerate and deepen the healing process, we should be able to increase the ranks of the "super shrinks" and provide a better, more reliable treatment to our patients. In so doing, we should also be able to enhance therapists' confidence in their skills, as well as contribute to their personal development.

Chapter Two
Inquiry, Assessment, and Case Conceptualization

All psychotherapy must begin with a thorough assessment, obtained via inquiry into the nature of the patient's symptoms and suffering. A specific and detailed examination of each area of disturbance is essential in order to discover the underlying mechanisms responsible for these disturbances. We want to assess, rather than assume, that we understand what the patient is experiencing. Taking a phenomenological approach to inquiry is particularly important. Rather than just accepting "I feel depressed," or "I am anxious all the time," as sufficient information, we would ask how the patient actually experiences this anxiety or depression internally; when it is worse, when it started, and how it is affecting the patient's functioning in various areas of her life.

While developing a detailed understanding of the nature and severity of the patient's presenting problems is essential, so too is the need to assess both the patient's willingness to engage in psychotherapy, and capacity to work in an emotionally intense, focused, and dynamic manner. As we conduct the inquiry into the areas of difficulty, we must also assess the patient's strengths and capacities—what he brings to the table that can assist us in the healing process. This is a reminder that we are treating a patient with a problem, not just a problem or diagnosis.

Detailed and concrete means for obtaining a detailed inquiry and, in so doing, developing a clear case conceptualization used to guide treatment, will be the focus of this chapter. Integrating the information obtained via assessment into a conceptual model of both the clinical problem, and interventions designed to address the problem, are essential components of such a conceptualization. While research demonstrates that those trained to develop a clear and comprehensive case formulation improved their outcomes significantly over control groups (Kendjelic & Eells, 2007), this vital skill is neglected in most training programs (Farber, 2009; Ivey, 2006). However, "a hypothesis about the causes, precipitants, and maintaining influences of a person's psychological, interpersonal, and behavioral problems" (Kendjelic & Eells, 2007, p. 66) is an invaluable guide to effective treatment. It should also be emphasized that such a formulation is a hypothesis, and one that needs to be tested out continually and revised when necessary.

The reader will learn how to use the patient's response to intervention, rather than history or DSM diagnosis, as the primary assessment tool used to guide to further intervention. Developing an internal focus, and encouraging the patient's active engagement in this exploratory phase of treatment, while identifying and removing obstacles to collaboration, will be highlighted with clinical examples.

Methods of Assessment

The Descriptive Approach

Despite their prominent use, research suggests that descriptive diagnoses, like those included in the DSM V, have little predictive value, and tell the clinician nothing about the cause of the patient's symptoms (Craddock & Owen, 2010; Shedler, Karliner, & Katz, 2003; Shedler, Magman, & Manis, 1993). Furthermore, there is no genetic or neuroscientific evidence to support the breakdown of complex disorders into separate and distinct categories (Insel, 2013). So, while some refer to the DSM diagnostic manual as the "Bible" for the field, it is only a dictionary of terms and categories based on a consensus about clusters of symptoms shared by a particular group of patients. Such classifications can actually be harmful. Recent research (Lam, Salkovskis, & Hogg, 2015) has highlighted the dangers of labeling patients in this manner. Clinicians who received a diagnosis, rather than a description of the patient, were negatively affected by it. They became unduly pessimistic about the patient's prospects, and treatment became less effective as a result. These findings suggest that therapists are just as prone to bias and prejudice regarding labels such as "borderline" or "schizophrenic" as the public is, and that patients suffer as a consequence of such labeling. This only increases the importance of avoiding such labels and dealing with the unique human beings we are attempting to assist.

The Historical Approach

Just as descriptive diagnoses fail to provide the information we need to understand and effectively treat our patients, developmental history alone has also proven to be an inadequate assessment tool. Many therapists make the mistake of beginning their inquiry in the past, presuming some sort of direct link between past events and current levels of psychopathology. In fact, there is little empirical evidence to support such a notion. Instead, the data seems to suggest that human beings respond to adversity along the bell-shaped curve (Bonanno,

2007; Zolli & Healy, 2013). While some individuals are deeply and permanently scared by early childhood events, others respond by becoming stronger and more resilient (Bonanno, 2007; Rendon, 2015). In fact, recent research suggests that "personal, psychic resilience is more widespread, improvable, and teachable than previously thought" (Zolli & Healy, 2013, p. 14). An exception to this may be multiple and repetitive childhood trauma, which seems to affect the brain and body in profound and lasting ways (Edwards, Holden, Felitti, & Andra, 2003; Felitti et al., 1998). Yet, even in these cases, responses to the trauma vary widely. Once again, it is worth noting the need to assess, rather than assume, that we understand how particular events have affected and shaped a given patient.

An Alternative Approach: Response to Intervention

Since neither descriptive diagnoses nor developmental history alone provide the kind of information we need to understand the source of our patients' difficulties or to determine the type of treatment they require, what can? The evidence suggests that the patient's response to intervention, in the here and now, provides the kind of timely information we need to formulate a dynamic understanding of our patient. In particular, monitoring the patient's response to our interventions reveals his *current* level of capacity to engage in the process of psychotherapy (Davanloo, 1990; Duncan, 2010; Malan, 1976).

David Malan and Michael Balint (Malan, 1980) discovered this surprising finding quite by accident, when doing research at the Tavistock Clinic in London decades ago. They wanted to study the possible effectiveness of short-term dynamic psychotherapy, assuming that only the healthiest patients with circumscribed problems of recent origin would be able to benefit from such an approach. However, very few of the patients on the waiting list fit these criteria! They forged ahead reluctantly, randomly assigning patients on the clinic's waiting list to either short- or long-term dynamic psychotherapy, and then studying the results. Much to their surprise, they discovered that the most penetrating and lasting change among those receiving short-term dynamic psychotherapy occurred in cases that were both complex and chronic. This was one of the first studies to suggest that history and descriptive diagnoses were not an accurate predictor of response to treatment (although Alexander and French came to the same conclusion in the 40s). Instead, they found three factors that were predictive of successful outcome in brief dynamic psychotherapy: (1) the therapist's ability to see the current problem as the most recent example of a recurring conflict in the patient's life, (2) the therapist's willingness to deal directly and swiftly with negative feelings in the transference, and (3) the patient's ability to respond to the therapist's intervention in an affect-laden manner within the first four sessions.

The Trial Therapy

Davanloo (1990), who collaborated with Malan in the 70s and 80s, adopted these strategies, and expanded upon them, by developing a method of assessment he refers to as the "trial therapy." In many ways, each evaluation constitutes a scientific case study. The ISTDP therapist gathers specific data regarding the patient's presenting symptoms and problems, obtaining as much detailed information as possible about the circumstances giving rise to them. The triggers to the patient's symptoms often provide essential information about the underlying cause of the disturbance. In this way, the therapist can begin to formulate a hypothesis about the underlying forces responsible for their creation. Then the hypothesis is shared and tested out, using the patient's response to confirm, refute, or revise it.

It should be noted that Davanloo (personal communication, 1989) developed this active approach to assessment and treatment after becoming frustrated and feeling guilty about the long and erratic course of most analytic treatments. He noted, as others had before and since, that patients who enter treatment in a state of crisis are often particularly open to intervention and can make deep, rapid, and long-lasting change in a brief amount of time (Lindemann, 1979). In such cases, the environmental crisis triggers feelings of such intensity that the patient's characteristic defenses have already broken down. This breakdown in defenses paves the way for the breakthrough of unconscious conflicts responsible for the patient's symptoms and suffering. With the unconscious in an open and fluid state, rapid reorganization is often possible. Having worked with Lindemann in a crisis clinic, and observing this phenomenon, Davanloo (1980) began to wonder if it would be possible to *create* an internal crisis in patients who were stuck in more chronic states of suffering. In order to accomplish this, he used active techniques, in which high levels of focus on the internal state of the patient were used. He found that exerting some pressure on the patient to be open, honest, collaborative, and emotionally engaged, while challenging him to abandon defensive strategies of avoidance, resulted in just the kind of internal crisis and upheaval required to gain rapid entry into the unconscious life of the patient (Davanloo, 1980, 1990, 2000). These findings have been replicated and confirmed by others in the field (Abbass, 2015; Frederickson, 2013; Malan & Coughlin Della Selva, 2007; Shedler, 2010).

Eventually, Davanloo (1980, 1990, 1995, 2000) developed a systematic, yet dynamic, method of assessment and treatment that involves the implementation of what he calls the "central dynamic sequence." This sequence of interventions consists of all the active ingredients in the therapy itself, designed to uncover and then resolve the unconscious origin of the patient's symptoms and suffering. Using the central dynamic sequence as a structure for the phase of inquiry enables the therapist to gather crucial data on the nature of the patient's disturbances, while simultaneously assessing the patient's ability to respond to each form of intervention. In other words, responses to each phase of the assessment, from the identification of symptoms and triggers; to the awareness and regulation of anxiety; type and tenacity of defenses; and the ability to access emotions, reveal the specific mechanisms or deficits responsible for the patient's disorder. The rapid identification of these underlying mechanisms allows the therapist to devise a therapeutic strategy designed to address the patient's areas of disturbance in a specific and targeted manner.

The central dynamic sequence consists of:

1. A detailed inquiry, into the nature, history, and severity of the presenting complaints, with a clear outline of the precipitating event or recent example of the presenting complaint;
2. Pressure to experience feelings involved in the triggering event;
3. Monitor and assess level and channel of anxiety;
4. Identify, clarify, and block or challenge defenses in the way of feeling;
5. Facilitate a breakthrough of mixed feelings in the Current (C) or Transference (T), with a link to the Past (P);
6. Make sense of memories, dreams, and associations that are de-repressed following the breakthrough of feelings; and
7. Consolidate insight, using the two triangles (conflict and person) to drive home the links between feelings, anxiety, defense, and presenting problems, as well as between past, present, and transference pattern of behavior.

In order to complete this sequence of interventions, and assess the patient's ability, or lack thereof, to engage in the various aspects of dynamic inquiry, sufficient time needs to be allotted for the process to take place. Davanloo (core training 1989–1991) suggested that we allow at least three hours for this initial assessment. In this way, the method can be applied systematically, but flexibly, based on the patient's response to each phase of inquiry. By the end of the initial evaluation, both patient and therapist should have a fairly clear sense of the nature of the problems being presented, whether they can work together, and whether this intensive, dynamic, emotion-focused work will be of benefit to the patient.

Malan's Triangles

Malan's triangles of conflict and person (1976, 1979) provide a kind of map of the patient's internal world (Figure 2.1), and graphically depict both internal emotional conflicts and the repetitive nature of conflicts with others. The triangles also provide a guide for the dynamic psychotherapist, attempting to assess both the underlying mechanisms responsible for the patient's difficulties, as well as his ability to engage in emotion-focused, dynamic work. "Menninger (1958) operationalized the notion of intrapsychic conflict by drawing a 'triangle of insight', in which impulses and feelings, defenses, and anxiety each occupy one of the three corners" (Coughlin Della Selva, 1996/2004, p. 6).

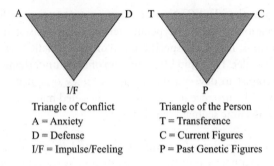

Figure 2.1 The Two Triangles

At the bottom of the triangle of conflict are the core emotions that have been selected for in evolution: love, pain, grief, rage, and guilt (Figure 2.2). These feelings, and their accompanying impulses, facilitate the kind of emotional attachment and bonding to others so vital for survival and optimal development. The triangle of person depicts the way in which these emotions and emotional conflicts, with their origin in the past, get replayed in the patient's current life, including in the relationship with the therapist. Both intrapsychic and interpersonal patterns of behavior are crucial to identify, understand, and ultimately interrupt, in order to create new and healthier modes of functioning.

Using the Triangles as an Assessment Tool and Guide

We endeavor to connect the two triangles in our clinical work with patients from its inception. The patient's problems exist at the top of the triangle, and typically involve high and unregulated levels of anxiety and/or excessive reliance on

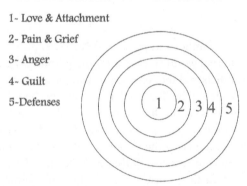

Figure 2.2 Attachment Affects

defenses against his true feelings, affecting current functioning. Since chronic avoidance of feelings causes and perpetuates the patient's problems, our goal is to get "to the bottom of the triangles" and discover/reclaim basic feelings and desires from the past which are continuing to influence the patient in the present. In order to do this we must (1) probe for feelings, while (2) monitoring anxiety and (3) blocking defensive avoidance. This is our essential "psychodiagnostic procedure." Responses to this kind of probing reveal the underlying nature of the patient's problem, as well as his ego adaptive capacity, or lack thereof.

PSYCHODIAGNOSTIC PROCEDURE

1. Pressure to feelings toward significant other
2. Monitor anxiety
3. Block defense

Patient's response to intervention is diagnostic and guides next step.

Response to Intervention

When we ask a patient about his feelings toward someone in his current life, for example, he can only respond in one of three ways. He can tell us what he feels, become filled with anxiety, or resort to defenses against his feelings. His response provides both information about his current functioning, and guides us in our intervention. If the patient can identify feelings, we will proceed with an exploration of the experience of these feelings. If the patient responds with high levels of anxiety, we will focus on down-regulating anxiety. If the patient responds with a defense, we will identify and clarify the function of this defense in an effort to help the patient relinquish the defense in favor of facing their underlying feelings. Tracking response to intervention allows for this kind of systematic but flexible responding on the part of the therapist.

RESPONSE TO INTERVENTION AS GUIDE

- If patient responds with impulses/feelings, go to portrait.
- If patient responds with defenses, do defenses work in order to acquaint patient with cost and turn him against defenses.
- If patient goes to resistance in the transference, respond with head-on collision.
- If patient responds with high anxiety and low capacity, do restructuring.

It is incumbent upon the therapist to ensure that "from the first moments of the therapeutic encounter, the client is experiencing the relationship as meaningful and positive" (Duncan, 2010, p. 38). The therapist's interest in understanding the patient's internal experience, his willingness to be involved and offer himself as a resource, while balancing encouragement and challenge, all increase the likelihood that the patient will get involved in the process and join the therapist in an active exploration of the problems at hand. Neutrality is discouraged here. Rather, a stand for the patient's well-being, along with a willingness to work hard and get involved in a joint effort toward that end, is most highly associated with positive outcome in psychotherapy (Abbass, 2015; Wampold, 2011). Using the triangles as a guide facilitates this process.

Again, it is the patient's response to this internal focus that will provide the most accurate and timely information on his willingness and capacity to engage in psychotherapy. Some patients have a hard time tolerating closeness and caring, and will try to push away or discourage such involvement with the therapist. Others insist they have no problem and that other people are the source of their distress. These responses to our initial inquiries provide the information required to design an intervention tailored to their specific needs. Persistence and patience, along with highly developed interpersonal skill and a systematic method of assessment and treatment are required to achieve these goals consistently.

Inquiry

Patients come to therapy because of current distress. While there may well be, and usually are, unresolved conflicts from the past contributing to the current problems, the patient's motivation stems from the problems he is currently experiencing. Perhaps the therapist's tendency to begin her inquiry with a focus on the past, rather than the present, is one of the factors contributing to such a high dropout rate in psychotherapy. "Their past, their diagnoses, and their genetics are easy to mistake as factors that completely determine their lives. But then we relate to dead concepts rather than living persons" (Frederickson, 2013, p. 2). Instead, it is most effective to assess the patient's problems and capacities in the present moment.

The ability to display an attitude of genuine interest and curiosity, while obtaining detailed information regarding the patient's presenting problems, is critical at this early stage of treatment. We need to obtain specific information on exactly what kinds of symptoms the patient is experiencing, when and where the symptom are triggered, when it all started, and how he has been coping up until now.

Specific Examples and Identification of Triggers

We begin by inquiring about the areas of difficulty, say a tendency to become depressed, or an inability to sustain romantic relationships, and then focus on the precipitating events to these difficulties. In particular, an examination of the circumstances surrounding the first instance of the problem, and/or the most recent example of the problem, is essential information to obtain. Information regarding the precipitants to the symptoms and disturbances contains dynamic significance and help us form hypotheses regarding the nature of the underlying disturbance to be addressed. This is the essence of a case formulation that makes sense of the patient's problems while providing a rationale for treatment.

This importance of identifying the precipitating factors to the patient's symptoms was especially relevant during a recent group supervision session, in which three trainees presented three male patients; each seeking help with debilitating anxiety and depression. Of interest, all three had been suffering for approximately three years. However, inquiry revealed that the precipitating events (and underlying conflicts) were quite different in each case.

In the first case, a man in his late 20s became severely depressed and nonfunctional after winning a top national prize and "beating" all his competition. This suggests that conflicts over success, being the center of attention, and winning were at the root of his symptoms. Oedipal issues would certainly need to be explored. Had his mother always favored him? Was his father a success or failure? Was he the younger brother who knocked his brother out of the top spot in the family? These are the kinds of questions we might ask to test out our hypothesis. Again, the patient's responses to these questions will ultimately provide the data with which we will either confirm or reformulate our hypothesis.

In the second case, the therapist had not conducted a detailed inquiry and was not clear about the precipitant. Despite this oversight, the therapist had been quite focused on the patient's marriage, assuming that anger toward his wife was being turned inward, resulting in depression. Since she had no solid data upon which to make such a conclusion, I urged her to conduct a more focused inquiry during the next session to see if they could discover what had given rise to the depression. Further inquiry revealed that his man adored his wife and had only become symptomatic when their first child was born. More detailed questions were required to sort out the nature of the conflicts giving rise to his symptoms. Did the couple agree to have this child, or did the wife get pregnant "by mistake"? Did he want the child, but then find he was jealous of the time and attention his wife devoted to the baby? What was the gender of the child? Where was he in the birth order of his own family? Was he the first born, who was usurped by a younger sibling, or the youngest of a large brood who never got enough love and attention? These are the kind of questions we need to ask in order to flesh out the nature of the underlying conflict responsible for the symptomatic disturbance. Then, and only then, can we help him take up the issue responsible for the symptoms, rather than merely manage the symptom or attempt to treat it out of context.

In the third case, a middle-aged man became so anxious and depressed that he asked to be hospitalized. Inquiry revealed that he had been highly functional all his life, up until three years ago, when the anxiety and depression began. He was married, with grown children, all of whom were doing well. He had trained as a surgeon and had developed a successful practice. After surviving an aggressive cancer at the age of 40, which resulted in the closing of his medical practice, he managed to create a whole new career for himself that was, once again, very successful. So why would he get depressed now, in his 54th year? The therapist, in hearing about how dependent he had become on his mother (they talked by phone each day), assumed that this was the source of the problem (rather than one of the results). The therapist was convinced that the relationship with his mother was dysfunctional, and somehow responsible for his suffering, though he could provide no compelling evidence to support such a conclusion. Further exploration revealed that the patient's father had died three years before, just before the symptoms began. In fact, *this* was the trigger to his depression. Inquiry into the nature of his relationship with his father, and the events surrounding his death, were in order. We seek to understand WHY the patient is suffering as he is at this particular time, rather than simply being concerned with HOW he is functioning.

Defenses Interfering With Inquiry and Assessment

During this early phase of assessment, only those defenses interfering with engagement, clarity, and specificity need to be addressed and blocked. If patients remain vague in their presentation, we cannot understand the nature of their problems. Rather than passively accepting general statements, we must probe further, while exerting some pressure on the patient to be specific. The notion of pressuring patients may seem anathema to those who take a supportive approach, but just such a strategy is usually very helpful and sometimes absolutely necessary. Since defenses hurt patients, and contribute to their suffering, as well as undermining successful therapeutic intervention, blocking defenses is an act of compassion (Frederickson, 2013).

In addition to vagueness, the tendency of some patients to externalize the cause of their suffering, or even their motivation to seek treatment, must be eradicated, so that an internal focus can be established. While there are usually external events that trigger the patient's problems, they do not *cause* the problem. This is a distinction many therapists fail to make. In fact, therapists sometimes join the patient's external focus and agree that her alcoholic husband or a cancer diagnosis is the problem. While the patient's husband might, in fact, have a drinking problem, and getting a cancer diagnosis is certainly stressful, these facts alone do not explain the patient's emotional and psychological problems. Instead, by investigating how these external events are causing an internal problem for the patient, we begin to develop the kind of internal focus required for psychotherapy to be effective.

Evaluating Anxiety

It is incumbent upon the therapist to assess the patient's level of anxiety early in the first session. While we will go into much greater detail on this important topic in Chapter 3, I will briefly outline what needs to be evaluated at this early stage of assessment. We expect patients to be anxious when they come to see a therapist. In relatively healthy patients, this anxiety is noticeable in their voluntary muscles, with tension in the hands and sighing respiration. If we do not notice physical signs of anxiety, we need to inquire in order to determine whether the patient is simply detached and uninvolved, or the anxiety is getting channeled in the smooth muscle (with symptoms like migraine headaches or ulcerative colitis) or into the cognitive-perceptual apparatus (with confusion, dizziness, blurry vision, or dissociation). It is essential to get this information early so that the therapist can tailor his interventions to the patient's level of anxiety tolerance and remain in the "safety zone."

Patients with anxiety in their voluntary (striated) muscles can usually tolerate the direct experience of unconscious feelings and fantasies without ill effect. Those who channel anxiety into their smooth (involuntary) muscles must be treated with greater caution. Restructuring of this anxiety pathway is the primary task in such cases. A gradual, step-wise approach ensures that the symptoms will improve, rather than get worse, as the result of ill-timed interventions. Patients who experience cognitive-perceptual distortions when anxious need a graded approach, designed to build their capacity before exposing them to unconscious conflicts. Assessing anxiety is a crucial aspect of the diagnostic evaluation, as it dictates the focus and pace of further intervention. We can only intervene in a safe manner if we keep our eye on anxiety, ensuring that it remains within the patient's level of tolerance. When anxiety is too high, the patient can't process and integrate what is being experienced. When anxiety is too low, no real change occurs.

Attending to Nonverbal Communication

It is generally accepted that 60–65% of all interpersonal communication is nonverbal (Burgoon, Guerrero, & Floyd, 2009). "Unfortunately the emphasis in the clinical setting is disproportionately placed on verbal behavior. Many nonverbal behaviors are unconscious and represent a more accurate description of the patient's attitude and emotional state" (Foley & Gentile, 2010, p. 38). Therefore, attending to and articulating the patient's pattern of behavior (again, often nonverbal), as it happens, has proven to be an effective strategy for creating the kind of immediacy associated with positive outcome (Hill, 2004; Hill, Wonjin, Spangler, Stahl, & Sullivan, 2008; Kasper, Hill, & Klvlighan, 2008; Sherer & Rogers, 1980). This type of focused attention interrupts the kind of automaticity that keeps patients stuck in habitual patterns of reactivity. Research (Langer, 2014) suggests that those who engage in mindful attention experience an enhanced sense of well-being and a decrease in subjective distress. Furthermore, this type of immediacy and mindfulness paves the way for new experiences and an enhanced sense of conscious choice.

Allan Abbass (2015), a master clinician and outstanding researcher in ISTDP, teaches his trainees to "listen with their eyes" as well as their ears. If we only attend to the verbal content of our patient's report, we can miss vital nonverbal communication alerting us to the unconscious source of our patient's difficulties. Watching them carefully, in order to SEE what is happening, moment to moment, can provide essential information that would otherwise be missed.

Defense Work

Once we have obtained a survey of the patient's difficulties and identified a specific example of the presenting complaint to explore in detail, we begin to explore the feelings involved. This "pressure to feeling" typically generates anxiety and leads to defensive avoidance, revealing the nature of the emotional conflicts responsible for the patient's difficulties. In particular, most of the patient's symptoms and suffering are the inevitable result of excessive reliance on defenses against her feelings. Given this, evaluating the nature and tenacity of these defenses, the relationship between defenses and symptoms, and the patient's ability to become aware of these mechanisms, must be evaluated carefully. Davanloo (1990) has created a clear and systematic method for assessing the nature and tenacity of the defenses. This process involves several steps, including (1) identification of defenses, (2) clarification of defenses, and (3) examination of the cost of defenses.

Identification and Clarification of Defenses

Most often, when asked about feelings toward others, patients initially respond with some kind of defense. After identifying the defense—what the patient is *doing* to avoid the feeling—we must clarify the function of the defense, i.e., to help the patient avoid awareness of distressing feelings. Both an identification of the defense and a clarification of its function are necessary before moving on to the phase of examining the consequences of these avoidant strategies. Damasio (1994, 2000) reminds us that we have no more control over our emotions than we do over feelings like hunger and fatigue. Our feelings and emotions are quite automatic and often unconscious. The only choice we have is whether to become aware of our feelings so we can experience them fully, or remain in the dark by relying on automatic avoidant strategies that end up causing further pain and suffering. When we resist the experience of painful feelings, we create suffering. When patients habitually suppress emotional pain and anger, they end up tired and depressed. Therapeutic work is required to help them see this mechanism clearly. Once they see how their defenses cause their suffering, they will be motivated to relinquish them in the quest for healing.

Cost-Benefit Analysis

While the patient is often aware of the benefit of the defense, she is rarely as aware of the costs they exact. Careful work is required to tie the defenses to the patient's symptoms and, in so doing, begin to turn her against them. It is essential that the patient can see the link between reliance on defenses against feelings and her symptoms. Once the patient sees the cost of her defenses, she has choice in the matter: to continue to make use of the avoidant strategies that create and perpetuate her symptoms, or honestly face the feelings and wishes she has been avoiding. Up until that point, the patient is operating on automatic pilot, with no real choices or options. Often these interventions must be repeated several times before the patient can clearly see the pattern in which avoided emotions cause symptoms and suffering.

Occasionally, patients are able to respond to the therapist's intervention by dropping defenses and engaging in an open, curious, and emotionally engaged manner. More often, patients defend their defenses rather than relinquishing them. In other words, they side with the defenses and extol their benefits. Defenses usually begin as an attempt to cope with high levels of anxiety regarding overwhelming feelings. However, defenses that may have been adaptive in the past often lose their utility over time and actually create more problems in adult life. For example, it may have been highly adaptive to suppress anger toward a tyrannical father. By learning to be silent and invisible the patient prevented attack. However, as an adult, the tendency toward timidity and passivity exacerbates his difficulties. Acknowledging the adaptive value of defenses, while highlighting the attendant costs, is usually effective in facilitating an awareness of their limited value.

When Defenses Create Resistance

In some cases, the defenses the patient has been using to avoid his own feelings create a wall of resistance between patient and therapist. In other words, the defenses that help the patient detach from his own distressing thought and feelings also create interpersonal distance with others. Defenses such as emotional detachment, passivity or defiance, rapid speech, externalization, and relentless self-attack form a barrier to closeness and undermine therapeutic collaboration. Unless and until the patient is willing to engage openly and honestly with the therapist, no real therapy can take place. Therefore, when present, resistance in the transference must be taken up directly.

Feelings and Impulses

Once we have conducted our survey of difficulties and have obtained a recent example in which symptoms were triggered, we inquire about the feelings toward others in the cited examples. Then we can evaluate the patient's ability to be "in touch with" his feelings. Once again, Davanloo has provided us with concrete and operational definitions to guide the process. In order to be considered "in touch with feeling," three key elements must be present: (1) cognitive label of the emotion; (2) physiological activation in the body; and (3) awareness of impulses associated with the emotion. A fourth variable, the patient's willingness and ability to share these feelings with others (the interpersonal aspect), must also be assessed in the interaction with the therapist.

Here we are referring to the basic human emotions selected for in the evolutionary process. These include love, sexual feelings, pain and grief, and anger and guilt. Our basic feelings are characteristic of the species and do not need to be learned. We are wired to love and attach to caretakers. Ruptures to this bond create pain and grief, and evokes anger at anyone responsible for such a rupture, including the attachment figure. However, the experience of anger and rage toward a loved one also triggers guilt and creates conflict. The result of this conflict often takes the form of an unconscious need to punish the self, driven by this guilt. Especially when ruptures to the bond are repetitive, and are not repaired, or there is no one with whom the child can share his feelings regarding these ruptures, all these intense mixed feelings are avoided with defensive strategies. Such strategies may preserve the bond, but end up hurting the child. Most often these warded-off feelings get acted out or internalized, causing symptoms and suffering.

These core emotions each have a kind of signature. They are each experienced in ways that are characteristic of the species and reflect hard wiring. The patient is either aware of each element of the feeling, or he isn't. Sometimes patients are aware of feelings, but are hesitant to share them, while others are in no position to share, as they have no idea what they are feeling. The particular "missing pieces" provide vital diagnostic information. It is also important to assess which feelings are readily experienced and which are avoided. While some patients are detached and seem unaware of all strong feelings, others have relatively easy access to some emotions, but very little to others. This is also of diagnostic significance and leads to a specific affective focus for the work.

Coherence

Patients often come to therapy with some awareness of their symptoms, but blind to internal mechanisms responsible for the creation and perpetuation of their suffering. In order to discover the unconscious forces responsible for the patient's symptoms, we must adopt an attitude of curiosity, and invite the patient to join us in a detailed exploration of recent examples of the problems to be addressed. Understanding the precipitants of the patient's symptoms can be both diagnostic and therapeutic. It is not uncommon for patients to be utterly confused about what is happening to them. They either have no idea why they feel as they do or have some mistaken idea about the origin of their problems ("It must be my hormones" or "It's my daughter who is making me miserable"). When a patient responds to a question by saying "I don't know," many therapists are stumped and don't know how to proceed. It is important to remember that patients who lack awareness of their inner life cannot tell us in so many words what is causing their distress. Instead, they may show us. I might respond by saying, "Do you want to know?" or "Would you like to understand yourself better and get to the bottom of these difficulties?"

I sometimes suggest that trainees try to be more like Columbo, the bumbling detective, rather than House, the arrogant know-it-all. "Ask, don't tell" is the best approach. This also aids in the development of a collaborative alliance, so essential for successful psychotherapy.

Once previously avoided feelings and impulses are experienced, the memories associated with these feelings come to consciousness in an unmistakable fashion. This allows us to discover the unconscious coherence between the patient's apparently senseless behavior and his unresolved emotional conflicts from the past. In other words, the memories, dreams, and associations that follow a breakdown of defenses and breakthrough of feelings help us make sense of the patient's conflicts and suffering. Once these conflicts are conscious, patient and therapist can reevaluate them from a new and healthier perspective. Then, what kept going wrong has a chance to go right (Malan, personal communication).

Spectrum of Disorders

All of the information gathered via inquiry helps us understand how the patient is internally structured and will assist us place him on the spectrum of psychopathology. On the left-hand side of the spectrum are patients who are highly functional and only have one area of conflict, say with romantic partners or authority figures. Their defenses are typically dystonic and anxiety is channeled into the striated muscles. These patients connect with the therapist easily and erect no barrier to being seen and known. These patients are relatively rare. More often, the patients who come to see us have multiple long-standing problems, along with entrenched and syntonic defenses, and unregulated anxiety. These patients, in the mid spectrum of psychopathology, constitute the bulk of most therapists' caseloads.

On the right hand side of the spectrum are patients with fragile ego structures, who experience cognitive-perceptual disruption in the face of anxiety. They tend to be incapacitated by their symptoms and experience significant impairment in daily functioning.

The patient's level of pathology determines the type and intensity of treatment they will require. Patients on the left side of spectrum respond to the standard technique of pressure to face and experience their true feelings, while those in the mid spectrum require restructuring of defenses before they can safely experience their complex mixed feelings toward others. More fragile patients on the right side of spectrum need a more ego-building and graded approach to this emotion-focused work.

Woman in a Fog—A Trial Therapy

The following case will be used to illustrate the process of a trial therapy, using the central dynamic sequence as a framework and guide. Davanloo (personal communication, 1989) suggests going into the initial session "blind" to the patient's history, in order to conduct our evaluation in the here and now, free of assumptions and premature conclusions.

A woman in her mid 30s came to see me for a three-hour consultation. I knew virtually nothing about her prior to our meeting, and started the inquiry with a blank slate. The patient entered the session about 10 minutes late and out of breath, as her train had been delayed. Since she was clearly flustered, I decided to begin by asking about her current emotional state. Her response gave me important diagnostic information.

Therapist: So how do you feel now that you are here?

Patient: Good. I think—it was nice taking the train in—it gave me some time to think about . . . ah . . . focus on my thoughts . . .

It is important to note that the patient didn't answer my question. Instead of telling me how she was feeling, she responded with a vague "good" and then moved on to her thoughts. I blocked the defense of intellectualization and asked the question again, in order to assess her ability to focus on and attend to her internal state, a prerequisite for dynamic psychotherapy. It is essential that the patient be helped to see the link between reliance on defenses against feelings and her symptoms.

Therapist: Before you go into that though, about your thoughts, are you aware that there is some anxiety right now, if you pay attention?

Patient: Yeah, I think I always have some anxiety (laughs).

Therapist: OK, but we don't want you ignoring that, laughing over it, because it's really important (blocking defenses). If you pay attention (inviting her to form a healthy relationship with herself), how are you noticing it? What is happening in your body that lets you know you are nervous?

Patient: I usually experience it as tightness in my chest.

Therapist: Is that there now? (Patient still not attending in the moment.)

Patient: A little bit.

Therapist: What else physically?

The patient responded well to this initial intervention, dropping the defense of intellectualization, and attending to her inner state of anxiety. She indicated that most of her anxiety was experienced as muscle tension, and noticed that it had been increasing lately. As she reported on her anxiety, a dismissive attitude toward her own feelings was noted. In particular, she tended to laugh off and minimize the chronic nature of her anxiety. I brought this to her attention. It is not enough for the therapist to see these defenses, but for the patient to see them and do something about them. If this is skipped over, the therapist will still be monitoring and managing defenses for the patient rather than encouraging her to develop this capacity. It is preferable to go slow in the beginning to help patients turn against defenses. Then, the process will go more quickly and smoothly in the end.

Linking Defenses to Presenting Problems

Therapist: But you say you're always anxious, which isn't funny—that's a terrible thing to have to walk around with.

Patient: Yeah, and it will swing back and forth between being anxious and then depressed. Sometimes it's both. A few weeks ago I was somewhere in between a panic attack and breaking down and crying.

Therapist: So somehow you know there is some kind of relationship between anxiety and depression, and you've had both, with some kind of upsurge recently, which has brought you here. So, let's start to look at what brought you here and what you are hoping to get out of our time together today (asking for specific details about the triggers to this upsurge in symptomatic distress).

Patient: Well, I think, I am in a place right now . . . maybe it's coming back to where I grew up . . . and in a place where I'm observing, rather than participating in it. I feel like, I'm just turning 36, and I feel like I'm just coming out of a fog, a 20-year fog, and I'm finding myself waking up from the fog and wondering, "Who am I? Who did I marry?" I have a 2-year-old daughter and I have some idea how I got here, but . . .

Therapist: So something about turning 36, coming back home, there is something about turning 36, coming back home, there is something precipitating an internal crisis, things are shifting around and you're asking yourself "What am I doing?"

Patient: I think it stems mainly from my marriage. I am really unhappy in my marriage and just really feeling that and thinking about that and what contributed to that.

Therapist: And what's happened in the last couple of months to bring that to a head?

Patient: Well, we've moved twice in the past year because my husband was laid off, so we moved once and stayed there for six months, then moved again and my whole world has kind of . . . there is a lot of instability. There has been a lot of anger about having to move (laughing). And I think it's brought up a lot of questioning, "Why am I here?"

Uprooting and moving for her husband's job was clearly the current precipitant to her distress. However, inquiry revealed that her tendency to ignore her feelings well pre-dated this recent problem and contributed significantly to her anxiety and depression. In fact, persistence in this internal focus yielded positive results, with information suggesting this pattern of living "in a fog" had been going on for 20 years, since adolescence. Given this, it would be a mistake to focus exclusively on the current problem with her husband. Rather, we began to see how this recent problem was simply the most recent manifestation of a conflict from the past that had been recycled over the years. Her habit of laughing off her feelings became our focus.

Pressure to Feelings

Therapist: His losing the jobs, uprooting, moving, has been the recent precipitant and there are a lot of angry feelings coming up toward him. Do you notice how you laugh every time you mention these angry feelings toward him? There are obviously feelings, but it isn't funny, right?

Patient: No.

Therapist: So what is the laughing then? (Assessing whether the patient is able to identify the purpose and cost of her defensive avoidance and dismissal of feelings.)

Patient: Trying to defuse it.

Therapist: How it that going to help you though? You have come here to have an honest look at what is going on inside, to develop an intimate relationship with yourself, to get out of this fog, to get clear about what you want, you feel, so if you keep laughing it off and skimming the surface, what will happen to your time here?

Patient: Yeah, it will be wasted.

This is a very positive response. Not only was the patient aware that she was doing something to avoid her own feelings, but that continuing to do so would result in a waste of our time and ultimate therapeutic failure. On the other hand, this alone won't get us very far. It's not enough to see what's wrong. There must be a commitment to doing something healthy instead. Coupling interventions designed to turn patients against defenses, while encouraging them to face what they have been avoiding, is most effective.

Persistence in our exploration of the ways in which the patient was dealing with her own feelings in the session revealed a long-standing problem in this area. Until and unless the patient is able to develop a healthy relationship with herself, she will be crippled in her ability to do so with others. The patient went on to reveal more information about this pattern, helping us understand its origin. At the same time, a repetition of this pattern in the therapy was blocked and a new, healthy way of relating to herself was encouraged. In this way, therapy was already taking place, even though we were still "officially" in the inquiry and assessment phase of treatment. Again, it is response to intervention that gives us the most accurate and current information about the nature of the patient's conflicts and her current capacity to engage in the therapeutic task. Therefore, we begin to intervene right away and often see progress happening rapidly. No time is wasted in helping patients begin to make healthy choices.

Therapist: And as long as that's the case, it's almost impossible to have a healthy relationship with someone else. I see there is some feeling coming up as we look at this unhealthy way you've been relating to yourself. What's coming up?

Patient: It's interesting when you say, "You don't take yourself seriously." I've been feeling this way since I was a teenager. I was really passionate about a number of things, but never took myself seriously.

As the patient started to examine a 20-year pattern of self-neglect and self-sabotage, deep feelings of pain and sadness emerged. Experiencing the painful consequences of these defenses helped motivate her to abandon them. Consequently, the work deepened and the alliance was strengthened.

Identification of Self-Defeating Pattern

Therapist: And it's been going on for a long time. So, it's almost like there are two parts of you—this really healthy, vital, passionate part of you that's been there since adolescence, in which you were really clear what you were passionate about, but there's this other part of you that hasn't supported you or taken you seriously. Is it just neglect, or . . . ? (Highlighting the conflict.)

Patient: It's almost sabotage, in a way. Self-neglect, but it's self-destructive, I think.

Instead of laughing off her distress or minimizing it, the patient declared that this pattern of behavior was self-destructive. So we already see a shift from taking a negligent and dismissive attitude toward herself, to the adoption of a very serious one instead. Details regarding the nature and origin of this 20-year-long self-destructive pattern followed. Whenever she started to experience success—in school or in sports—she would quit and give up. Even when she had enthusiastic support from coaches, she would abandon the sport in which she was excelling.

As we explored the origin of this pattern of self-sabotage, fresh information emerged spontaneously from the patient. These memories came on the heels of strong emotion and were a clear indication of healthy strivings and a fortified alliance. She was beginning to see how she had played out her inner conflicts in all spheres of her life, not just with her husband.

Difficulties With Closeness

Therapist: You're alerting us to something else really important, so I want to underline it. You have a way of detaching, not only from your own feelings, but from others—you don't go all in, always holding something back. So I sense a double sadness right now—the loss of the job and the sadness that you weren't fully there when you were there and let something precious go.

Patient: Exactly. Just last night I was out to dinner with old friends from high school and it was that same feeling of sadness that I wasn't really there when I was with them. Last night I was so appreciative of these women, from whom I felt so distant and emotionally detached. I had such trouble making deep and abiding friendships.

Therapist: Right, so that's the other primary issue. So are you aware, that even here with me, especially when you're talking—like now I'm talking and you look at me, but when you're talking your eyes are all over and it looks like it's difficult to be fully present and connected. Are you aware of that? A tendency to keep a distance not only from your own feelings but from others.

Patient: Yeah, yeah, I've noticed that.

Therapist: When did you get afraid to be close and start to erect a wall?

Patient: As far as I can remember, my parents divorced when I was finishing 6th grade and going into Middle School.

Therapist: Where were you living?

Patient: Outside Denver. But, yeah, that's definitely when the self-destructive behavior began and the inability to focus on meaningful friendships with girls and really focusing on boys. It was just one after the other.

Therapist: What happens to the feelings you have toward your father?

Patient: I just remember being so angry. And at another point, I remember walking out of the high school and there was a girl on my team who lived nearby and you could see her house from the field. I remember looking down and seeing my father coming out of her house in his pajamas. I was devastated. You've got to be kidding me—he is sleeping with one of my teammate's mothers?

The patient was talking about being angry with her father, but was getting tearful and weepy. Her tendency to cover up anger with tears and sadness was the very mechanism responsible for her depression. However, she had trouble connecting with the anger toward her father from so long ago. She spontaneously mentioned having no trouble feeling this anger toward her husband. She went on to identify a recent situation in which anger toward her husband was triggered, but not expressed. Since this was the precipitant to her seeking a consultation at this time, it was essential that we examine these feelings carefully.

Patient: My birthday was yesterday. He knew, but he was boarding an airplane and he didn't say anything. He was just chatting.

Therapist: So how are you feeling, if you pay attention?

Patient: Annoyed and pissed.

Therapist: Can you feel that inside, if you don't smile over it?

Patient: Tight.

Therapist: OK, is that anger or tension and anxiety?

Patient: Anxiety.

Therapist: It's anxiety and constriction. So if you allow yourself to feel the anger, how do you feel that anger inside, right now?

Patient: Right now? Um . . . well, I have a vision of a lion breathing down.

Therapist: Yeah, and can you also feel the power of that that wants to come up and out like a lion?

Patient: Yeah!

Therapist: So, in your imagination, if that came out—this primitive animal rage—what do you see yourself doing? What is the impulse toward him?

Patient: Roar. Tear him up. Clawing him.

Therapist: Where?

Patient: His face.

Therapist: What's it like to begin to acknowledge this?

Patient: Kind of releases the tension. I have been tearing him apart with words—making "biting" remarks, criticizing him and being on his case.

Therapist: So this is what we have to look at. Instead of playing this out, which is destructive, let's look at this. In your imagination, if you totally lost control and the lion came out, what do you see happening in your imagination?

Patient: Um . . . teeth gnashing, roaring, and probably dismembering him.

Therapist: Yeah, so how do you see that, how do you do that? Dismembering, how?

Patient: Disemboweling him (biting her lip).

Therapist: And there is also biting. If you don't censor yourself, to protect him.

Patient: It's this shutdown I start to feel.

Therapist: So that came right after wanting to bite him. So there was something about that—biting him where?

Patient: His neck.

Therapist: Go for the jugular, which would do what?

Patient: Kill him. Then, uh . . . then I just feel so guilty about it, being so angry with him. I feel guilty about that.

It was essential to help this patient access all her mixed feelings toward her husband so she could deal with them in a healthy way and not simply act them out in a self-destructive fashion. Initially, anxiety replaced anger. Then, following the impulse to bite, the patient started to shut down, instantly repressing the wish to kill her husband. These defensive mechanisms needed to be blocked in order to facilitate the direct experience of feelings and impulses, and to prevent a return or exacerbation of symptoms. In order to facilitate the experience of mixed feelings toward him, it is of the utmost importance to face the impact of the rage on him—to look at his face and the damage done.

Therapist: So when you look at him dead, what do you see in his face, in his eyes? What position is he in?

Patient: He's just lying on the ground.

Therapist: What's happening now?

Patient: I'm having a hard time. It's like I am shutting down.

Therapist: Shutting down, right? Rather than to face and feel the guilt over your destructive rage toward someone you love, you just go to self-punishment—shut down, kill off your own feelings, your own vitality. You go cold yourself rather than to feel those mixed feelings. You feel guilty because you also love him. 'Cause if he actually died and you got a phone call today that his plane crashed and he's dead . . . what kind of feelings? (Here we begin to see the driver of her self-sabotage—punishment over guilt about rage toward loved ones who have betrayed or neglected her.)

Patient: I mean, I just, I have completely shut down those feelings for him.

Therapist: So you mean it would be "hallelujah!"

Patient: Yeah—like that would be the answer. I have definitely been having those feelings and fantasies.

Therapist: What kind of fantasies? How do you kill him off in your mind?

Patient: This is terrible. He rides his bike to the train station and if he's a few minutes late I think, maybe he was killed.

Therapist: Then, how do you imagine him dead? He is hit by a car?

Patient: A bus (with great emphasis).

Therapist: A bus. And he has been on a bicycle. So how does he end up, what is the picture and how does he actually die?

Patient: Well, ah, he is essentially crushed.

Therapist: I see, he actually gets run over and crushed.

Patient: It's a very violent hit.

Therapist: This massive rage that just flattens him, crushes him and he is killed. So, when you imagine that, his bloody, smashed body on the pavement, what do you see in his eyes and on his face?

Patient: (Patient starts to cry.) Oh, I just see how sweet he is.

Therapist: Just let yourself feel that. There is a very painful feeling of guilt and, under that, love for this sweet man.

Patient:	Yeah.
Therapist:	So, when this feeling comes up, what do you want to do?
Patient:	Hold him.
Therapist:	How do you hold him?
Patient:	Cradle him. Say I am sorry for being so mean.
Therapist:	Just let yourself feel that—deep feelings of guilt and remorse for how mean and cruel you have been—pushing away someone who loves you.

With the therapist's help, the patient was able to face and experience all her mixed feelings toward her husband, including rage, guilt, and love. In so doing the patient could suddenly and clearly see the ways in which she had been acting this out in an automatic, unconscious fashion—pushing him away, belittling him, killing off his confidence, and fantasizing about replacing him with her old boyfriend. The guilt she experienced regarding her hostility toward him triggered deep feelings of love, with a wish to repair the damage done. Further, links between past and present were made spontaneously. She started to see that she had identified with her father, and was treating her husband and her mother the way he had treated her. These emotional insights were very painful to her and provided a deeply felt desire to turn it around. This breakthrough of feeling was achieved in the first hour and a half session. We had an hour break for lunch and started the next session with an examination of the impact the morning's work had on her.

Session After the Break: Making Links and Consolidating Insights

Patient:	I found as I was walking around that, just walking, my gait felt a little freer. I was thinking that, right before I got married, I did this body work, like Rolfing. The woman who I worked with always said, "You have to loosen your hips up—you are so tight." And I could really feel, walking around here, that it dawned on me, there is this connection. She would say, "You are so beautiful, you should allow your femininity to come through," but I couldn't do it. Now, I could just feel it in my walk.
Therapist:	Right—so that's the same word you used when you said, "I feel like I can own these feelings now."
Patient:	Yeah, and it felt good to me. There have been times when I am a certain way or act a certain way for other people. But walking around just felt good to me.

It should be noted that the patient looked quite different after the break. Her hair, which had been tied back, was loosely falling over her shoulders. Her whole appearance was softer and more feminine. This coincided with her report of the internal experience of looseness and freedom within her body. This was a significant shift, not only in the feelings she was having in her body, but the meaning of it. In the past, she has been highly reactive to others, either complying or defying their wishes. Now she was talking about owning her own feelings and having a sense of being herself—for no one else.

Patient: Peaceful. Then, things just started coming to me and pieces were all falling together. I had a sudden urge to call my mother and connect with her. I was thinking about how it must have been so hard for my mother. I wanted to apologize. I was such a difficult adolescent. I just feel bad. Now that I'm a mother. I can't even imagine. I used to sneak out at night. I feel terrible to put her through that.

Therapist: Just like your father did.

Patient: Yeah! For so long I've been angry with her for not being there for me. When my Dad left, she had to go back to work and my siblings were already off in college—so I was left alone with it all. I was blaming her—and my Dad—but, because he's so unavailable and incapable of sitting down and talking about it, she's been the one to talk to. I think the shift I noticed, out there walking around, instead of blaming her, was feeling more of a shared experience. We were both in a really difficult place.

Therapist: And you were both left by your Dad. So, of course you had angry feelings, sad feelings—so did she—and it sounds like you wish you could have gone through that together.

Patient: It's a similar dynamic with my husband—instead of, especially in this last year, when he's been laid off, we've just been at each other, as opposed to sharing.

Therapist: Oh, so that's really important to see that parallel—going after each other rather than going through the feelings together.

Patient: Yeah, really being friends to each other and lovers.

Therapist: So, there is a shift. You feel that awakening for some desire for closeness, with your mother and your husband.

Patient: And I think it was—there seems to be a similar terror—like I had the same kind of wish but fear of wanting to be close, but being terrified of being close. It's the same that I had with my Mom. Right now, it's interesting to view—to experience and look at my marriage as being a more similar dynamic to my mother than. . . .

Therapist: That's the good news, because that's a healthier relationship and it was a healthy shift when you finally said good-bye to Patrick and that whole dynamic, saying "I'm not going to do that anymore." But then, for some reason, you find you're afraid to get too close and you push away those who are more capable of love and connection. Why would you do that?

Patient: I think because my parents' divorce was so sudden. It was just kind of seemed to be chugging along and normal and relatively happy.

Therapist: So on some deep unconscious level, deciding "I'm never going to let that happen again."
Patient: Yeah.
Therapist: To let down my guard, be close and happy, because out of the blue something like this can happen.
Patient: Yeah.
Therapist: But, what's the alternative?
Patent: I've lived the alternative and it's miserable.

As the therapist helped the patient to attend to her inner life—to feel these painful and anxiety-provoking feelings and impulses—instead of suppressing them or acting them out in a destructive fashion, we were able to get to the root cause of the conflict. The links between unresolved feelings from the past regarding her parents' divorce, and what she was playing out in her current life, became crystal clear. Instead of berating herself, shutting down, distancing from loved ones and criticizing them, she felt compassion for herself, her mother, and her husband. Furthermore, she was determined to do things differently in her own life, rather than repeat the past. She could see how protecting herself by keeping a distance and pushing away a loving husband, was simply a continuation of a self-destructive pattern that originated in adolescence. Having faced the guilt over her rage, positive feelings and memories began to surface.

De-Repression: New Memories Surface

Of note, during the morning session, the patient reported that she couldn't remember ever feeling passion for her husband, and wondered if she had simply made a safe choice for a nice guy who was little more than a friend and companion. Having gotten through defenses to her true feelings, old but vivid memories returned.

Patient: I'm just kind of remembering times, before it started to disintegrate, I'm starting to feel more of the security and peacefulness.
Therapist: What were some of those memories, of the times you felt that—secure?
Patient: I'm thinking about the first time we made love. I have this memory of lying in bed together. It was just something about his body that seemed calm and present. It was just kind of simple and uncomplicated.
Therapist: What is the feeling you get in touch with when you go back to that?
Patient: I still, it's like, I feel it in my chest—but it's not the tight constricted feeling, it's more a warm feeling. The other thing I remembered after the morning, when I had trouble remembering when we were passionate with each other. I remember, on our honeymoon, how we were just devouring each other.

Therapist: What do you remember about devouring each other? What it was like to feel that kind of desire?

Patient: It felt wonderful and I—the whole honeymoon, I wanted so badly to get pregnant. I had never felt that way before but . . .

Therapist: A deep opening of receptivity—letting him inside you and wanting his child.

Having distinguished the past from the present, and getting in touch with loving, passionate feelings toward her husband, the patient had a new perspective from which to view her life.

Consolidation of Insights

Therapist: So it seems like you have put a lot together and have also had a pretty deep experience of all the mixed feelings under that sense of being shut down, right? So, how do you feel about what we've been able to do today and where do you feel you are?

Patient: I think this morning was . . . I was really surprised by the feelings that came up and, uh, and, in some ways, glad I married someone more like my mother than my father.

Therapist: You can thank that healthy part of you, right?

Patient: And, yeah, understanding that, or working a little bit on the self-sabotage that I've created or perpetuated against myself. I don't want to live the rest of my life doing that.

Therapist: And we could see that the engine to that—like why would you suddenly start doing that after your parents divorced? It was a self-destructive way to deal with the feelings about that. You weren't being supported in any way to express or share.

Patient: Yeah, um . . . yeah. I think my—I feel like I have more clarity on what the dynamics are at play—which is incredibly helpful.

Therapist: How do you feel about having supported yourself to get what you wanted and reach your goal?

Patient: Physically I—I don't feel much of the tension. And, it's hard to describe but it feels—I feel—freer.

Therapist: Can you actually feel good about yourself and proud that you did it and in a short amount of time?

Patient: Yeah, yeah. And I kind of feel, what's the big deal if I just go home and—I think I can just go to Patrick and say, "This is what I'm upset about." I don't have to be defensive.

Therapist: You can do it—with him, with your Mom—to let friends back in?

Patient: Yeah,

Therapist: Great. Pretty amazing work you've been able to do today. It's been such a pleasure to be able to work with you.

Patient: Thank you. I think what was really powerful for me was when you would point out that I would laugh—that was really powerful for me. Thank you for making me aware of that.

Therapist: You're welcome.

Securely attached children express love and affection freely. The can also express reactive pain and rage when affectionate bonds are disrupted (Bowlby, 1969). These affects alert caretakers that the child is in distress and requires attention and attunement. When such attunement is lacking, or the child's basic needs and feelings are thwarted, neglected, or punished, intensely mixed feelings toward attachment figures is stimulated. Without help and support to experience and process such intense mixed feelings, the overwhelming anxiety and guilt over rage toward loved ones that is generated often goes into a self-destructive pathway. Feelings that can't be expressed either get repressed or acted out, creating symptoms and suffering.

"The Woman in a Fog" is a good example of this very dynamic. In the process of a three-hour "trial therapy" therapist and patient were able to identify and resolve her core conflict regarding feelings from the past triggered by recent events with her husband. In the past, these feelings had been avoided in a self-destructive manner. She had good, secure, early attachments and had lots of strengths. However, when her parents suddenly divorced, she was left alone with intense mixed feelings toward both her parents that were more than she could manage. Her mother, who had stayed home to raise the children, was now suddenly thrust back into the working world and worrying about providing for her family, while dealing with her own sorrow and rage. Her father simply took off and wasn't available to process any of these feelings. At the same time, all her siblings were away in college. Being left alone to deal with these feelings greatly increased the likelihood that they would get expressed indirectly, in a self-destructive manner.

Without intervention at this crucial time in her life, she might have simply repeated the past, divorced her husband, and exposed her son to the very kind of rupture she experienced in her own family of origin. By facing and experiencing her feelings about the present and the past, new options for healing were made available.

The Therapist Factor

In order to achieve the best and most consistent results, we need to practice what we preach and demonstrate the kind of clear and direct style of communication we are seeking from our patients. This means that the therapist must ask specific and targeted questions, rather than vague, open-ended ones (as many of us were taught to do years ago). If the therapist asks general questions, we can hardly make hay out of the fact that the patient responds in kind.

In contrast, if the therapist asks specific questions and the patient doesn't answer the question, or does so in a vague and noncommittal fashion, that tells us something important about him. Sometimes the patient even goes so far as to say he has no problem. The obvious question of why he is sitting in a therapist's office needs to be asked! Often patients show us the problems they cannot articulate. Such was the case here. The patient came into the session reporting a problem with her husband. Careful attention to the patient's pattern of behavior revealed a more pervasive problem of self-neglect and self-sabotage, which became the focus of a very brief and successful treatment. This highlights the importance of learning to read, and then verbalize, what is being communicated nonverbally. In addition, the abilities to assess and monitor anxiety, block and restructure defenses, and facilitate the deep, visceral experience of complex mixed feelings toward others, including the therapist, are vital skills for the dynamic therapist to develop in order to intervene as quickly and effectively as possible.

Summary

The notion that there are discrete disease entities responsible for emotional disorders is increasingly questioned, although it remains all too common in our field. Seeing a patient as "a borderline," for example, is tantamount to conflating the person with her symptoms. In fact, quite a lot of evidence has been accumulating to suggest that disorders such as depression, anxiety, and even schizophrenia and bipolar disorder seem to "merge imperceptibly with no demonstrable borders between them" (Barlow et al., 2011). The alternative to the descriptive diagnosis of discrete disorders is a "trans-diagnostic approach" (Barlow et al., 2011; Kring & Sloan, 2010), designed to target the underlying mechanisms responsible for symptoms. Then, a therapeutic approach, based on the science of what works to activate and resolve the unconscious conflicts responsible for the patient's symptoms and suffering, must be utilized to facilitate healing and resolution.

Intensive Short-Term Dynamic Psychotherapy is just such an approach. This model of treatment integrates all six factors associated with brain and behavior change. Outcome research suggests it is highly cost and clinically effective across a wide spectrum of patients.

Rather than treating symptoms alone, the dynamic therapist endeavors to treat the underlying cause of the symptoms and, in so doing, boost adaptive functioning and facilitate cure. By including specific interventions associated with brain and behavior change in adults, including a tight focus, identifying and intensifying anxiety-laden conflicts, helping patients recognize and turn against defenses, and facilitating the visceral experience of previously avoided feelings, therapeutic outcomes can be significantly enhanced.

In addition to assessing the nature, severity, and history of the patient's disorders, it is essential to assess her current capacity to do this kind of emotion-focused work. That assessment must include the patient's ability to tolerate and regulate anxiety, the nature and tenacity of defenses, the ability to experience and observe her feelings on multiple levels, and a willingness to cooperate and let the therapist close enough to help. Assessing the patient's strengths and capacities, in order to work at her highest level of tolerance, and in order to create a strong alliance with her healthy strivings, is essential in getting the treatment off to an effective start.

While the therapist's presence, engagement, and enthusiasm about the process are essential ingredients for success in psychotherapy, it is also of paramount importance that she employ a specific treatment model. Having a theoretical model in mind enables the therapist to organize and make sense of a great deal of data, which could otherwise be overwhelming. Further, "Without a treatment, there can be no collaborative effort to establish goals of therapy, and the therapist and client cannot agree on the tasks needed to accomplish the goals . . ." (Duncan, 2010, p. 62). In the case of dynamic psychotherapy, our focus is on the internal conflicts giving rise to the patient's symptoms and suffering. In order to discover what these forces are, a very specific and tightly focused inquiry must be performed. Further, we need specific approaches to disentangle these conflicts, such that new and more adaptive strategies can replace them. This point is one worth reiterating. Without a clear and comprehensive case conceptualization, based on our theoretical model, we will not be able to approach treatment in a systematic and thoughtful manner (McWilliams, 2011; Pebbles-Kleiger, 2002; Shedler, 2014). It is important to note that conceptualizations are hypotheses that are fluid and constantly being modified, based on the patient's response to intervention. An example of an initial consultation was included to elucidate this process.

Chapter Three
Anxiety: Assessment and Regulation

In this chapter, anxiety will be defined in concrete and operational terms, with a particular focus on the internal experience of anxiety and its regulation. Anxiety is a biophysiological response to (often unconsciously) perceived challenges and threats to emotional safety, autonomy, and connection. As such, it is experienced physically, in the body. Anxiety is not a thought ("I'm so worried I won't have enough money to retire"), or a stimulus ("abandonment"), but a visceral, bodily experience. Given this, it is essential that therapists learn to observe nonverbal signs of anxiety, rather than relying solely on the patient's verbal report. Methods for assessing, tracking, and regulating anxiety, in order to maintain an optimal level of activation, will be outlined and illustrated in this chapter. Doing so deepens the healing process and speeds recovery.

Freud's Second Theory of Anxiety

It wasn't until relatively late in his career that Freud came to recognize the internal cause and function of anxiety. In his paper, "Inhibitions, Symptoms and Anxiety," Freud (1926) outlined his second theory of anxiety, suggesting that anxiety works as a *signal* that feelings and impulses experienced as "dangerous" have been activated and are threatening to come into consciousness.

Since human beings are dependent for so long, any thought, feeling, or action that can threaten the bond with caretakers is experienced as threatening, activates anxiety, and tends to be avoided thereafter (creating defenses). Any feeling or impulse, even loving ones, can be associated with anxiety, if early caretakers respond in a negative way to such emotions. It is not only anger that can be forbidden. Feelings of love and tenderness are often rejected and prohibited as well (Sutie, 1999). Observing and tracking the patient's level of anxiety as various affects get activated provide the clinician valuable information about the nature of the patient's emotional conflicts.

This was really the beginning of attachment theory (Della Selva, 1993). It is in this context that we must understand anxiety. Anxiety does not exist in a vacuum. It is not a disorder in and of itself, anymore than a fever is. Rather, both anxiety and a fever are signs of an underlying disturbance. In the case of anxiety, the signal indicates that something is off kilter within the patient's internal emotional system, in his relationships to others, or both.

Anxiety regarding mixed feelings toward loved ones is almost inevitable. No one can hurt us most deeply or evoke more intense anger than those we need and love. When we feel enraged with the same person we love and depend upon for our very survival, anxiety and guilt will be stimulated, and conflict will be experienced. It is easy to see how we are designed for these conflicting feelings and impulses, since we have evolved to have three brains in one head! On a primitive, reptilian level, we may feel the impulse to lash out and attack a loved one who has hurt or threatened us. At the same time, the limbic system has been wired for love and attachment, motivating us to protect loved ones from harm. Add to that the neo-cortical awareness that such violent behavior is morally wrong, and the conditions are ripe for an intense conflict over mixed feelings toward others to develop. Helping patients to become aware of, tolerate, and process these complex mixed feelings, without undue anxiety or the need to rely on destructive defenses, constitutes a large part of the therapeutic task. This process enables patients to get on friendly terms with their feelings, so they can use the energy and information they provide to take constructive action.

What Triggers Anxiety?

Therapists, as well as patients, often get confused about the distinction between the external *stimulus* generating anxiety and the internal *experience* of anxiety itself. This gives rise to errors in causation. To speak of "separation anxiety" is to merge the experience of anxiety (again, a biophysiological response) with its trigger—separation. In addition, these phrases fail to recognize that the strong *feelings* evoked by the separation, rather than the separation itself, are often the cause of anxiety in adults. While dependent children can die if left alone, this is rarely the case with adults. Separation from a loved one is not dangerous in and of itself, but the feelings that the separation evokes can certainly trigger anxiety and be experienced as quite threatening.

It is a therapist's job to help his patient understand what is actually causing her anxiety. A patient might say, "I am afraid of my professor. He yelled at me in class and now I'm not going to lectures." Just such a case was the recent trigger for a debate between some CBT therapists and their dynamic colleagues. The CBT therapist in this case accepted the patient's version of the problem (fear of professor) at face value. Given this understand of the problem, the recommended solution involved teaching the patient breathing techniques to reduce anxiety, so that she could attend lectures, and then confront what she had been avoiding. Despite the fact that the patient was able to learn these breathing exercises and use them in the therapist's office, she continued to avoid going to class.

The dynamic therapist reviewing this case suggested looking inward, at the patient's *feelings* toward the professor. In fact, a focus on the patient's feelings toward the professor in the safe confines of the therapist's office resulted in an increase of anxiety. Since the professor was not in the consulting room—or anywhere near the place—the fact that the patient was still nervous, suggested that she was actually anxious about her feelings toward him. Treatment efforts focused on helping the patient identify and process feelings of anger toward the professor. Once these feelings were approached and experienced (and eventually tied to an authority figure from the past), the patient's anxiety disappeared. Of note, this rapid reduction in anxiety was experienced only after the "forbidden" feelings and impulses were consciously experienced. Since her anxiety was tolerable, continued movement toward anxiety-provoking feelings and impulses was indicated. In this way, the therapist was able to intervene at the patient's optimal level of activation and, in so doing, achieve rapid resolution of the presenting problem. It is important to note that, in such cases, anxiety no longer needs to be managed, because it is no longer triggered. The patient was now on friendly terms with her feelings and understood their origin. No longer anxious about her anger, she could use these feelings in a constructive manner when necessary. She returned to class and had no trouble completing the course.

The Benefits of Anxiety

In the past, both psychoanalytic and behavioral approaches warned against the dangers of evoking anything more than very mild anxiety during sessions, with the idea that anxiety could somehow harm the patient and undermine treatment (Barlow, 2010). Perhaps as a result of such a cautious approach, early research found few positive effects from psychotherapy (Bergin, 1966; Bergin & Strupp, 1972). While Yerkes and Dodson (1908) discovered a vital link between anxiety arousal and performance early in the 1900s, it took many decades for this information to be integrated into our understanding of therapeutic change (Diamond, Campbell, Park, Halonen, & Zoladz, 2007; Lupien, Maheu, Tu, Fiocco, & Schranck, 2007; Moran, Taylor, & Moser, 2012). While high and unregulated levels of anxiety can cause great suffering, moderate levels of anxiety heighten awareness and enhances performance (Yerkes & Dodson, 1908). In fact, moderate levels of anxiety are *required* for neural growth and new learning in adults—an idea that has started to gain traction in the literature once again (Ogden et al. 2005; Siegel, 2001, 2009b). Recent neuroscientific studies (Doidge, 2007; Lupien, Maheu, Tu, Fiocco, & Schranck, 2007) have underscored the need to induce moderate levels of anxiety for brain change to take place in adults (Figure 3.1). Most therapists know how to reduce anxiety, but

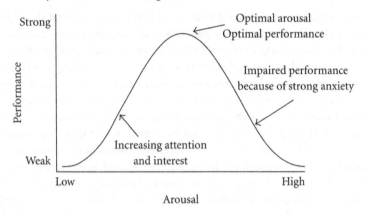

Figure 3.1 Optimal Level of Anxiety
Source: Yerkes & Dodson (1908)

few have been taught to actually simulate anxiety by increasing pressure on patients to get emotionally involved in the process. Just such an approach is necessary to get detached and emotionally controlled patients into the optimal range of activation, where change can happen.

Research Findings

Recent research supports the notion that anxiety is reliably reduced once the feelings giving rise to the anxiety are experienced freely (Pitman, Slavin-Mulford, & Hilsenroth, 2014; Wilborg & Dahl, 1996). Pitman, Slavin-Mulford, and Hilsenroth (2014) demonstrated that "high levels of psychodynamic-interpersonal techniques early in treatment were significantly and positively related to the amount of reliable change in anxiety symptoms" (p. 393) over the course of treatment. These techniques included: (1) the process of identifying the patient's feelings, wishes, and fantasies; (2) linking current feelings to unresolved feelings from the past; (3) highlighting recurrent interpersonal patterns; and (4) helping patients understand themselves in a new way, allowing for fresh alternatives. Results of this study suggested that an examination of the therapeutic relationship was most effective *after* the feelings, wishes, and fantasies from the past had been elucidated. In this way, the patient was able to see what he was attempting to reenact in the present, what was unresolved from the past. At termination, 76% of these patients, who suffered from both anxiety disorders and had an Axis II diagnosis, scored in the normal range on anxiety (assessed by the BSI). Once again, this suggests that therapeutic strategies designed to activate the feelings giving rise to the patient's anxiety are effective in achieving lasting change for those experiencing high and poorly regulated anxiety.

By increasing the patients' ability to tolerate the anxiety inherent in approaching previously avoided feelings, wishes, and goals, we are helping them live more powerfully. When we encourage patients to avoid or down-regulate anxiety unnecessarily, they may experience some temporary relief, but often continue to suffer in the real world. An interesting study on the treatment of panic disorder with agoraphobia (Craske & Barlow, 2008) underscored this finding. They discovered that reducing anxiety through breathing exercises and relaxation actually *undermined* recovery. Conversely, exposure to anxiety-provoking feelings and impulses proved far more effective in the long run. Just such a result was recounted in the previous example of the student "afraid of her professor."

Both clinical and research evidence suggest that helping patients increase their tolerance for anxiety, rather than reducing anxiety alone, is the most effective treatment strategy. In this way, patient and therapist can move ahead, to the underlying feelings and conflicts responsible for increased anxiety. The authors (Craske & Barlow, 2008), noted that patients with panic and agoraphobia had significant conflicts between their desire for autonomy and dependency. Dealing with this underlying conflict, rather than the symptom of anxiety alone, increased treatment effectiveness. The fact that this study was conducted by therapists who identify themselves as practicing Cognitive Behavioral Therapy speaks to the increasing ubiquity of interventions that are both dynamic and emotion-focused. This fact also underscores the need to examine what therapists actually do, rather than what they call it.

Assessment: Evaluating the Level and Degree of Anxiety

How do we make sure that patients are experiencing anxiety at their own optimal level, where change is most likely to take place? Yogi Berra, that great 20th-century philosopher, suggested, "You can observe a lot by watching." Davanloo (1990, 2000), did just that, by videotaping therapy sessions and studying the process. In so doing, he made significant discoveries about anxiety and its signaling function. He has identified three main "channels" of anxiety, each of which reflects the patient's current level of anxiety tolerance and has important diagnostic significance. These pathways of anxiety include: (1) striated or voluntary muscle tension, (2) smooth or involuntary muscle activation, and (3) cognitive/perceptual disruption.

CHANNELS OF ANXIETY

- STRIATED MUSCLES: Hand Clenching and Sighing Respiration
- SMOOTH MUSCLES: Migraine, IBS, Hypertension
- COGNITIVE DISRUPTION: Dissociation, Dizziness, Fainting/Fugue States, Visual and Auditory Changes

---

Ultimately, the best way to assess these pathways of anxiety, as well as the patient's ability to tolerate the anxiety involved in the process of uncovering, is to focus in and pressure/invite/encourage the patient to experience the feelings giving rise to this anxiety. "The *pressure* to emotionally engage, mobilizes complex feelings related to past attachments and this, in turn, mobilizes anxiety and defense in the office" (Abbass & Town, 2013, p. 434). In this way, the therapist is able to obtain the most timely and accurate assessment of the patient's current level of anxiety tolerance. If, and only if, anxiety is being experienced as muscle tension, can the underlying feelings and impulses be explored in a safe and therapeutic manner.

If there is no "signal anxiety" in the voluntary muscles, the patient is either defending against feelings with detachment and isolation of affect, or his anxiety is too high and is affecting smooth muscle or interfering with cognitive-perceptual clarity. Failure to make this crucial assessment can result in an exacerbation of symptoms. Careful inquiry and observation is required in order to keep anxiety in the optimal range.

Striated Muscle Anxiety

Patients who experience or "channel" their anxiety into the striated or voluntary muscles are typically aware that they are anxious, and associate muscle tension with that anxiety. The ability to be consciously aware of anxiety, and to bind anxiety in muscle tension, demonstrates a fairly high level of ego adaptive capacity. Sighing respiration and hand clenching are the cardinal signs of anxiety activation in the striated muscles. Striated muscle activation is a green light (ten Have de Labije & Neborsky, 2012), suggesting that it is safe to explore the feelings triggering that anxiety. Patients who channel their anxiety into striated muscles are able to benefit from the standard technique designed by Davanloo (1990) to "unlock the unconscious." By focusing on the experience of feelings underneath the anxiety and blocking defenses, the therapy can operate at an optimal level for new learning and neural growth.

While muscle tension is typically a sign of high capacity, chronic tension can still have debilitating effects on health and well-being. Patients who are chronically anxious and physically tense often develop somatic pain, as well as fatigue and depression, as a direct result of using so much energy to contain their feelings and impulses. Research suggests that facilitating the visceral experience of the feelings underneath this tension is both cost and clinically effective in the treatment of chronic headache, backache, pelvic pain, and fibromyalgia, as well as anxiety and depression (Abbass, Lovas, & Purdy, 2008; Abbass, Town, & Driessen, 2012; Sarno, 1999, 2006; Schubiner, 2011; Town, Hardy, McCullough, & Stride, 2012).

Smooth Muscle Anxiety

The second channel of anxiety is that of the smooth (involuntary) muscles, including those in the gastrointestinal tract, blood vessels, and airways, resulting in symptoms such as migraines, asthma, irritable bowel syndrome, and hypertension. Patients with somatic channels of anxiety are often completely unaware that they are anxious, and mistake their anxiety symptoms for medical conditions. While the patient's pain and suffering are very real, there is often no organic basis for their chronic condition (of course, this must be evaluated carefully and not assumed). Such patients are often referred to mental health professionals after countless medical tests fail to uncover a biological basis for their symptoms.

In order to diagnose the emotional factors contributing to physical symptoms, it is essential to track the patient carefully. In particular, observing the sudden onset of symptoms as painful emotions are approached is the key required to help patients make the link between anxiety associated with emotions and physical symptoms. Since patients who channel their anxiety into smooth muscles confuse their physical symptoms with emotional activation, a step-wise restructuring approach is required to built capacity for anxiety and affect tolerance. Pressing for the experience of feelings is only safe once the patient's anxiety is experienced in the striated muscles. Otherwise, pressure to feelings can result in an exacerbation of symptoms.

Cognitive-Perceptual Disruption

Finally, the third pathway of unconscious anxiety involves cognitive-perceptual disruption, including visual blurring, ringing of the ears, alteration or constriction of the visual field, mental confusion, dizziness, dissociation, and even hallucinations. Catching the drifting and confusion characteristic of cognitive-perceptual disruption as soon as it is evident is essential to prevent destructive and regressive defenses from infecting the therapeutic process. Without such intervention, we may lose contact with the patient. Silence is to be avoided in such cases, as anxiety and paranoia will only increase in the absence of the therapist's authentic presence. Instead, reaching out to the patient actively, and speaking to him about his anxiety, is both necessary and therapeutic. Anxiety is rapidly reduced when pressure to explore the feelings is eliminated, while an exclusive focus on the physiological experience of anxiety is encouraged. Once anxiety has diminished and cognitive clarity has been restored, links to the feelings and conflicts responsible for the spike in anxiety must be made. This kind of cognitive understanding of the patient's internal emotional life is required to build capacity and develop insight. We want to help these patients "mentalize" so they can think about their emotional responses rather than becoming confused and symptomatic (Fonagy, Gergely, Jurist, & Target, 2005).

Anxiety Tolerance

In order to intervene effectively, therapists must assess the level and channel of anxiety, as well as the patient's capacity to tolerate anxiety without resorting to defenses. A balance between experiencing and reflecting is necessary for the optimal experience of anxiety, as well as therapeutic progress. Careful attention to the phenomenon of anxiety must start from the inception of treatment, and be used throughout, as our guide to the safe exploration of feelings and conflicts. Is the patient aware of anxiety and how it is being experienced in the body? Does he have a clear and accurate understanding of what is causing the anxiety or does he have some fundamental misunderstanding about the triggers and precipitants to anxiety? Can he tolerate anxiety consciously or does he need to defend against it with muscle weakness or cognitive confusion? These are some of the questions that we need to ask and answer, in order to be able to work at each patient's current level of tolerance.

One very bright psychiatry resident, who was taking a course in Short-Term Dynamic Psychotherapy, seemed to pick up on the importance of tracking anxiety in the body very quickly, leading to dramatically improved outcomes for his patients. I asked him how he achieved these results and he said, "I just follow the anxiety. When I hear that sigh, and see those hands get clenched, I ask about the feelings underneath, and hit pay dirt every time." This is good advice for all therapists—follow the anxiety! The anxiety is actually telling you where the pain and distress lie. Since this is what patients need our help with, we must approach the anxiety-laden issues, rather than avoiding them. When patients are afraid of their own feelings, they have little emotional freedom or flexibility. Conversely, developing an increasing level of comfort with our own feelings enables us to tolerate and regulate them without resorting to destructive defenses, and emboldens patients to deal effectively with others. Furthermore, patients experience an increased sense of mastery and competence when they are able to face their fears and anxieties directly (Weinberger, 1995). We deprive our patients of this experience if we tread too lightly and avoid their anxiety-provoking fears and wishes.

Striated Anxiety and the Standard Approach—A Clinical Example

This patient, a young woman in her mid 30s, requested a consultation to discuss her concerns about a seeming lack of feeling regarding the death of her mother. When asked, she was not aware of any sign or symptom that she was avoiding or repressing such feelings. Still, she was concerned about her own lack of feeling, and wanted to explore what might be happening inside. Since the unconscious often speaks to us nonverbally, the therapist must always keep her eye on the patient's body, while listening to the content and tone of what she is saying. In this case, her nonverbal behavior held the key to understanding the factors involved in delayed and derailed mourning.

Therapist: How can I help?
Patient: I want to focus on the death of my mother because I just lost her. That's a bit tough. And, well, we had a period during the spring where she got more and more ill—she died of cancer. What I would

like to get into is my reaction of her death because I kind of well, thought a lot about it beforehand. We had a warning, we knew there was nothing to do and it was a matter of time, and she got more and more ill and I kind of, me, my father and sister, stood together and managed together. That might be an important key word—that we tried to manage it together. We managed so much, that when she died, I was surprised by my reaction.

Therapist: What was it?

Patient: It was not as much reaction as I expected it to be. I cried a little bit and that was it. I thought, "Can this be it?" Something must be wrong. Maybe I'm afraid that I'm not in connection with my own feelings. That is scary because I used to be very connected.

Therapist: So have you been concerned for a while that you are not as connected as you used to be, or is it just in the situation with your mother?

Patient: It's . . . I haven't thought, I don't feel disconnected in general, but in relation to my mother. "Why don't I react? What is happening to me?" I can't get a grip on it. (Starts to cough.)

On a conscious level, the patient did not understand the mechanisms responsible for her lack of feeling regarding her mother's death. However, her body offered us a signal and an important clue. As we approached the topic of her mother's death, she began to have a coughing fit—alerting us to some conflict regarding suppressed feelings. This was brought to her attention.

Link Between Symptoms and Suppressed Feelings

Therapist: But you have a cough.

Patient: Yeah, yeah.

Therapist: And your mother died 5 weeks ago, of cancer. What kind?

Patient: Lung. (Patient immediately starts to tear up.)

Therapist: Right then you made some kind of connection?

Patient: It was because this pain is in my lungs now. I can feel that very much.

Therapist: What does it feel like? The feeling, if you don't get scared about it, is painful?

Patient: Yes.

Therapist: Hard to breathe?

Patient: Yes. (Patient is actually feeling anxiety about the grief and is constricting her chest, with the difficulty breathing the inevitable result of such a process.)

Therapist: Some feelings are coming up now. So what is coming up?

Patient: Sadness. (But starts coughing again, rather uncontrollably.)

Therapist: Let's see if you can let yourself feel that sadness and grief. It looks like you get anxious about it and cut off the feeling—then you start coughing—do you see that?

Examination of the link between the patient's symptoms (a cough) and suppressed feelings regarding her mother's death was enough to activate previously repressed feelings of grief. Since the patient channeled all of her anxiety into striated muscle tension, it was considered safe to move forward to a focus on the experience of her mixed feelings toward her mother. The ways in which these feelings were accessed and integrated will be detailed in Chapter 5.

Smooth Muscle Discharge and Restructuring

As demonstrated in the previous case, constriction of the chest muscles leads to physical pain and coughing. However, as soon as the patient was able to experience the grief and anger that had been suppressed, her symptoms disappeared. In other cases, physical symptoms are created or exacerbated by a smooth muscle pathway of anxiety. In the following case, anxiety was channeled into the patient's gut. As a result, she experienced frequent bouts of diarrhea. Careful monitoring of anxiety was required to prevent a worsening of symptoms. A restructuring approach, in which links are made between suppressed feelings and impulses and physical symptoms, was indicated. We typically begin the examination of feelings toward current figures associated with symptom activation, rather than central attachment figures, as that can prove too anxiety provoking. As demonstrated in the following vignette, feelings toward the therapist are also too anxiety provoking to examine at first. Several rounds of restructuring were required to build the capacity for the patient to face these feelings without going over her threshold of anxiety tolerance.

The Anxious Meditator

This nursing student came for therapy complaining of an inability to regulate anxiety effectively, despite 10 years of intense meditation practice. While she was noticeably tense in her voluntary muscles at the start of the interview, pressure to feel revealed a significant somatic channel of anxiety. Anxiety needed to be evaluated and monitored on a moment-to-moment basis to ensure safe and effective intervention, at her optimal level of tolerance.

Therapist: Tell me what brings you.
Patient: I guess a lot of things bring me. I am studying to be a nurse and I'm working with a really rough population, so I think just for my own mental health it's important to be in therapy.
Therapist: Now, where is that?

Patient: With juvenile sex offenders and families that have experienced sexual abuse. Pretty daunting. And, like in my own life, working with anxiety. Like something is missing. I have been doing Zen practice for years, which has been awesome, but there is something I'm not reaching.

Therapist: OK, let's stop there, because you mention anxiety. Are you feeling anxious now?

Patient: A little bit.

Evaluating Level and Channels of Anxiety

Therapist: OK, so tell me what do you notice. What are you feeling physically, first of all, with the anxiety?

Patient: I feel my throat gets a little closed. One of the things I'm always working with is tension and energy at the base of my skull. There is a lot when I'm sitting. Yeah, just a general tightness in here.

Therapist: So mostly up here, in this part of your body?

Patient: But I do have diarrhea a lot.

Therapist: Do you? OK, that's important. Any pattern that you notice?

Patient: Well, like I noticed, on the first day of my internship, I had diarrhea constantly, and then it calmed down, but then my mind speeds up and my whole body is racing.

Therapist: Uh huh. Let's see if this has to do with different levels of anxiety, because here you said, yes, you had some, but almost indicating it wasn't that high. Like, on a scale from 1 to 10, what would you say this level is?

Patient: A three.

Therapist: Like a three. OK, so when it's a three it's in muscle tension and constriction in here, but my guess is that when it gets higher, then it goes into the GI system. So, like first day of internship, it's what level?

Patient: Eight or nine.

Therapist: So then it goes into the gut with diarrhea and do you have pain?

Patient: No.

Therapist: Just loose and frequent. And what about a 10? What would be a situation that would be off the scale?

Patient: The most anxious? Uh, I'd say that's the most anxious I've been in a long time, but when I get really anxious my whole body can get tremors and shake.

Therapist: So, let's just use this experience you are having right now. You have some anxiety right now—it's not that high, but it's there—about coming here today. So you must have some feelings that are stirring that anxiety up. What are you aware of—what kinds of feelings do you have coming here today?

Patient: Um, well, originally I felt curious and kind of excited, but as I am sitting here, I can feel my eyes getting a little glassy—like when you said, "There must be something under there." I felt like I got a little glassy and a little spacey.

This vignette speaks to the value of exerting pressure on the patient to experience feelings, while carefully monitoring her ability to respond, as a means for obtaining the most accurate and timely assessment of anxiety tolerance. Though she initially exhibited striated muscle anxiety, a somatic channel into the gut, with frequent bouts of diarrhea, was subsequently reported. Further inquiry into feelings toward the therapist revealed a pattern of cognitive disruption when anxiety was very high. This underscores the need to prioritize what we observe, over what we hear in verbal report. The patient did not report cognitive disruption, but careful monitoring of her response revealed it. Subsequently, the patient needed to be watched closely, to make sure that we do not go over her threshold of tolerance, triggering diarrhea or dissociation.

Anxiety Regarding Transference Feelings

Therapist: OK, great. I think this is the third level then. At a relatively low level of anxiety there is muscle tension; higher and it goes into the gut; super high and you go "Bleep"—a little cognitive space out. Good that you noticed that, so there is something about our looking at feelings here and now, between you and me, that jacked up your anxiety very suddenly. Have you been aware that sometimes your anxiety can spike?

Patient: Oh, definitely, definitely. The glassy feeling is definitely familiar. I think—I notice it a lot when I'm in situations with authority—like sitting down with a professor. I don't feel that way with my teacher right now—my spiritual teacher—but I can have that sense of powerlessness here—like I want to impress you.

Therapist: So you have a lot of feelings toward these authority figures, which comes up immediately here with me?

A cognitive recap of the process was employed at this juncture to reinforce what has been learned so far. This involved linking both triangles. Patient and therapist were able to understand that an invitation to close contact with the therapist evoked strong mixed feelings toward authority figures. Given her tendency to channel anxiety into the smooth muscles, and to get glassy eyed and somewhat dissociated as anxiety increased, pressure to experience feelings was modified accordingly. A graded, step-wise approach, designed to increase the patient's capacity to bear these feelings without undue anxiety or the use of destructive defenses, was used in this case.

Cognitive-Perceptual Disruption and the Graded Approach

When anxiety is too high and activates either the smooth muscle system or cognitive-perceptual functioning, we need to employ specific methods to reduce it. These include: (1) a focus on the physiological experience of anxiety in the body; (2) taking the pressure of the feelings, thoughts, or desires that are generating the anxiety; (3) talking and cognizing about what is happening on an emotional level; (4) returning to inquiry; or (5) switching focus from the anxiety-provoking stimulus to something else. While this may sound paradoxical, it is most often the patients' attempts to *avoid* their anxiety that prevent its successful regulation. Just allowing it to be there, without the story; simply resting attention on the sensations involved, usually leads to a rapid reduction in the felt experience of anxiety. A focus on the body is very useful here. A focus on the body can be achieved by asking questions such as: "How are you feeling that anxiety right now, physically?" "It looks like anxiety is very high and you are starting to hyperventilate. Do you feel constriction in your chest?" "Let's pay attention to what is happening inside so we can help you regulate that anxiety." Just keep asking, "What else do you notice?" and "Is it higher, lower, or the same, now that we pay attention to it?" until the anxiety is reduced and you see some muscle tension or hear a sigh.

Once the experience of anxiety has been down-regulated, and the patient's thinking and perceptions have cleared up, a cognitive recap of the process is essential to drive home insights into the triggers to the patient's anxiety. We might review the process by saying, "We now see that even mentioning the word anger in relation to your mother generates a great deal of anxiety in you." We can then return to inquiry with something like, "Is it only anger toward your mother that is so anxiety provoking, or do you get anxious about anger toward others as well?" Another option is to wonder how the patient learned to be so terrified of anger. Helping patients reflect upon and understand the nature of their emotional conflicts is often experienced as calming and centering. It's troubling enough to suddenly be filled with intense anxiety. A lack of understanding regarding the trigger only exacerbates anxiety. Developing insight about the precipitant can be highly therapeutic.

The Man Who Never Kissed a Girl

This 39-year-old single man came to see me for an initial consultation after reading my books. I knew nothing about him prior to our meeting, and assessed his difficulties and capacities by using response to intervention as my primary assessment tool.

Therapist: So how can I help?
Patient: Um, uh, well, sort of, I suppose two areas, lots of areas really, but I suppose two come immediately to mind—my work, which is sort of ground to a halt, really.

Therapist: What do you do?

Patient: I'm a bookkeeper—but, um, and, uh, you know it's been going on for all my working life, really. I suppose, 12–18 months ago, the partnership I was in—you see, I'm a kind of consultant and you have these contracts—they said, "We're not going to continue the contract with you. You can keep some of the work but we're going to take other bits back." Eventually that partnership broke up anyway, so technically, people say, "What do you do?", I said, "I'm self-employed" and I do have a number of consultancies out there . . . uh, but I suppose, just the energy to do the work . . . um . . .

A simple question about the patient's line of work resulted in some cognitive slippage. The fact that he became a bit confused and started to drift off during the first moments of the interview, without any pressure from the therapist, suggested that the patient's anxiety was very high, and his capacity for awareness and regulation was quite low. This required immediate attention.

Evaluating Anxiety

Therapist: What's happening just now? If you pay attention, what is coming up as you begin to talk about the struggles you've had at work?

Patient: Just a sort of disorientation.

Therapist: Great. I'm glad you noticed it. So how did you start to feel disoriented?

Patient: Well my head, it started to feel slightly filmy (fuzzy thinking and visual clouding).

Therapist: Yeah, so what do you associate that with, what kind of emotional state?

Patient: An anxious state.

On the positive side, this patient was aware that his "disorientation" was a manifestation of anxiety. However, his previous lack of awareness that anxiety was building up had prevented him from regulating it effectively. Inquiry revealed a tendency to ignore anxiety at low levels. Consequently, anxiety increased until it was at such a pitch he lost track of his thoughts. While most patients are anxious about coming to see a therapist, his level of anxiety was exceptionally high and disruptive. As long as the patient cognitively disrupts when anxiety is triggered, you essentially have no patient in the room. Reaching out to the patient, talking and helping him stay connected to his bodily experience, and to the therapist, is essential in preventing any further dissociation.

Therapist: What did you start noticing physically that let you know "I'm anxious"? Physical sensations you were having?

Patient: Just there (pointing to the center of his body).

Therapist: What's in there?

Patient: Just breathing a bit harder and the stomach is a bit . . .

Therapist: Yeah, what is in your stomach?

Patient: Uh, sort of butterflies, sort of, a little bit, getting there—not the real sicky butterflies.

Therapist: It's not roiling and you're not nauseous, just a little bit in your stomach. And anything else you notice physically?

Patient: No. My shoulders are a bit . . .

Therapist: Tight? Tense?

With encouragement to focus on the physical experience of anxiety, the patient was able to shift from confusion and muscle weakness to muscle tension and activation. This was a good prognostic sign. As we paid attention to his anxiety, and focused on a felt desire to be present and engaged, the patient's anxiety decreased. At the same time, his cognitions cleared up. This was a signal that it was safe to begin exploring the thoughts and feelings that had triggered the anxiety about coming to see me. This could only be done productively when the anxiety was in the striated muscles. When he was feeling weak and disoriented, nothing could be explored effectively. Anxiety had to be downregulated first, so we had a clear thinking patient in the room. Remember, it is response to intervention, rather than the initial presentation, that is most predictive of therapeutic success. His ability to respond rapidly to my interventions was a very good sign.

Understanding the Trigger to Anxiety

Therapist: Then suddenly you noticed it started to get into your head—feeling a bit confused and disoriented—and also you were saying there was some sort of sensation.

Patient: I suppose I was looking at you and the bookshelves and I suppose I was checking, you know, checking you out. Getting what you were like. I know, I've read both your books.

Therapist: So you started a relationship with me even before you got here. Let's look at how you are feeling about being here with me.

Patient: I suppose the hope, really, from reading the books, and I suppose what I've always known intuitively that my problems relationally, sexual stuff, is related to the past, but also that, there is a lot of emotion trapped, a lot of anxiety, and sometimes I even wake up in the morning and I have that shoulder thing. I thought you might ask, "When did this happen?" and it's just been going on for years and years and years. What attracted me about your books was the focus on affects and emotion and just really grabbing onto that.

Therapist: Right, so there is some hope, some desire to get connected to yourself?

Patient: Yes.
Therapist: To get connected to those feelings, free yourself up.
Patient: Yes, completely.

Activating Approach Goals

In addition to focusing on the physiology of anxiety, designed to bring anxiety down to a manageable level, activating the approach system is an effective way to rebalance the system (Grawe, 2007). If we simply lower anxiety, desire and motivation can go with it. In this particular case, the patient had been immobilized by anxiety such that everything in his life had "ground to a halt." In order to move forward, in therapy and in life, this man needed to connect with a felt desire to approach valued goals. There is no growth without anxiety. However, without access to desires that propel us into action, growth is prevented and stagnation results.

Therapist: OK, so let's look at that, what your goals are, not just what the problems are, but what you really want to get out of this time.
Patient: Oh, the goal I would love to have, it sounds really simple, is just to access some of that emotion. I would say that, probably since my mother got dementia and my Aunt dying 18 months ago, I did access a little bit—when I say that, I mean two cries for 15 seconds each, just these little spurts, but other than that, for years and years. But, on the other hand . . .
Therapist: So what you really want is to connect with yourself emotionally.

As important as it was for this man to connect with himself emotionally, feeling his emotions was really just a means to an end, and not an end in and of itself. Access to the information and energy contained in these feelings and desires was required in order to motivate him to pursue his goals. Since he had been depressed and dispirited for a long time, working exclusively on his problems would have limited value. As Grawe (2007) reminds us, "First he must rebuild the impoverished brain regions because their easy activation will be necessary to enable the patient to pursue positive goals in a self-initiating, self-governed manner . . ." (p. 16). Activating the felt desire for meaningful goals, while blocking the tendency to revert to old patterns that maintain the avoidant strategies and create the problems, was necessary to facilitate therapeutic change.

Therapist: To be able to really feel what you feel, experience it, release it. So, what will you get—if you got this sense of connection with yourself, what does that give you that you really want in your life?
Patient: Well, peace, strength, a sense of purpose—to be able to do what I really want to do. To live my life.

Therapist:	Exactly, in an authentic way, to live a life in alignment with who you are and what you really feel. So you have this goal but there are things getting in your way—things blocking you in realizing that—so you want help from me to get through those blocks.
Patient:	Yes (tears coming to his eyes).
Therapist:	So what just happened now? There is some feeling coming up just now.
Patient:	Everything you said is just how I feel, so I suppose my anxiety in coming here . . .
Therapist:	But the feeling right now? There is a feeling coming up in this moment.
Patient:	I'm not really sure. A feeling of relief. It was as you were talking, you understand (getting tearful).
Therapist:	Something about being understood is touching something in you.
Patient:	Yes.
Therapist:	You feel moved in some way and tears come to your eyes. Are you aware of it?
Patient:	Yes.

The therapeutic interventions employed here were successful in helping the patient achieve one of his initial goals—to connect with his own emotions. Further, sharing these feelings in order to have the experience of closeness with another, another of his goals, was also achieved. In this way, the patient was having an emotional experience and not just a cognitive understanding of his difficulties. Of course, this was not without conflict. Actually getting some of what he wanted intensified his conflicts. In fact, by helping to activate the desire system, his conflict over whether to approach or avoid what he desired comes into view in an unmistakable way. It turns out he would become so anxious around women that he was unable to think or speak clearly. The last time he approached some attractive women in a wine bar, his words got completely muddled and he ran out of the place in a state of panic. At the age of 39, he had never dated or kissed a girl. Interventions were successful in increasing his capacity for the awareness and regulation of anxiety, so that he could approach his own feelings, and close contact with the therapist, without undue anxiety. Within the first 20 minutes of the interview, he was able to get to some of the feelings of pain and longing that had been trapped by anxiety and repression nearly all his life.

Building Anxiety Tolerance

In addition to the intensity of felt anxiety, we must also assess the patient's ability to tolerate anxiety for growth. Here we are referring to the patient's ability to withstand internal discomfort in an effort to reach desired goals, without resorting to avoidant strategies. Some patients can tolerate a high level of anxiety without symptomatic suffering, while others tolerate very little and behave like hothouse flowers, unable to withstand any challenge or adversity without wilting. In these cases we will work to increase the patient's tolerance for anxiety without resorting to defenses. Both aspects of anxiety—level of intensity and level of tolerance—must be assessed and continually monitored to ensure a safe and effective process, taking place at the patient's optimal level of activation.

In the following case, the patient was both psychologically minded and extremely articulate. She could talk "about" all sorts of things quite freely, as long as she did so in an intellectual manner. However, talking in an emotionally detached manner is rarely therapeutic. Consequently, I began to exert some pressure on her to connect to her feelings, and to let me close enough to help her. As pressure intensified, the patient's relaxed manner was replaced with high and unregulated levels of anxiety. This case illustrated the need to remain vigilant, up- and down-regulating anxiety as needed to determine and maintain the optimal level of activation.

The Broken Bird

This 60-year-old woman came for help with emotional detachment and an inability to open her heart to love. She had been in a 10-year Jungian analysis in which her defenses against emotional involvement were never confronted. As a result she reported never feeling anxious in sessions, but also getting no help with her presenting problems. In order to help her with this problem of emotional distancing from others, it was necessary to spot it in operation in the therapeutic relationship and challenge her to do something different, here and now.

Inquiry

Therapist: Tell me what brings you.

Patient: I was thinking, on the way here, I walk over, it takes me 20 minutes. I don't have to hold a key or a bag, it's really wonderful. I was thinking, if someone said, "Tell me about you," it seems I have everything. I work the job, self employed . . .

Therapist: But inside?

Patient: But I feel this emptiness and sadness. It's so strange when that comes up. Ten years ago I had a series of very interesting dreams and I went to see a therapist and the first thing she said was tell me a dream. I told her about one. We have parrots and the parrot was in my coat. We were walking on the street and I fall and I crush the bird and when I take it out it only has a wing left. One wing with blood on it and it was really painful. Later I realized that was my heart. It was warm and soft with a little blood on it. Then Carol said, "What's wrong with your heart?" And that's where we started 10 years ago. There was something wrong with my heart. I wasn't where I wanted to be. I was really angry. I was angry at bank tellers, and with my mother, and in relationship with everyone.

Therapist: So that was 10 years ago, but let's start with what brings you right now? What motivated you to pick up the phone?

Patient: Yes, it is, as soon as I say that about the bird, the emotion comes right up.

Therapist: Tell me what it feels like inside. There is a lot of pain.

Patient: I don't really know what the sadness is.

Therapist: But just tell me what it feels like.

Patient: Perhaps it has something to do with growing up, with childhood of course.

Therapist: Before you tell me what you think it is about, could you just describe how it feels inside—like if I was from Mars and I didn't know what it was like to be human and what that would feel like? Where is it located?

Patient: It was in the heart, right here. It always wells up from here. I said I want to stay out of my head and get into my heart, but it's very hard not to go to my head. I find the heart is very protected. It's very hard to go there and open up. I don't even know what cause my sadness. If I knew I would be glad to tell you.

While the patient's intellectualizing defenses were effective in keeping anxiety under control and out of awareness, they also created her presenting problem. Left unattended, her emotional detachment would also create a resistance to treatment. Given this, the therapist increased the pressure on the patient to connect to her own emotions and to allow the therapist close enough to help. In so doing, anxiety could also be assessed.

Therapist: You said you don't want to stay in your head but to let yourself feel instead. Still, we see all the ways you detach from your feelings and also keep a distance from me.

Patient: I want to get to it (sitting up and sighing deeply).

Therapist: If you pay attention to it, can you detect anxiety? Because you've had a couple of big sighs just now.

Patient: I feel anxiety right now. We are talking about it now. How come? I think it's because we're talking about it.

Therapist: How does it feel physically?

Patient: The chest gets tight, the heart goes faster, and it shoots upward into my head.

Therapist: So what happens with that?

Patient: I feel it in my body—it gets tense.

Therapist: And what happens in your head with the anxiety?

Patient: I can't think actually.

Therapist: So that's important to see that it can interfere with your thinking. You go blank or lose track?

Patient: Think I don't want to go there—the brain shuts down—gets cloudy. Push things away.

Therapist: Is it beyond your control? Just shuts down? Does it affect your vision? Do you have tunnel vision or blurry vision?

Patient: That's so strange because I know when the sadness comes, I know how that feels, but I never paid attention to anxiety—how that comes up. Normally in the sessions anxiety doesn't come up. (In her analysis there was not enough attention paid to emotions or to closeness, so her anxiety was not evoked.) It's triggered by something and my eye twitches.

Therapist: Any visual changes?

Patient: Visual? I don't see anything. I don't see clear. The head sort of shut down like cotton ball, like a cloud—a cloud comes and you don't see any blue—it goes on in there. This is really clear. Wow—it covers my brain and the temperature rises and heat come up my neck and I feel hot. What were we talking about?

When anxiety exceeded her level of tolerance it interfered with cognitive and visual clarity. No therapeutic progress can be made when the patient can't see or think straight. In cases such as this, anxiety needs to be down-regulated before the work can continue. Then a cognitive recap of the process can take place.

Therapist: I'm not so sure it's what we are talking about, but what we are doing—to look at your feeling—to get close—a huge alarm bell goes off, with anxiety and shutdown.

Patient: Anxiety shoot up. Right.

Therapist: As if you are physically and emotionally terrified to let anyone close, and for you to be in a vulnerable position. Is that right? This is what you are afraid of and guard against.

Patient: I think I just checked out (indicating increased observing capacity).

Therapist: So let's slow down the process and pay attention to what goes on inside. Usually you stay busy and don't get close enough to anyone to let this happen.

Patient: Well, I get angry—that's the sensation—when the anger comes up, you can't think, you get hot, you can't think. The body gets all—I get very defensive.

Therapist: How do you experience that anger?

Patient: You know, it feels like fire coming up inside. That triggers the sprinkler system that puts out the fire. So the thing releases and try to put it out. Wow. What if I don't send out the signal to send the cloud, cold, frozen area, numbing it? If I just let that go, what would happen?

Exploration of the process revealed the source of the patient's high anxiety. While I initially thought that closeness was the trigger, the patient was even more specific. When others, including the therapist, tried to get close to her, reactive rage was activated. This rage was experienced as terrifying, so she distanced herself from her own feelings, and from the other, in order to avoid it. Although these defenses worked to keep her anxiety-provoking feelings under wraps, they also created difficulties in self-understanding and relationships with others. The ensuing work on this conflict resulted in considerable insight. She was able to see that anger triggered anxiety that was "watered down" by the sprinkler system of tears. Further, she wondered what would happen if she allowed herself to experience that rage directly, rather than "sending in the clouds." This comment served as a signal to the therapist that she was ready to approach the feelings beneath her anxiety.

Therapist: If that happened here with me, because there is rage too, if that came out, the tiger, the vicious part. What you are so afraid of, if that rage came out?

Patient: What I see—what I get in touch with just a little bit of that rage. I don't think I ever get in touch with that rage. What comes out is sadness. That comes out now. When you talk about the rage, that the water tries to put away. If the water doesn't come out, what is that rage? Actually . . .

Therapist: The tears are the sprinkler system. You are really afraid of the rage.

Patient: Then the tears come. Suddenly, the emotions switch and there is a detour.

Therapist: Because you are afraid of that rage—because you say you can feel it, and if that came up and out toward me, what would happen? Can you feel it in your body?

Patient: Yes, wow!

Therapist: Do you want to have a look at it?

Patient: I would love to have a look at it. That is why I have come here.

Therapist: We began to explore the possibility that, if you can learn to trust your heart, you don't have to work so hard to be a good girl. In a way, all that thinking and figuring out has gotten in the way of you just connecting with your heart and with others, because now you say you feel lighter and happy. So there is an opening up to be connected with yourself and here with me.

Patient: You, I see you! When I come back, it is a different you than the you when I first came in. When I first came in I was assessing you with my brain. I look at you and make a quick judgment—I say, "OK, she's attractive." I try to assess the age—does she look kind? I didn't really go too far, but this time, coming back, you look warmer. You look more relaxed. Your face looks sweet and my eyes actually see better! Literally I see more of your face. Isn't that funny?

Therapist: Well, your anxiety is down. You're present and you can really be here.

Patient: Yes, my vision is better!

Therapist: Absolutely. And those feelings—your feelings color your perception. So, you were anxious and guarded when you came in, so of course, that colored your vision and now, what you see in me is a reflection of how you are feeling.

Patient: You look different, I swear. You seem more relaxed to me.

Therapist: That could be. I was just meeting you too—it goes both ways, but you seem to recognize that the state you are in—open or closed— fearful or warm—affects your vision.

Patient: Literally.

Therapist: I can see it in you too. You look lighter in your face—more relaxed.

Patient: Yes. This is a different face. I come out a different person. And you do too!

As forbidden feelings and impulses broke through the repressive barrier, the patient's anxiety dissipated and her vision cleared up in a dramatic fashion. The therapeutic process involved a corrective emotional experience, as well as providing insight into the mechanisms responsible for her presenting problems. Despite a history of extensive trauma, this patient had managed to function at a very high level. She immigrated to the US as a young woman and established a successful business. She was creative and had many friends. It was only in close relationships that unconscious feelings, and anxiety associated with traumatic attachments, became unmanageable. When highly anxious she regressed, became cognitively confused, and experienced both visual blurriness and muscle weakness. A graded approach was required to help her gradually face and integrate the feelings she had been avoiding. Then the patient was able to recover memories that made sense of her difficulties. She entered treatment in a state of confusion—not knowing what was wrong with her heart—but left our first three-hour session with a deep understanding of herself that allowed for new possibilities. Techniques designed to up- and down-regulate anxiety, in order to work in her optimal zone of activation, were critical to our success. Later sessions will be included in subsequent chapters.

When Defenses Increase Anxiety

Repressive defenses, such as denial, minimization, rationalization, and displacement, are usually quite effective in reducing or even eliminating the awareness of anxiety in patients who rely on them. In contrast, regressive defenses, such as projection and somatization, tend to backfire and exacerbate, rather than reduce, anxiety. Patients who project their hostility onto others become increasingly fearful and vigilant. Those who somaticize can work themselves into a frenzy of worry, only increasing their anxiety. In cases such as these, defenses must be blocked in order to regulate anxiety adaptively. Instead of slowing down when anxious, some patients race forward and get overwhelmed. Being able to slow things down so that the patient can function in his optimal range is a vital skill for therapists to develop.

In the following case, an anxious and depressed man came for therapy to address concerns about his sexuality, and a lifelong difficulty in maintaining romantic relationships. It became readily apparent that he had a tendency to blame and doubt himself until he was nearly ready to collapse. He tended to flood with anxiety rapidly. It was up to the therapist to slow down this process, in which excessive reliance on destructive defenses only increased his anxiety. Such vicious cycles can be torturous to patients, and, left unchecked, can undermine therapeutic progress. This is one of those cases in which going slower in the beginning will make things go faster and smoother in the end.

The Man Who Was Afraid to Love

Therapist: Tell me what brings you.

Patient: Relationships. My sexuality. I am gay. Usually relationships start beautifully, but after a year I don't want to have sex anymore and push my partner away. My last relationship of five years just ended.

Therapist: Same pattern there?

Patient: After some previous therapy I thought it would get better and I would want to have sex again but it didn't work. We had lots of problems. He was 20 years younger, so it was complicated. Oh, I am so anxious!

Therapist: What's happening inside?

Patient: I feel shaky, my hands and arms.

Therapist: Do you feel weak?

Patient: Trembling (crosses arms).

Therapist: And in the center there?

Patient: I am cold.

Therapist: It seemed to spike just when you spoke about your ex.

Patient: The problem is that I have been in therapy for 12 years and whenever we approached my angry feelings, we would hit a wall. I just got blocked.

Therapist: That's where you got stuck in the therapy?

Patient: She said my sex problem was really about anxiety regarding closeness.

Therapist: What do you think?

Patient: I agree. I am flooded with anxiety.

Therapist: I wonder how you were feeling about coming here to see me today?

Patient: I was really looking forward to coming here. I actually have a warm, positive feeling.

Therapist: How do you feel that inside? What are the sensations?

Patient: I could cry. It makes me feel sad (sigh).

Therapist: And does the anxiety come down when you let those feelings come up?

Patient: Yes.

Therapist: So the anxiety goes down. First there is a warm, positive feeling and then it taps into some sadness. What does it feel like in your body?

Patient: Memories come of my mother. She told me she didn't like me from birth. I was ugly and she couldn't feed me. The birth was traumatic.

This patient entered the initial session with such high anxiety that he was physically shaking. Attention to the physiological experience of anxiety was successful in reducing its intensity. As anxiety diminished, feelings toward the therapist were activated, along with temporary relief. However, he shifted rapidly to old and traumatic memories of his mother, which restimulated high levels of anxiety and distress. Patients such as this can use therapy as another means of self-torture, rather than an opportunity for healing. In order to prevent this, the patient's regressive defenses needed to be blocked.

Patient: Then the anxiety comes back and I start to shake. I am mentally collected but emotionally withdrawn.

Therapist: Feelings come up in relationships that trigger high levels of anxiety. Then you shut down and withdraw. We are starting to see the pattern in relationships that causes so much difficulty.

Patient: I am ready, but hitting the wall.

Therapist: Can we look at this together?

Patient: Yes, I am trying.

Therapist: What happens if you don't try so hard?

Patient: I feel too much.

Therapist: What if there is nothing wrong with that—nothing wrong with you? What if you don't need to be fixed? Can we just accept you, rather than making you wrong? Can you accept and embrace all your feelings, instead of working against yourself?

Patient: I get scared (crying).

Therapist: Let's see if you can just allow this feeling to come up. This is what you need and want but don't allow—to accept yourself as you are and to have an intimate relationship with you and others.

Patient: (Crying.) Yeah—it's so scary. There is so much sadness and I'm so afraid, it could blow my head away. I also associate this anxiety with another memory. My Mom told me I was crying and crying when I was little. My father would hit my butt so I would be quiet—and it worked.

Therapist: Is this where you want to go right now?

Patient: Yes, I scare myself. I get terrified when I start to cry.

The patient was beginning to observe his own pattern in operation. In particular he was able to see that he was increasing his anxiety, and torturing himself instead of allowing a feeling of sadness to be experienced. This awareness provided him with a choice—to continue to treat himself in this torturous fashion or allow for something new and different to transpire.

Patient: I am shaking all over. It's a fight inside me. I am trying to do something different

Therapist: If you don't try right now, but just pay attention to what is happening inside.

Patient: My arms are calm. The anxiety is in the center now.

Therapist: If you just rest your attention on that anxiety in your body and don't fight it.

Patient: (Big sigh.) It's better, actually. It's like I can feel the baby shaking inside.

Therapist: Can you embrace it? It looks like something shifted.

Patient: I feel calm now.

Therapist: How does that feel—to calmly connect to you?

Patient: It's like I could relax. It's actually something uncommon. (Starts to laugh.) It's a nice feeling of being safe—not, I don't have to do anything—this is the feeling. I feel like I have some strength now—not weak.

Therapist: Calm and strong.

Patient: Yeah! It's amazing. I really feel something strong within me.

Blocking defenses that increased anxiety and distress, while focusing on feelings in the here and now, resulted in the patient's anxiety plummeting. In its place was a newfound feeling of calm, strength, and safety. These interventions were effective in down-regulating anxiety, halting self-flagellation, and creating alliance between the healthy part of the patient and the therapist, as well as creating a corrective experience.

Differential Diagnosis: Is It Anxiety or Cognitive Impairment?

Many patients who have trouble with concentration and attention are diagnosed with ADHD or even dementia, even though anxiety may be the culprit. In the following case, a 73-year-old woman with a long history of anxiety and depression came for a psychotherapy evaluation. Fortunately, she was seen by Oyanne Vorkin, a talented ISTDP therapist in Norway. Others in the clinic had suggested that the patient was experiencing cognitive decline as the result of some sort of organic process. While the patient certainly seemed confused and disorganized at the start of the interview, careful monitoring of anxiety and blocking of defenses against her emotions resulted in a dramatic clearing in her cognition. This kind of interview is highly diagnostic, and is an invaluable aid in discovering the underlying cause of the patient's cognitive confusion.

Patient: I am here to get out of anxiety, a deep depression, and a feeling of aloneness. I have friends but it's not like it used to be . . . just dropping by . . . I lived in Bergen for several years and in a way . . . a lot happened when my husband died. That was several years ago, but . . .

The patient was rambling on and losing focus. The first task was to determine why her thinking was so confused. Was she in the early stages of dementia, or just anxious? Her response to intervention revealed the source of these difficulties.

Therapist: So you want my help now to get out of anxiety, depression, and aloneness. Can you give me a recent example?

Patient: Then I have to talk about my daughter. That is the hardest.

Therapist: Is there a recent example?

Patient: The hardest now, what I said about my father. I have seen psychologists and psychiatrists before but he was never in the picture. That is actually strange.

Therapist: I'm sure we'll return to your father later, but to get a clearer picture of how you're doing now, could you give me an example of the difficulty with your daughter and that loneliness?

Patient: Well, my daughter . . . the thing about mother . . . she said . . . because there was something strange happening the day she died.

Therapist: Yes, but . . .

Patient: When she died, my daughter said, "The day Granny died was the best day of my life." I really don't know. I understand what she meant. She sees that my mother ruined a lot for me. I have been through a lot.

Therapist: And we will get back to your history. But right now, how are you doing right now with your daughter?

Patient: It is very painful. My daughter probably has a lot to do with it. But now there has been a year where I've been very ill, very low, it just happened all of a sudden, like boom. I just went—everything went black.

Therapist: What happened?

Patient: I had a breast removed and I've had a heart attack.

Therapist: When?

Patient: In 1995.

Therapist: Twenty years ago?

Patient: No, not 1995, 2005.

Despite several attempts to maintain a focus, the patient continued to jump from topic to topic and seemed very confused. Drug and alcohol abuse had also been reported in her chart, so the therapist decided to ask about current usage to assess whether this might be contributing to the patient's confused mental state.

Therapist: You have mentioned alcohol and pills. I wonder if that adds to your confusion?

Patient: (Sigh.) No. It wasn't. What are you asking? You are mentioning things I haven't talked about, and that's what has to come out. I want it out. I just can't put it into words.

Therapist: Maybe I can help you a little. It was when I mentioned alcohol and pills.

Patient: Yes. I got very silent then.

Therapist: What made you so quiet right now?

Patient: Right, that was strange.

Therapist: Are you uncomfortable talking about pills?

Patient: Maybe it is.

Therapist: Maybe it's easier to get off track?

Patient: I wouldn't exclude that.

The patient's sigh and increased diversionary tactics indicated that a rise in feeling, triggering anxiety and defense, was in operation. This was a very good sign. The therapist tested this out by wondered if she was feeling uncomfortable discussing her drug use, and the patient agreed. She then wondered if she was avoiding this by getting off the track. Again, the patient agreed, albeit in a somewhat roundabout fashion.

Therapist: So let's get back to what happened that precipitated this depression.

Patient: I think it's just the relationship to my daughter that I thought was too bad.

Therapist: What happened?

Patient: Nothing happened for a long time. She didn't answer the phone, didn't want me to call, didn't want to talk to me.

Therapist: Do you think that has something to do with your anxiety increasing?

Patient: I think that made it difficult, because . . .

Therapist: Wait, it looks as though something is happening to you. You hunch over, look down and start to disappear a little. What kind of feeling is coming up?

Patient: Yes, why doesn't my daughter want anything to do with me?

Therapist: Yes, that is the question (block defense). There is a very strong feeling toward you daughter.

Patient: Very strong. Terribly strong.

Therapist: What is the feeling?

Patient: It's terrible. What's wrong with me?

Therapist: You start to ask questions (block defense), but if we just zoom into that feeling you are having as you talk about your daughter. Can you feel that?

Patient: Grief.

Therapist: Where do you feel it?

Patient: All over.

As the patient allowed herself to feel the grief beneath her anxiety, her thinking cleared up, and the plot thickened.

Pressure to Feelings

Patient: It's hard. At the senior center everyone says, "My son came to visit. We had such a good time!" I am thinking my daughter never comes to see me. I lived near her for 10 years. She is the one who arranged it, so I could babysit for her children. Which I did. But the family she is in now—I am going to be straightforward—they are snobs!

Therapist: It looks like some other feelings are showing up in you.

Patient: Yes, now I am a little . . . feel like . . . anger.

Therapist: Toward your daughter?

Patient: Yes, because I think she should just be herself. She was so in love when she remarried. If she's still like that, I don't know, I can't get anything out of her. Maybe I'm the kind of person who is not supposed to know about her children, but I love her so much. She has probably experienced that I've been holding onto her over the years and that has been painful for her.

Therapist: You have such strong mixed feelings toward her—you have huge grief, anger over what she's done, and a great love for her. You are also able to take her perspective and realize things have been difficult for her as well.

Patient: The tears are there, I can feel them. I don't know how you got me out of it, because now I can feel that I'm crying. I haven't cried over this.

Therapist: You haven't cried. You have been tensing up and getting anxious and confused instead.

Patient: All the time.

Through a process of careful tracking, inquiry, and response to intervention, the therapist was able to determine that anxiety and defenses (resulting in depression) were most likely responsible for this woman's confusion. Since depression often mimics dementia in the elderly, taking the time to do an in-depth interview can be especially helpful in arriving at a proper diagnosis. All too often we dismiss the elderly and offer medical, as opposed to psychotherapeutic, intervention. In this case, when the patient was helped to face her mixed feelings toward her daughter, her confusion disappeared and she was able to think clearly—not only about herself and her inner life, but that of her daughter.

Summary

Anxiety is a biophysiological response to an emotional threat. Anxiety is often triggered when we invite patients to pay attention to their emotions and to connect with us, in a close and caring way. This allows us to assess and regulate anxiety as it is experienced from moment to moment. It also enables the clinician to conduct the therapy safely and effectively, at the patient's optimal level of anxiety tolerance.

Anxiety can be channeled into voluntary striated muscles, involuntary smooth muscles, or cognitive-perceptual disruption. Assessment of the channel of anxiety, and level of anxiety tolerance, is used to determine the pace and intensity of emotional activation. When the tolerance is good, and anxiety is in striated muscles, we can proceed directly to the mobilization of emotion. Conversely, if the patient's tolerance is low, and anxiety is channeled into smooth muscle pathways or into cognitive-perceptual disruption, a graded approach, designed to increase capacity, is required. Specific techniques designed to reliably up- and down-regulate anxiety, while bolstering capacity and speeding the process of healing, were outlined and illustrated.

Chapter Four
Defense and Resistance

We can define a psychological defense as any behavior, thought, or feeling that is employed in an effort to avoid painful or anxiety-provoking thoughts, feelings, and impulses. In order to understand how and why patients employ defense to avoid their own feelings and impulses, we must consider the long period of dependence characteristic of the species. Because children are dependent on caretakers for their very survival, they must adapt to the interpersonal conditions provided by parents and other authorities. Avoiding and defending against any thought, feeling, or behavior that would endanger these attachments, or the child's sense of safety and autonomy, is adaptive (Della Selva, 1993). However, the very defenses that may have literally saved the child in the past, often cause harm and perpetuate suffering in the present, as an adult. In any case, when relied on excessively and rigidly, defenses often cause or perpetuate the very suffering the patient comes into our office to resolve (McCullough Vaillant, 1997). Given this, interrupting the habitual use of defenses is an act of compassion and is an invaluable aid in the fostering of growth and development.

The desires that bring the patient to our door are manifestations of healthy strivings—to be a whole and authentic self, and to attach in a secure manner to others (Blatt & Fonagy, 2008). Since, almost by definition, our patients have conflicts and impairments in one or both of these areas, they are also anxious and hesitant about the whole enterprise. We refer to the patient's avoidant strategies as defenses. Defenses can only be understood within the context of the conflicts of which they are a part. Defenses do not exist in a vacuum, nor can they be effectively treated as such. Patients can, and often do, defend against painful realities; against their own anxiety-provoking and guilt-laden feelings; and against close emotional contact with others, including the therapist. Much of the skill involved in psychotherapy, especially in the early phases, involves dealing effectively with defenses that can all too readily become a resistance that can undermine the therapeutic process. Without access to therapeutic interventions specifically designed to overcome defense and resistance, therapies can easily stall or simply fail to get off the ground in the first place.

As previously noted, dropout rates in psychotherapy are still alarmingly high. While in some cases, dropping out of therapy may be a sign of good judgment on the patient's part, a lack of skill in motivating patients to abandon defense and resistance is often a major contributor to treatment failure. Learning to assess the nature and tenacity of defenses, and to intervene in such a way that helps the patient relinquish them, are essential elements in any effective psychotherapy.

In this chapter, different types and levels of defenses will be outlined and illustrated. In addition to "formal defenses," such as denial and rationalization, this chapter will examine character defenses, such as passivity or defiance, and tactical defenses against emotional closeness. In addition to working with specific defenses against specific feelings, understanding how defenses can be knit together to form a resistance or barrier to closeness, including with the therapist, will be elucidated. Techniques and strategies designed to identify the nature of the defenses at play, assess the degree of syntonicity involved, and dismantle and remove these barriers to connection and healing, will occupy a good deal of our attention. Clinical examples will highlight these skills and processes, which are so crucial for deep, rapid, and consistently effective intervention.

Understanding Defenses

History of the Concept

Sigmund Freud (1894/1962) was the first to suggest that human beings use various types of unconscious strategies to protect themselves against anxiety and emotional distress. His daughter, Anna Freud (1979), wrote the classic text on these "formal defenses." These defenses included denial, rationalization, displacement, and projection; all designed to avoid conscious awareness of "painful or unbearable ideas or affects" (Freud, 1979, p. 42). The patient's symptoms and suffering were viewed as the inevitable result of excessive reliance on defenses against painful realities and the feelings these realities evoke. As the Buddhists suggest, pain multiplied by resistance equals suffering. Defenses may offer temporary relief, but come at a significant cost to the happiness, health, and well-being of those who resort to them. In the end, defenses weaken the individual who habitually relies upon them. In contrast, ego strength has been understood as the ability to face one's own feelings and impulses *without* the need to defend against them. Given this, "Ms. Freud advocated examining the defensive system to assess the functioning of the ego" (Coughlin Della Selva, 1996/2004, p. 55). Therapists often assume patients "need" their defenses and are "doing the best they can." Others (Ferenzi & Rank, 1925; Reich, 1972), have "suggested that defenses needed to be confronted and eliminated in order to increase the kind of affective involvement in the treatment process necessary for deep and permanent change to occur" (Coughlin Della Selva, 1996/2004, pp. 55–56). Putting some pressure on the patient to be affectively involved in the process, while calling defensive avoidance into question, helps the practitioner assess, rather than assume, whether the patient "needs" a particular defense or is strong enough to relinquish it in order to face his true feelings.

The Cost and Benefit of Defenses

Research (Cramer, 2000, 2006) suggests that defenses are ubiquitous in human functioning, but come at a substantial cost to our emotional, interpersonal, physical, and occupational well-being. While we all use these types of avoidant strategies at times, excessive and habitual reliance on them undermines the overall functioning of the individual who employs them. In fact, most of our patient's symptoms and presenting complaints are the direct, though inadvertent, result of an excessive reliance on defenses against painful and anxiety producing feelings. For example, patients who tend to be people-pleasing chronically suppress their own needs and feelings, and often get tired and depressed as a result. These symptoms are the inevitable consequence of this chronic suppression of emotion. Reliance on defenses against the patient's true feelings affects others as well. In other words, defenses have interpersonal, as well as intrapsychic, consequences. To continue with this example, patients who chronically repress their own feelings and desires are unable to speak up and make their needs and feelings known, making it quite unlikely that their needs will be met. This scenario only increases the likelihood that the patient will end up sad, depressed, frustrated, and hopeless.

The dynamic interaction between the patient's defenses, and the kind of response he tends to elicit from others, is referred to as cyclical psychodynamics (Wachtel, 1997) or, more commonly, a self-fulfilling prophecy. These phenomena are vital to understand, so that we don't repeat and reenact the patient's problematic pattern of interaction in therapy. Instead, we attempt to provide a corrective emotional experience (Alexander & French, 1946), understood as a kind of counter offer (Balint, 1995) to the patient's expectations of others. In order to accomplish this, the therapist must block the patient's invitation to interact in an automatic fashion that is harmful, while offering a healthy alternative. For example, instead of responding to the patient's passivity and subservience by taking control and being too active, the effective therapists points out the way in which he presents himself and is inviting the therapist to interact with him, while offering a healthy alternative: "By taking a passive, subservient, sort of one down position here with me, you invite me to take over. Is that in your best interest? Is that the way you want to continue here—or would you be willing to put in 100% of your effort so that we can work together as a team?" In another case, the therapist might point out the patient's tendency to neglect herself, and suggest a healthy alternative: "Do you notice how you talk about the needs and feelings of everyone but you? You have come here for your own reasons. Would you be willing to take this time to focus on yourself and what is going on inside of you?" In both examples the patient is asked to relate to herself and the therapist in a new and healthy way. Once again, this kind of intervention is a manifestation of the therapist's clear and consistent stance for heath, healing, and growth, and against anything that would harm the patient or undermine her healthy development.

The Effect of Defensive Functioning on Health and Well-Being

The notion that the excessive use of defenses is associated with elevated levels of psychopathology has been supported by research. In fact the data suggests a fairly direct relationship between defense use and psychopathology (Cramer, 2002). This is particularly the case in regard to "immature defenses" (such as denial and projection), which have been associated with high levels of personality dysfunction (Hibbard & Porcerelli, 1998; Valliant, 1994); symptomatology (Muris & Merkelbach, 1996); and depression (Flannery & Perry, 1990; Kwon, 2000, 2002). Given this, it makes sense that psychotherapy should have removal or restructuring of defenses as one of its primary goals. Treatments that focus on symptom reduction alone tend to result in high relapse rates, while those dealing with the patient's defensive structure produce more robust and lasting results (Josephs, Sanders, & Gorman, 2014; Vaillant, 1993). These findings underscore the vital role of defense restructuring for long-term recovery from psychiatric disturbances (McCullough Vaillant, 1997; Solbaken & Abbass, 2013).

Additionally, defenses often exact a physical toll on those who make frequent use of them (Pennebaker, 1997). Chronic tension and suppression of feelings and impulses often results in physical pain (Sarno, 2006; Schubiner, 2011). Pain is one of the leading causes of disability worldwide, and is a drain to the medical system, as well as on the lives of those who suffer from it. Dr. Sarno (1999) has suggested that talking to patients about their emotional pain is the most conservative form of medicine we can practice, and should be the first line of intervention, before expensive and high risk procedures are considered. However, most doctors have not been taught how to assess or treat the emotional factors that are often associated with chronic pain. In fact, even mental health professionals fail to develop these skills. Alternatively, by learning to identify and treat the underlying emotional causes of pain (the chronic suppression of anxiety-provoking feelings and impulses), therapists can help patients become free of pain, while regaining their emotional and physical health. Research suggests (Abbass et al., 2010; Abbass, Campbell, & Tarzwell, 2009; Abbass, Joffres, & Ogrodniczuk, 2008; Hsu et al., 2010; Sarno, 2006; Schubiner & Betzhold, 2012) that such emotion-focused interventions are both cost and clinically effective.

Are Defenses Necessary?

Within the field, there is a wide disparity of opinion on the utility and neces-
sity of defenses in human functioning. Some seem to think that psychological
defenses are necessary for optimal functioning, going so far as to suggest it
would somehow be dangerous to "strip patients of their defenses." At the other
end of the spectrum are clinicians who assert that defenses are always harmful,
and are not in the least bit necessary (Firestone & Catlett, 1999). A more moderate view holds that defenses have both benefits (though usually temporary)
and costs (Brenner, 1976; Cramer, 2006; Vaillant, 1993, 1998, 2015). Research
supports this moderate view. It appears that the use of defenses "at the norma-
tive level" protect individuals from undue stress and anxiety, while both high
and low levels of defense use are associated with increased levels of psychopathology (Cramer, 2006; Vaillant, 2015).

Defenses and Psychotherapy

So what does the research say about the effect of psychotherapy on defense
use? An early study (Strauss & Harden, 1981), conducted at Austin Riggs, was
designed to study this very question. The researchers found that a decrease in
the defenses of denial, projection, and identification was highly associated with
a reduction in "bizarre-disorganized" symptoms in a group of patients with
Borderline Personality Disorder. Of note, the most improved patients showed
the most dramatic reduction in the use of these defenses. In another study
(Hersoug, Sexton, & Hoglend, 2002), patients with anxiety and personality
disorders used significantly more mature defenses after therapy than before.
Research suggests that change in defensive function is a vital measure of recovery, and predicts both symptom reduction (Bond & Perry, 2005) and long-
term outcome (Laaksonen, Sirkia, Knekt, & Lindfors, 2014; Valliant, 2015).
There seems to be consensus in the literature that the use of immature defenses
decreases, and that of mature defenses increases, as the result of effective psychotherapy (Cramer, 2006).

A recent examination of the effectiveness of ISTDP on an inpatient unit
designed for patients considered treatment resistant (failed to benefit from
at least three previous treatments), revealed dramatic improvement in both
symptoms and interpersonal functioning after an eight-week course of therapy
(Solbaken & Abbass, 2013). Of interest, one-third of the patients who achieved
these dramatic gains (scoring in the normal range on the BSI and IIP) never
had a major breakthrough of unconscious feelings and memories. Instead, their
improvement was attributed to the therapeutic focus on restructuring defenses
and regulating anxiety (Solbaken & Abbass, 2013). Since, almost by definition,
treatment resistant patients have character defenses that prevent the kind of
emotional engagement required for psychotherapy, it makes sense that helping
patients to turn against these defenses and open up to themselves and others had

a profoundly healing effect. Interrupting the automaticity of character defenses appears to be a necessary precondition required to prepare the patient for a new and corrective emotional experience. By helping patients replace regressive defenses with more mature defenses, emotions became increasingly accessible and tolerable. As a result, significant therapeutic benefits were obtained in this previously resistant group of patients.

Davanloo's Approach

So, how do we help patients abandon the defenses that both protect and harm them? Davanloo (1980, 1990) has developed a straightforward strategy to defense work involving three steps: (1) identify the defense, (2) clarify the function of the defense, and (3) examine the consequences. Once the patient can identify the defenses he has been relying on in order to avoid painful and anxiety-laden feelings, and can articulate the costs to him, we must emphasize that he now has a choice—to persist in relying on defenses that perpetuate suffering, or to courageously face and experience the feelings he has been avoiding. Letting the patient obsess about this, or sit on the fence for any length of time, does him no favors. Alternatively, trying to force the patient to face what he is still avoiding is a misuse of our power. The conflict is *within* the patient and is not ours to take on. However, once the patient is conscious of this choice, we must put some pressure on him to *do something about it*. Insight alone is rarely sufficient for change (Atkinson, 2004). Determination and courage are required to make changes in habitual modes of functioning. We offer ourselves as a partner in the process, if and when the patient chooses to abandon his defenses and experience his true feeling.

In addition to providing an operational definition of defense work, Davanloo (1980, 1990) has also emphasized the importance of the therapist's stance. Rather than adopting a neutral stance, he has advocated taking a position that is decidedly *for* the patient's health, and *against* anything that is destructive. While honoring the patient's choice, he makes *his* position clear—that he is there to help the patient face the truth, no matter how painful, in order to heal. He also makes it clear that he will not collude with defense and resistance, or passively stand by while the patient continues to make destructive choices. Inherent in this stance is a respect of the patients' autonomy. It also requires the therapist's willingness to abandon an omnipotent stance. The fact is, no therapist can change a patient without his cooperation. This reality is made explicit in the practice of ISTDP, with the ultimate choice, and responsibility for that choice, squarely in the lap of the patient.

We sometimes forget that patients come for therapy for all kinds of reasons—not all of them therapeutic. They come to get out of trouble at work or at home; they come in a passive fashion, waiting to be fixed but without the determination to do any work; or they come to complain and get support for their status as a victim. If we are not aware of these motives, we can inadvertently create a collusive alliance with the patient, rather than a healthy, collaborative one.

Working With Defenses

Just as assessment of the level and channel of anxiety provides the therapist with vital diagnostic information about the patient's level of ego adaptive capacity, so too does the assessment of defenses. Does the patient rely on repressive or regressive defenses? Are these defenses dystonic or syntonic? Do the defenses operate as a resistance to contact with the therapist, threatening to undermine treatment efforts? All of this information is vital in determining the type and intensity of interventions required to help the patient dismantle his defensive system. Again, defenses are any thought, feeling, or behavior that is employed in an effort to avoid painful and anxiety-provoking feelings and impulses. Rationalization, minimization, displacement, and justification are just some of the intellectualizing or repressive defenses patients often employ. Patients who rely on such defenses typically have fairly good ego adaptive capacity. The fact that they can use their intellect to mange their feelings—sometimes referred to as "mentalization" (Fonagy, Gergely, Jurist, & Target, 2005)—suggests good capacity.

It should also be noted that, while exacting a cost to those who rely upon them, repressive defense are typically effective in reducing or even eliminating the awareness of anxiety from consciousness. In contrast, regressive defenses, such as somatization, projection, acting out, dissociation, and denial tend to actually increase the anxiety of those who employ them. Consequently, patients who rely on these defenses, sometimes referred to as "immature defenses," have low levels of ego strength and require restructuring in order to face their feelings and impulses without negative consequences. Therefore, careful examination of the nature and flexibility of the patient's defenses reveals essential information about the capacity to do the work of dynamic psychotherapy. In addition, this information can serve as a guide to intervention.

Just as defenses can be used to avoid the internal experience of painful and anxiety-provoking feelings and impulses, they can also be employed interpersonally in order to maintain an emotional distance from others. We feel when in close contact with others. If we can't tolerate the strong feelings, longings, and desires that close contact arouses, we will have to create emotional distance in order to keep these feelings under wraps. Effective intervention requires attention to the type and nature of defenses operating at "the front of the system" (Abbass, 2015). In other words, if the patient is defended against emotional closeness with the therapist, addressing defenses against the internal experience of grief about a loss will have little effect. Just because a patient is sitting in the room with you does not necessarily mean you have a patient who is open or available to therapeutic intervention. If the patient is sitting with his eyes to the floor, is wearing his coat and hat, and has his arms crossed, his willingness to engage openly with the therapist must be taken up immediately. Some patients are not quite so obvious about their lack of availability. For example, a patient might enter the office with a smile and seem to cooperate on a conscious level, but steer the conversation away from anything significant or any affect-laden material, rendering the interaction superficial and without therapeutic impact. In these cases, we must appreciate the anxiety involved in looking in those dark places, but remind the patient that keeping himself alone with his fears and staying blind to their source will perpetuate his suffering.

In order to help patients relinquish defenses that cause symptoms and perpetuate suffering, we must help them identify defenses, understand their function, and assess the cost entailed. Once the patient is helped to see that the ways they avoid anxiety-laden feelings actually cause or exacerbate their difficulties, their motivation to abandon them in favor of experiencing their true feelings is enhanced.

Defenses come in many sizes, shapes, and colors. One way to avoid inner conflicts is to have a conflict with reality! In other words, if I deny what has happened, I don't have to deal with my feelings about what happened. When patients deny or distort reality—what we might regard as a defense at the level of the stimulus—we must work to clarify reality, before examining the patients' feelings about these events. Asking specific questions and persisting in obtaining specific responses aimed at clarifying just what happened, when, where, and with whom, is often required to discover the reality our patients are dealing with. Patients and (all too frequently) their therapists often resist, argue with, avoid, or deny reality. If we defend against reality, and refuse to face what is so, we will be hampered, if not crippled, in dealing with reality in a powerful and effective way. How can we help our patients to deal with life on life's terms if we shy away from the truth?

Vagueness as a Cover for Painful Realities and Feelings

One of the most prominent means of avoiding a painful reality is simply to remain vague and general about what has transpired that causes us pain. However, the devil is in the details. Rather than collude with our patient's vagueness, inquiring about the specific details involved in situations giving rise to the patient's symptoms is the first rule of effective psychotherapy. The following is a stunning example of the tenacity required to extract this information from resistant patients.

Woman in Denial

A woman in her 40s, strikingly beautiful, intelligent, and highly accomplished in her professional life, came to therapy because she was feeling depressed. In our first session, she tended to be vague and general in her comments, ignoring her own feelings and needs while focusing excessively on her husband and his story. I pointed this out and began to wonder if this pattern of self-denial and self-sacrifice was contributing to her depression. While she complained about his lack of ambition, a sting of business failures, and his controlling manner at home, she did nothing about it, but remained both subservient and compliant in their relationship. She came into our third session with more vagueness about the cause of her distress.

Patient: It was a really rough week.
Therapist: How so?
Patient: With my husband.
Therapist: What happened?
Patient: I just hate to think about it.
Therapist: But you have raised it here. Shall we look into it?
Patient: It was just so upsetting.
Therapist: What happened?
Patient: He was really harsh with my daughter.
Therapist: Could you give me a specific example?
Patient: Well, he just really yelled at her.
Therapist: What did he say?

It is clear from this transcript just how strenuously the patient was avoiding a painful truth, and how persistent the therapist needed to be in order to obtain the details required to understand the nature of the situation being described. Doing so also triggered the feelings being avoided. It is not up to the therapist to force patients to examine their life in detail, but to make it very clear that avoidance of such clarity has distinct consequences.

Cost of Maintaining Defenses

Therapist: But, from what I understand, something very distressing did happen. What will happen if you continue to avoid this?
Patient: Nothing. The problems will just go on.
Therapist: And not only for you, but for your daughters too.
Patient: That's what I'm beginning to realize—that by protecting him, I am not protecting them.
Therapist: Is that what you want, or can we have an honest look at what he actually said to your daughter?
Patient: He called her a lazy, fucking whore.

At this point the patient, who had been relatively calm while discussing this incident in vague terms, burst into tears. She was able to avoid her feelings about what happened as long as she remained vague about the specifics, and refused to "believe" what had happened. Once she began to face reality, other specifics came to the fore, including an incident in which her husband threatened to kill the family dog, and another in which he brandished a gun. Now that she was willing to face what was actually happening with her husband, she was able to take constructive action. As long as she denied reality and viewed her husband as the sole source of the problem, nothing would change. When she saw her own role in creating and maintaining the problem, she was empowered. Following this pivotal session, she contacted a lawyer, got a protective order, and left the house with her daughter.

Internalization and Displacement

Depression has been called the common cold of mental illness. Depression is often the result of excessive use of defenses against the patients' feelings, wishes, and desires. In particular, feelings toward others get repressed and internalized. The energy it takes to contain all these feelings can be exhausting. When such avoidant strategies are long-standing and habitual, the patient is literally cut off from herself on an emotional level, with little awareness of what is driving her behavior. In such cases, most of our work is aimed at helping the patient acknowledge and experience these previously avoided feelings, without undue anxiety or the need to defend against them. In order to accomplish this, we must be armed with effective techniques for identifying the defenses that are in the way of feeling. It is essential that patients be able to distinguish feelings from defenses, as to see how an excessive reliance on defenses has caused or at least perpetuated their symptoms and suffering. Once this dynamic is clear, patients are in a position to choose to continue in this old manner, which will maintain suffering, or to face their feelings honestly and retrieve emotional freedom.

In the following case, a patient had become depressed after discovering her boyfriend was having an affair with her best friend. While she could easily access pain and grief over this double loss and profound betrayal, she seemed to have a great deal of difficulty experiencing her anger toward those who betrayed her. When asked how she felt toward her boyfriend, she responded with defenses, which blocked her access to her feelings and created her depression.

The Jilted Lover

Therapist: How do you feel toward him?

Patient: I think it was awful, but I guess he was tired of me.

Therapist: Those are you thoughts and judgments—it was awful and he must be tired of me—but that's not a feeling. What is the feeling toward him?

Patient: It was probably my fault. Maybe I'm not sexy enough for him.

Therapist: Now you are blaming and attacking yourself. Do you see how you avoid your feelings toward him by turning on yourself?

Patient: I'm not sure I understand what you mean.

Therapist: I am asking how you feel toward him, but you tell me about you—that you are not sexy enough, he must be tired of you, etc. This is not a feeling toward him, but a criticism of yourself. Do you see that?

Patient: Yes, I guess it is.

Therapist: How do you end up feeling when you do that?

Patient: Terrible.

Therapist: Yes, it's bad enough that your boyfriend and best friend betrayed you, but in a sense, you side with them against you. Now it's 3 against one and you don't have a prayer.

Patient: That's true.

Therapist: So you protect them and attack yourself. No wonder you are depressed!

Patient: You're right, I really end up making it worse.

Therapist: Now that you see this, you have a choice. You can continue to avoid your feelings toward the two of them, turning it on yourself and maintaining your depression, or you could honestly face and experience your true feelings toward them.

Patient: I would rather face it, because this is a terrible way to live.

In this case, defenses against feelings toward others was the primary culprit in the patient's depression. While in touch with the pain of loss, this patient avoided her feelings of anger toward her boyfriend by internalizing it and attacking herself. These defenses were largely responsible for her depressed mood and energy. The patient needed help to distinguish her feelings from her defenses. Once she saw how her defenses exacerbated her suffering, she was motivated to abandon them in favor of having an honest look at her true feelings. The fact that she engaged readily with the therapist and erected no barrier to closeness, and was able to turn against her defenses without too much difficulty, suggested a fairly high level of capacity.

Somatization

The Woman With Asthma

When armed with specific techniques designed to assess and treat the underlying emotional conflicts responsible for the patient's difficulties, powerful effects can be obtained in short order. A woman in her early 60s had been treated unsuccessfully for anxiety and depression for decades. She came to me for a consultation. Familial and interpersonal strife seemed to be the trigger to her anxiety and ensuing asthma attacks.

Therapist: How would you like to use our time together?

Patient: Well, I figure if an opportunity is presented to me to meet with someone who might help, I'll jump on it!

Therapist: That's great. So, you are really interested in doing whatever you can to get help, so why don't you tell me what is troubling you right now?

Patient: There's been a lot of conflict at home with my son. He was all messed up on drugs and just got out of rehab. He wanted to come home, 'cause he had nowhere else to go. I was nervous about it but couldn't say no. What I did say was that he could stay as long as he was clean and sober. Then, don't you know, he starts using again. I even think he was dealing, 'cause I could hear him on the phone. Oh my!

Therapist: How are you aware of feeling right now, as you tell me about this?

Patient: Oh—I can hardly breath!

Therapist: What is happening in your body right now?

Patient: My chest is getting all tight and I am having some shortness of breath. You see, this is what happens! I end up with an asthma attack. That night, I had to go to the hospital.

Therapist: Let's slow down, because this is really important. Your son violates your trust, which must stir up lots of strong feelings, but all you are aware of is anxiety and constriction in your chest, which makes it hard to breathe. Then you are the one who ends up in the hospital.

Patient: That's right.

Therapist: I wonder what kind of feelings you have toward him.

Patient: I just get so nervous. What's going to happen to him?

Therapist: He's not here now, but still you are getting anxious. This suggests that it's your feelings toward him that are generating that anxiety. Should we have a look at those feelings?

Patient: You see, I am so angry at him, so furious, that I even thought to myself, "I am glad we don't have a gun in the house 'cause I am so mad I could shoot him!" (making a gun shape out of her right hand).

Therapist: Where would you shoot him?

Patient: Right in the chest!

Therapist: How do you see that?

Patient: He would be gasping for air and clutching his chest.

Therapist: Isn't that exactly what happened to you? Do you see how you protect him from your rage and turn it in on yourself? You are the one who can't breathe.

Patient: That is wild.

Therapist: How is your breathing right now?

Patient: It is smooth and easy. I can breathe! This is amazing.

A single consultation proved to have a profound effect on both the patient and the trainees who witnessed the consultation. In fact, the resident who had been treating this patient immediately sought out supervision and training in ISTDP, and has become a highly effective therapist in her own right.

Are Defenses Syntonic or Dystonic?

In addition to assessing the type of defenses being used, evaluating the level of identification with defenses determines whether they are dystonic—viewed as behaviors that end up hurting the patient—or viewed as an essential part of the self, or syntonic. In order to determine level of syntonicity, we employ a psychodiagnostic procedure that involves a) focus on feelings, while b) monitoring anxiety, and c) evaluating/blocking defenses as they arise. There are only three possible answers to the question about feelings toward others. Patients with high levels of motivation and capacity put up no resistance to such inquiry and are able to identify their true feeling. They can see how avoidance of their feelings exacerbates suffering and quickly relinquish defenses. Such a response indicates that defenses are dystonic. In other cases, patients respond by becoming increasingly defensive. They defend their defenses, and extoll their value. In still other cases, patients are so highly identified with their defenses they fail to distinguish between who they are and what they do. Such a patient might say, "That's just the way I am." We refer to such defenses as syntonic. Patients must be helped to see that they are doing something to avoid feelings that ultimately cause their difficulties. By focusing on the cost of defenses, we seek to render syntonic defenses dystonic.

Turning the Patient Against Her Defenses

In the following example, this very depressed and demoralized patient was brought in to see me for a consultation by her concerned husband. Her defenses of self-attack, including cutting herself, proved to be highly syntonic. Systematic work on this defense was required to render it dystonic and, in so doing, to increase the patient's desire to heal.

The Woman Who Cut

Therapist: Tell me what brings you.
Patient: Um, I guess, in March, I experienced this depression that got bad enough that I thought I'd start therapy, but it didn't work, and then I started to get anxiety and cutting myself.
Therapist: What kind of cutting?
Patient: Scratching to draw blood (motions to her legs).
Therapist: On your legs?
Patient: Up here on my arms. Actually, it's all over now.
Therapist: And this never happened before?
Patient: No.
Therapist: It's the first time. You seem to be making a link with anxiety—as if it's some way to discharge anxiety.

Patient: Yeah, it was, but also, when I was depressed—there was a period when I just felt nothing—just so . .

Therapist: Numb and detached.

After getting some more background, I brought the focus back to the here and now, in order to assess her current level of anxiety and depression, as well as her ability to attend to and regulate these inner states. Since her depression seemed to be a result of defenses including detachment, it was of the utmost importance that she be able to observe this mechanism at work.

Assessment of Anxiety

Therapist: Certainly you notice that you get anxious and depressed for sure, so let's start right now and check in. Are you aware that you are anxious right now?

Patient: Yes.

Therapist: So how do you notice that? What is happening in your body that lets you know you are anxious?

Patient: I can't stop moving (discharge).

Therapist: That's what you are doing (helping her distinguish the internal experience of anxiety from the things she does to avoid that experience), but inside what is telling you that you are anxious? What are those sensations?

Patient: That I just want to get up and leave.

Therapist: That's what you want to do (defense), so how you actually feel inside, in your body.

Patient: How do I feel? It's funny. I feel physically anxious but I feel very sad, very empty.

At first, the patient confused her feelings with the defenses of discharge and flight. It took a couple of rounds of clarification to help her distinguish between the internal experience of her anxiety and the mechanisms she used in an effort to avoid this experience. Her tolerance for anxiety was quite low, and her reliance on defenses rather high. However, after two rounds of clarification, she spontaneously revealed a feeling of sadness beneath the anxiety. This constituted a positive response to intervention, and was a good prognostic sign. This also provides an opening for the exploration of the underlying forces creating her distress.

Focus on Feelings

Therapist: Great—you are aware that under the anxiety you have a lot of feeling—there is sadness just underneath the anxiety.

Patient: Yes, there is.

Therapist: OK, so how do you experience the sadness?
Patient: Well, I try not to.

Turning Patient Against Defenses That Hurt Her

Therapist: So rather than feel the sadness you tense up and turn it into anxiety and that's not working so well for you. We don't know why, but for some reason you are scared of your own feelings, in this case sadness.
Patient: Right.
Therapist: Even when you are successful, you end up empty, so none of these are good options. Let's look at what you really want? What is your goal?
Patient: Just to be able to function.
Therapist: Really, that's it?
Patient: (Patient laughs—a good sign.) Not happy, just content.
Therapist: Why not happy?
Patient: Well not happy like laughing all the time, but at peace.
Therapist: So how do you feel when you say, "That's what I want for myself. I want to feel peaceful and happy."?
Patient: Um, I just don't see it happening.

This patient was so depressed, and her avoidant defenses were so strong and syntonic, that her desire for something new, healthy, and healing needed to be activated in order to stimulate conflict and motivation for change. The healthy part of her was literally paralyzed by the strength of these defenses. Consequently, there was no energy in the system. The therapist must persist in this effort until the patient can actually experience a felt desire to achieve therapeutic goals. A simple cognitive declaration is not sufficient. This woman had been in a vegetative depression for about eight months. Her helplessness and hopelessness re-emerged at every turn. It was absolutely essential for the therapist to block these depressive mechanisms, while simultaneously focusing on a positive approach goal (a therapeutic "one-two punch"), so that energy could enter the system and provide the fuel for the work ahead.

Highlighting Internal Conflict

Therapist: So right away, your brain says "you're not going to have it," but how do you feel it inside—that desire for what you really want for yourself (separating the patient from the defense of hopelessness)?
Patient: I don't. I think I feel like I don't deserve it.
Therapist: Again, as soon as you say it, an obstacle comes up. You get anxious. At first, a sadness comes up, and you get anxious. Now you say you

	want to be happy, and you get anxious. So something is going on where you distance from yourself.
Patient:	Yes.
Therapist:	What you feel in your heart—for some reason—you move away from, so you are kind of divided against yourself.
Patient:	Which stems, maybe, from the sadness, but I am afraid to find out what that sadness is about. I think I'm very afraid of that.

Now the third element of the triangle of conflict came into view. The patient was avoiding (D) her feelings (I/F) because she was afraid (A) of them and the memories associated with them. On some level, the patient had been willing to be anxious and depressed, rather than face her true feelings about what had actually happened in her life. Once she was able to see that her avoidance of these feelings was causing and perpetuating her symptomatic suffering, her motivation to abandon these defenses in favor of facing and experiencing her true feelings was ignited. It was essential that the therapist help the patient make this shift, rather than trying to do it for her. Therapists often work too hard and try to provide the energy and motivation the patient is lacking. However, such a position allows the patient to remain passive and detached.

Therapist:	Afraid to know you.
Patient:	Yeah.
Therapist:	Afraid to find out what those feelings are about.
Patient:	That's what I found out in these months—I go away from whatever situation or thought—I say, "Just don't go there."
Therapist:	And what we are seeing is that that pattern of avoiding when you feel anxious is interfering with what you want—to be happy and content. To be happy and content most people have to get to know themselves and be in contact with their feelings. If you are scared of yourself, afraid of your own feelings, you're going to be a jumbled mess.
Patient:	Sure. I think my fear is greater than my desire.

It is essential to get agreement about the therapeutic task, as well and the problems and goals, in order to establish a strong collaborative alliance with the patient. Therapists often miss this crucial step and end up working at cross-purposes with the patient. In the following vignette, I made it clear that the task required for the patient to get from the problem (anxiety, depression, and cutting) to her goals (to be peaceful, content, and happy) was to face what she has been avoiding. Until there is agreement about the therapeutic task, and the patient is willing to engage on an emotional level, no real therapeutic movement can be made. Once she agrees, we can move on to a more detailed inquiry into the onset of her symptoms.

Trigger to Depression and Self-Harm

Therapist: Now, you said, March is when something shifted.
Patient: February—end of February, the depression started.
Therapist: Do you know what triggered that?
Patient: No, I had bacterial pneumonia and was out of work for two weeks. My husband's theory is that I had more time to think.
Therapist: That's your husband's theory. What do you think?
Patient: I don't really have a theory. I think, I don't know, I guess, not being able to be who I was. My daily living changed. I have four kids. I wasn't able to take care of them. They just automatically became more independent.
Therapist: How old are they?
Patient: 10, 12, 15, 18. I think that made me feel very guilty, and the guilt just built up, and then I felt more depressed and more guilty because I couldn't function.
Therapist: These sound like thoughts—more like ideas—rather than feelings. Like you have been trying to figure it out with your head, but it's not something you have come to know in a visceral way.
Patient: Right.
Therapist: In fact, what you are saying is that you have some sense of what it's about but are afraid to face those feelings.
Patient: You're right.
Therapist: That sadness. What are you afraid of?
Patient: It may change things—change me—change the relationship I have with somebody.
Therapist: Who?
Patient: A family member—an aunt, uncle or brother. Parents.
Therapist: So you are afraid that if you have an honest look at what you really feel something might change—some relationships might change.
Patient: I don't like change.
Therapist: It will be hard for you to live then, because life is about change.
Patient: (Laughs—another good sign that her syntonic defenses are becoming dystonic.) I don't deal well with change. Sometimes I do, but not with this big stuff, and I guess this is something I wouldn't have any control over.
Therapist: What?
Patient: The reactions or, I don't know, I want to know what is there before I get there.
Therapist: This is interesting, because it sounds like you're in some conflict, right? A part of you is saying, "I don't want to know. I don't want to know about this feeling. Put the blinders on." And another part of you is saying, "I would like to know," so you are in some conflict. A part of you wants to know. Who wants to live in the dark? Driving

around with blinders on—you'll get in a wreck. It's not going to work very well.

Patient: I think that's—shortly after I was sick—I don't remember much of my early childhood—which is OK with me. Like up until 12—we moved and there was a new school. I remember that, with new friends and stuff. I figured, what I don't know doesn't hurt me, and I was fine not knowing but then we were back in my home town, driving around, and something triggered something—a memory—and I remember this street in Gainesville—I haven't been there in years.

Therapist: You grew up there?

Patient: I just remember this place and remember seeing this doctor and I didn't like it. Then, that night, part of me, just a small part of me thought, "I think that's what I'm running from—memories like that." Instead of fighting them, maybe just to be open to them, you know. Maybe it would help me, instead of blocking them all the time. So, at that point, I started thinking, maybe I do want to know more. (Patient is tearing up and looking very sad.)

The patient's defenses were beginning to weaken as the result of focused attention to turning her against defenses that were responsible for her suffering. As she took tentative steps toward letting go of these defenses, the feelings and memories she had been so adamantly avoiding began to surface. The movement was not dramatic, but slow and steady. Given how profoundly depressed she had been, and how syntonic her defenses were, these responses to intervention were actually quite positive. The patient was not merely saying she wanted to approach rather than avoid her feelings, but she was actually *doing* it—beginning to feel the emotions triggered in February, as well as revealing their precipitant.

Helping the Patient Turn Against Defenses and Revive Hope

Therapist: As you say that, it looks like some sadness comes up.

Patient: 'Cause I have given up a little bit.

Therapist: You are sad when you say you've given up on yourself. That's really sad that you've given up and haven't supported yourself. That is sad. So what would it be like to support yourself to get what you want?

Now she was sad, rather than resigned, about the fact that she has been detached as well as neglectful and frankly abusive toward herself. Still, the motivation to change was weak and needed to be strengthened.

Blocking Helplessness

Patient: I don't know how.

Therapist: Do you do it for other people, right? You're a mother of four.

Patient: Yeah, I do.
Therapist: What do you see right now?
Patient: If I can do it for them I am able to do it. It's in there somewhere.
Therapist: Your face kind of lit up, what were you thinking of?
Patient: That's good. If I can do it for them, I can do it for me.

This last interchange was of great significance. The therapist did not buy her presentation as an incapable woman. In other words, she did not confuse the patient with her defenses. Instead she reminded the patient of her strengths— in particular, the ability to care for and nurture others. Then she spontaneously harnessed that capacity, to utilize it in her own behalf. Recognizing this ability felt good to her, and provided additional fuel for moving forward.

This clinical vignette provides us with a reminder of the fact that only the healthy part of the patient, in concert with the therapist, can heal the injury. The patient cannot heal from a position of woundedness and weakness. Her strengths and capacity had to be brought to bear in order to achieve therapeutic ends. In this case, access to this healthy part of her was, in and of itself, therapeutic. Reviving hope is essential with depressed and hopeless patients. We do not achieve this by being cheerleaders, or lending them our hope, but by activating the dormant desires and strengths within them. This is a vital step in the process of helping the patient separate from defenses and turn against them, in favor of authentic relating to self and other.

Tactical Defenses: When Defenses Create a Barrier to Closeness

In addition to formal defenses, designed to prevent the patient from experiencing anxiety-provoking feelings, wishes, and fantasies, Davanloo (1980, 1990, 2000) has identified another set of defenses, referred to as "tactical" defenses. Tactical defenses are used interpersonally, to keep others at an emotional distance. Since feelings are evoked in close contact with others, if a patient can't tolerate his feelings, he won't be able to let anyone close. He develops interpersonal strategies to keep others at bay. Examples of tactical defenses include eye gaze avoidance; laughing and smiling; taking a helpless, weepy, victimized position; or talking so quickly there is no room for an interaction. Many, if not most, of these tactical defenses are unconscious. It is incumbent upon the therapist to identify these defenses, and get them out of operation as soon as possible, since they interfere with the development of a collaborative alliance, optimal affective activation, and genuine presence. Crossing legs and arms, keeping hats and coats on throughout the session, changing the subject, jumping from topic to topic, and contradicting oneself, are other examples of tactical defenses, used in to keep the therapist off track and at an emotional distance.

Left in place, these defenses become a wall between therapist and patient, preventing any genuine contact between the two. In addition, when rigid and chronic, these defenses create a kind of false self, and interfere with the patient's ability to make authentic contact with his inner life, and with others. As such, they are viewed as a major impediment to successful treatment. These defenses, which create a resistance to closeness, must be taken up as soon as they are apparent, as they will undermine treatment efforts if left in place. Unless the patient is willing to relinquish these defenses, and resistances against emotional closeness, the therapist will remain useless to the patient, who will continue to suffer.

Character Defenses

In addition to specific defenses against specific anxiety-provoking feelings, needs, and desires, some patients use defenses automatically and routinely, whether they are emotionally activated or not. In such cases, what may have started out as a defense against particular feelings, wishes, and inclinations becomes overgeneralized and integrated into the character of the patient. These rigid and pervasive postures and attitudes are referred to as character defenses. In other words, these defenses are characteristic of the person and show up everywhere, with everyone. Such character defenses prevent the patient from making contact with his own true feelings, as well as with others. In other words, these defenses operate as wall between the patient's head and heart, and his true and false self, as well as a wall between him and others. These pervasive and habitual defenses they must be identified and removed for therapeutic intervention to penetrate what has become "character armour" (Coughlin Della Selva, 1996/2004; Reich, 1972).

Phoenix Rising

Therapist: Tell me what brings you and what you'd like me to help you with.

Patient: So, I basically was depressed—and have been depressed all my life. I saw a report card from my first grade teacher alluding to my depression, though I have no memory of that. It's just been such a pervasive part of my experience that I never thought I would lose it, though I always hoped I would.

Therapist: How would you describe it—this depression—how you actually experience it?

Patient: Pervasive hopelessness—the expectation things won't go well for me and that I don't deserve for them to go well.

Distinguish Thoughts From Emotions

Therapist: Those are some thoughts you are having but it looks like you are feeling sad right now, so let's pay attention to that. How do you feel this emotional pain inside?

Patient: Unlovable—unworthy.

Therapist: Those are thoughts again, not a primary affect. So there is a mix of feelings and thoughts that are pretty negative about you. And also about the world and life—that things won't work out for you. That can only make it worse, wouldn't it?

Patient: Yeah.

Therapist: So if we can just have a look at that sadness. How do you experience it right now?

Patient: It will be hard for me to describe.

Therapist: If you just pay attention to your body—that is where we feel. What is happening in your body that tells you you are sad?

Patient: Well, certainly tears . . . um . . . kind of caved in feeling in my chest.

Therapist: Caved in . . . does it feel painful and achy or just hollow?

In this case, the patient reported chronic, lifelong depression. Inquiry revealed that this state was largely the result of excessive reliance on character defenses of passivity and compliance, as well as the habitual use of repressive defenses. The patient was highly identified with these defenses and viewed herself as essentially unlovable and unworthy. Therapeutic intervention was required to help the patient separate herself from her defenses. A failure to do so can result in the patient experiencing the therapist's challenge to defenses as an attack on the self.

We also see that this patient mistakes her defenses for her feelings. Helping the patient to identify feelings, and distinguish them from the defenses she uses to avoid them, was the first step in the process. Then helping her see how the pervasive use of these defenses actually caused her symptoms and suffering was required to help her turn against them. Again, a failure to distinguish between feelings, anxiety, and defenses can result in patients experiencing challenge to the defense as a personal attack. Achieving clarity and agreement here will prevent any such misunderstanding.

In this case, it took three rounds of intervention before the patient could begin to distinguish between *thoughts* like "I am unlovable" and "Things won't work out for me," and her internal *emotional* pain. Once she was able to see that thoughts are not feelings, we could begin to examine how avoiding feelings by going to thoughts creates symptoms.

Link Between Defenses and Symptoms

Patient: I ache everywhere, all the time, so that's another facet of my existence that has become the norm (patient has fibromyalgia and other pain syndromes).

Therapist: And maybe transferring some of that emotional pain into physical pain so that you ache all over?

Patient: Yeah.

This preliminary work resulted in an agreement about the mechanism responsible for the patient's lifelong depression and physical pain—excessive reliance on defenses against feeling her emotions on a visceral level. This lead the way to an agreement about our task—to abandon these defenses so she can experience and share previously avoided feelings. Although the patient was able to agree with the task on an intellectual level, she quickly reverted to these habitual strategies. Once patients know they are avoiding feelings by resorting to defenses, and that doing so hurts them and undermines therapeutic progress, challenge to the defenses is in order. Just talking about this is of little value. We urge the patient to do something instead. She had mentioned having a difficult time trusting anyone, so this was also broached directly.

Difficulty With Closeness

Therapist: The other thing that you bring up right away, which is associated with feelings about being here, are all the feelings around closeness. It's hard for you to get close, to depend, or need anyone. Is that right?

Patient: Yes . . . well, I am always hopeful that the next person will be someone I can trust and get close to, but I've had some bad experiences. I am afraid of trusting more than is warranted.

Therapist: Do you mean in therapy, you've had bad experiences, as well as in life?

Patient: Mostly in life in general. I have been in analysis for 10 years . . . though it seems like 12. It's been tremendously helpful to me, but recently there has been a change that has been really hard for me, even though I think it shouldn't be that hard.

Therapist: But it is.

Patient: Yeah, he is getting older and cut back his schedule to three days— eliminating our Monday meeting. Weekends are really difficult for me and I got through them by telling myself I could see him on Monday. So, that simple change has had a lot of emotional ramifications. That is the crux of the analysis, I guess. I am not sure I can trust him anymore.

Therapist: You go to, "I can't trust him," but has he been trustworthy over these past 10 years?

Patient: Yes.

Therapist: OK, so you obviously have some strong mixed feelings toward him that have gotten triggered by this schedule change.

Patient: Yeah, I guess so . . . (long pause). Maybe what it comes down to is that I do feel angry with him for a partial abandonment, but I don't trust him to be able to hear that.

Therapist: Have you told him?

Patient: I think I have. In fact, that's all we talk about now.

Therapist: Are you face to face?
Patient: Yes, I asked for that. I didn't like the couch and wanted more contact.

Pattern of Compliance

Therapist: But I notice here, you tend to avoid eye contact and spend most of the time looking at the floor. So this is a dilemma, because you are also here to check me out. Am I someone who can be helpful— am I trustworthy? How are you going to know if you don't look at me? Number two, even when you are here, you keep yourself alone, which sounds like is a problem, and feeds into loneliness and sadness.

Patient: Yeah, I always have the feeling with my analyst that he doesn't like me looking at him.

Therapist: So, are you compliant?

Patient: Yes (laughs).

Therapist: You are there for your own need but trying to make him comfortable? Is that a problem in your life? You said you don't trust anyone to take care of you, but it sounds like you don't take very good care of you.

Patient: Yeah.

Therapist: How about if we do it differently?

Patient: That sounds good.

Therapist: So if both you and me pay attention to you—why you are here and what you want? So, what you are saying so far, is that you need some help with this anger—both toward this analyst—and others in your life. And this may be related to the pervasive depression— the tendency to turn it back on yourself with you are not lovable, you are unworthy and so on—rather than facing your anger toward those who have let you down. That also interferes with closeness, because if you keep these feelings inside, it will create a barrier. So, the other thing that happens is that you get a lot of physical pain—not only depressed—but pain from suppressing all these feelings.

Defenses and Somatic Symptoms

Patient: Yes.

Therapist: Anything else physically?

Patient: Yes, headaches and TMJ.

Therapist: Related to holding all that anger inside.

Patient: Yes, as soon as the analyst told me about cutting back, the teeth grinding got so bad, I was destroying my molars and had to get them completely rebuilt.

Therapist: Oh my—this is really self-defeating, on the most intrinsic level. He gets spared and you are the one with all the pain. Is this something you are willing to look into together?

Patient: Yes.

The patient had spent her whole life sacrificing herself in order to care for and connect with others. In order to do so, she had repressed and internalized all her angry feelings toward others, harming herself while protecting the other. In this example, her rage toward her analyst was internalized, causing such excessive teeth grinding that she required major dental work. This example was used to illustrate the cost of her defenses, in an attempt to turn her against them. In so doing, the therapist was challenging the healthy part of the patient to stand up to the self-destructive forces within her. This was especially important in this case, as the patient had a strong tendency to be compliant with others.

Head-On Collision With the Resistance

In the previous case, work on defense and resistance was successful in helping the patient relinquish them in favor of authentic connection with herself and therapist. In other cases, a focus on defense and resistance results in an increase of their use and strength. In such cases, the patient seems to dig in his heels and becomes increasingly distant and uninvolved, or defiant and sarcastic. In other words, they use defenses as a resistance to the therapist and her treatment efforts, creating emotional distance. Since defenses against emotional closeness prevent patient and therapist from making a genuine emotional connection, they must become the focus of treatment. This type of resistance sabotages treatment efforts and must be confronted directly. Therefore, a "head-on collision" with the resistance (Davanloo, 1990; Kalpin, 1994) is required. This procedure involves a series of interventions involving the following steps: (1) outlining the therapeutic task; (2) clarifying defenses and resistance and the consequence of same, in the therapy and the patient's life; (3) acknowledging and confronting the patient's need to suffer and fail; (4) undoing therapist omnipotence; and (5) emphasizing the patient's choice and encouraging him to DO SOMETHING about the resistance and avoidance of closeness that will prevent healing from taking place.

It is important to recognize that increased resistance is actually a good sign. The rise in resistance is a reflection of an increase in painful, anxiety-laden feelings, pushing for expression. When the therapist puts pressure on the patient to "be real" and open up emotionally in order to get help, his attachment system gets activated. All the pain, rage, guilt, and grief associated with past relationships become mobilized and threaten to break through the repressive barrier. This threat fuels the resistance to letting the therapist into his intimate life. The conflict between old loyalties and new possibilities, between courageously facing painful feelings and avoiding them, gets intensified by the therapist's targeted interventions. As a result, the patient's conflict becomes crystalized in the transference relationship, where it is taken up directly. Working with feelings in the here and now of the therapeutic relationship increases the likelihood of a corrective emotional experience, so essential in the healing process. The visceral experience of feelings and impulses in the transference also operates as a trigger to the unconscious, leading to rapid de-repression of significant memories, shedding light on the origin of the patient's conflicts.

Woman Heading for a Heart Attack

This 66-year-old woman had been in therapy almost continually since the age of six, following her father's sudden death. She had acquired a good deal of intellectual insight during these treatments, but nothing had changed. She continued to be plagued by anxiety, depression, crushingly low self-esteem, relationship difficulties, and a host of physical ailments. Consequently, her list of medications was as long as her arm. While physically present and quite verbal, she remained emotionally detached in our first session, both from her own inner experience and from the therapist. These defenses were used habitually and affected every area of her functioning, from self-care to work and relationships. Consequently, they are considered characterological defenses. As such they were ubiquitous and affected our interaction. Unless removed, these defenses would guarantee another treatment failure.

Identification and Intensification of the
Patient's Internal Conflict

Therapist: Are you willing to be emotionally open here, so that I can get to know you?

Patient: Well, I mean, I am willing to be present and I am trying but I am also feeling defensive or something. (Patient motions with her hands that she is erecting a wall between herself and the therapist—a sign of the unconscious alliance.)

Therapist: It's really great that you notice that—fantastic. First of all, you realize there is anxiety, which creates these symptoms, and then you go "wooww," which is a pushing away from contact—like "Don't get too close to me." So are you aware that that is what the anxiety is about—letting someone close to get to know you in a deep and intimate way?

Patient: Oh yes, I don't think I've ever had that experience actually. Except with a long-term therapist, but that is like a professional experience.

The therapist started by giving the patient credit for recognizing her anxiety, as well as the defenses she used to reduce it. The therapist then pointed out the interpersonal consequences of these defenses—that of preventing closeness.

The patient corroborated this link between anxiety, closeness, and distancing, adding new and relevant information that ended with the rather devastating admission that she had never allowed anyone close to her in a deep and intimate way. Unless she allowed herself to feel the pain of self-imposed exile and declared her will to end it, the therapist would be rendered useless, like all those before her.

Challenge to Defense

Therapist: So you are really aware of that.

Patient: Very.

Therapist: But you still do it. Then, you end up keeping yourself walled off and alone. So, that must be a lonely place.

Patient: Oh yes, definitely a lonely place.

Therapist: Are you aware you have feelings about that coming up?

Patient: Yes, right here (points to her chest).

Therapist: What is the feeling?

Patient: I could cry. But you see I don't like to cry in front of people.

Therapist: Again it comes up right away here, and it highlights this conflict that you come here for help, and help with emotional problems, that are obviously of a deep nature. In order for me to help you, I have to be able to get close to you and close to those feelings, but another part of you is saying, "No way, I'm not showing you anything." So we see that you are working at cross-purposes here—part of you wanting to come and get help and another part of you is saying no way. This self-destructive part of you that smokes and drinks and is out to destroy you is already visible here.

Linking the patient's presenting problems to the pattern already in evidence in the therapy was required to intensify the tension between her healthy strivings and an entrenched pattern of self-destructiveness. Acknowledging this pattern was insufficient for change. It was essential that the patient feel the painful cost of her defenses, and then do something about them. As long as she continued to bury her pain, she would not heal.

The therapist must abandon any fantasies of omnipotence for therapy to be effective. She alone cannot cure the patient. Only a joint effort between a highly involved patient and committed therapist will result in healing. The therapist must emphasize this point—that the patient's participation is required for a positive result. This is one of the areas where therapists often stumble. They are, in a sense, too supportive of the patient's defenses—understanding them and validating them, instead of helping the patient turn against them. Perhaps this is one of the reasons that the majority of therapists reported a lack of skill and confidence in their ability to get patients actively involved in the treatment process. This is not always an easy task!

Challenging the Patient's Will

Patient: Right, exactly.
Therapist: So you are aware of this. It's amazing, in a sense how aware you
            are—that you have these feelings that you want to avoid and, in
            order to do that, you have to keep a certain distance, because it is in
            relationship that these feelings come up. So you are aware of this,
            and you are even aware of how self-defeating it is.
Patient: Oh, yes.
Therapist: But you still do it.
Patient: Right.
Therapist: So it is a choice. This is where the issue of your will . .
Patient: It's absent.

This is another turning point. Will the therapist buy this rationalization or,
remembering an earlier declaration of intention ("I am here!"), speak to her
conflict and her choice? If the therapist takes the bait and behaves as if the
patient is helpless, the therapy will stall. However, if she speaks to what is best
in the patient, allying with her strength, determination, and desire for healing,
while calling her lack of will into question, progress can be made. If we adopt a
potential rather than pathological view of the patient, siding with the patient's
healthy strivings, while simultaneously urging the patient to abandon old, outmoded avoidant strategies, therapeutic progress can be made.

Link to the Past

Therapist: I'm not sure it's absent. You are aware, so you are making a choice—
            will I dare to open up and get help or do I choose to keep to myself,
            keep my suffering? (I could see the patient was having a strong
            response to my intervention.) So what is happening?
Patient: I flashed to my Mom. She was a professional martyr. So, I think,
            "Oh my gosh." Though outwardly . . .
Therapist: We are not really interested in the outer part, but if we look at the
            part of you that is attached to the suffering, that keeps you alone,
            keeps you down, destroys your health, keeps you from getting help,
            your association is to your mother, who was a martyr. So this is a
            connection you haven't seen before? You thought I want to be dif-
            ferent from my mother.
Patient: Yeah, but then you look in the mirror and say, "Oh my God, I am my
            mother." I understand that. You know she had an alcohol problem
            and was depressed (and the patient has followed suit). My father
            died when my brother, sister, and I were very young.
Therapist: How old were you?
Patient: Six, I had just turned six. And she basically—there were problems
            before too—but she just tanked after that.

Therapist: Got very depressed, you mean?

Patient: Yes, and drank. We ended up taking care of her and we got a very strong message, with an Irish Catholic background—we just don't show emotion—at least not in my family, especially, you didn't complain. Although, I always did complain, but my role in the family was as the jokester.

Therapist: You have a tremendous amount of understanding, but it really hasn't helped you that much because, when push comes to shove, to open up to these feelings and have some compassion, rather than to be so nasty, or to open up and let someone else in, those walls go up. But I see there is a lot of pain there, so are you willing?

Patient: I am going to try my darnedest, that is for sure. I have a 15-year-old daughter and you can tell I'm not a teenager. My husband and I adopted her when I was 50 and you know "I have to live, I have to live, I have to live," but I'm doing everything not to.

Therapist: How awful—to expose your daughter to the very kind of loss you experienced as a child . . .

Patient: And even worse, because she is adopted.

Therapist: Another loss for her.

Patient: Oh no, I can't do it (crying).

In many ways the therapist was simply confronting reality—that if the patient continued to remain detached from her own feelings, and from the therapist, therapeutic efforts were destined to fail once again. If a different outcome was to be achieved this time around, a different process was required. The patient was encouraged to take some constructive action. In so doing, the therapist was urging the healthy part of the patient to stand up to the internal forces responsible for perpetuating her suffering. It is important to point out that the work on defense and resistance must take place within the context of encouragement to connect emotionally with the patient. If the therapist simply points out defense and resistance, without creating space for the healthy alternative, she can "turn into a nag and the analysis into harassment" (Greenson, 1967, p. 147).

In this case, the patient was able to see how she was repeating a painful pattern from the past and threatening her daughter with the same kind of devastating loss she had experienced as a child. With this awareness came deep waves of painful feeling. By feeling that pain, her motivation to abandon the defenses that kept her distant from others and perpetuated her suffering, was enhanced. She declared her determination to "try my darnedest," rather than pretend she had no will to mobilize, as she had earlier in the session. By abandoning defenses that served as a resistance to the treatment, the collaborative work of therapy was bolstered. Of course, the positive response to this kind of head-on collision with the resistance proved therapeutic. For a depressed and resigned patient to grab hold of her choice is reparative, in and of itself.

Transference Resistance

In the previous two cases, characterological defenses resulted in a lifelong history of self- defeating behavior that affected every area of the patient's life. These character defenses created a resistance that would ultimate sabotage treatment efforts, if not removed. The previous vignette illustrated the therapist's attempt to acquaint the patient with these defenses and their attendant costs in an effort to turn her against them. While useful, these interventions were not sufficient to undo a lifelong pattern of self-imposed suffering. In the next session, to be detailed in Chapter 5, a head-on collision with that resistance was required in order to break through it. The result was a breakdown of resistance, a breakthrough of previously unconscious feelings and memories, unleashing the unconscious alliance, which propelled healing forward.

In other cases, patients erect a defensive barrier with the therapist that are specific to the situation, and serve as a resistance to feelings in the transference. The ability to determine which type of defense or resistance is in the way of productive collaboration, as well as developing skills in helping patients remove them, are key components of effective intervention. In the following case, the therapist's initial confusion about whether she was dealing with character resistance or transference resistance contributed to the difficulties involved in getting the therapy moving forward.

This patient, referred to as "The Linebacker," had been quite successful in her life. She was an orthopedic surgeon, with many friends and a loving partnership. Her problems were fairly circumscribed and involved interpersonal conflicts at work that undermined both her enjoyment of, and success in, private practice. In our first two sessions, the extensive use of intellectualization, rationalization, and argumentativeness interfered with the development of a solid alliance, and threatened to undermine the process. Initially, the therapist got entangled in some in these defenses, co-creating a power struggle. When emotionally activated, the patient had a lot of difficulty stepping back and observing herself. Instead she was highly reactive and fairly rigid in her responses. She seemed to be on guard from the moment she entered the office, adopting an attitude akin to "the best defense is a good offense." At first, this struck me as evidence of character resistance, as in the previous case. However, attempts at a "head-on collision" with this resistance were unsuccessful. In reviewing our pattern of interaction together, material emerged suggesting that our struggle had actually been a manifestation of a specific transference resistance.

The Linebacker

Therapist: So we are trying to understand what is getting in the way here. Do you see that your tendency to argue and split hairs, to focus on external factors, to avoid my eyes and remain stiff and immovable, all contribute to a barrier here?

Patient: This is so weird. I am usually very animated, so I don't know why I am like that here. Maybe in other areas of my life I am the one in control. Then I feel looser and freer.

Therapist: So, is it just here with me that this is happening or am I part of a certain subset?

Patient: It happens with people in authority or with those who have more power than me.

Here it became clear that this tendency to go on the offense and get into power struggles with others was not universal or characterological, but was specific to interactions with authority figures, suggesting that this pattern of behavior actually constituted a transference resistance. Consequently, a focus on feelings toward the therapist, rather than a head-on collision with character resistance, was indicted.

Clarification

Therapist: This is very important. You are saying you are not universally terrified of closeness but are hesitant to open up to people in some position of authority.

Patient: Yeah. I try to manage the impression I'm making and end up tripping over my words. Lately, I just say as little as possible so I don't end up tripping over myself.

Therapist: As if you are afraid of what might come out with these authority figures.

Patient: Yes.

Therapist: And, in many ways, that has been present here from the moment you walked in to see this authority figure.

Patient: I suppose so. It's the same feeling and it starts as soon as I turn in your parking lot.

Pressure to Feelings Toward the Therapist

Therapist: What is that feeling toward me?

Patient: Uncomfortable. It's interesting because it's a duality. I am excited and it's good to see you. It's not like I dread it.

Therapist: But the feelings are mixed.

Patient: Very mixed. There is disharmony and that's always been a problem. That can lead to anger and negative consequences.

Therapist: So there is an anger that comes up here with me, as I am a member of this group.

Patient: It's frustration—an adrenalin rush; tightness in my chest.

Therapist: So there is anger and anxiety, with tension and constriction. What would happen if you didn't clamp down and that anger came out toward me?

Patient: I would stomp out.

Therapist: That would be a way to avoid the anger, wouldn't it? So if you don't avoid it, what would happen?

Patient: Things would escalate. It might get physical.

Therapist: What is the impulse in your arms?

Patient: To punch and hit. (Laughs.) This is bizarre.

Therapist: It's hard to look at.

Unconscious Alliance—Transfer of Images

Patient: It's really hard to look at. There was too much hitting and yelling in the past (starts to cry). Screaming between my mother and father; between my brother and me. Certainly at times being physically stopped, because I could have killed my brother.

Therapist: Your brother comes to mind?

Patient: He was almost 10 years older than me. Sometimes he would play with me, but then, for no reason, out of the blue, he would tackle me and hold me down. I would try to fight him off and would start screaming but then he would put his hand over my mouth or take a pillow and put it over my face.

Therapist: So he could have killed you too.

Patient: He would go berserk and just go nuts. I remember saying to him, "Just kill me." When my parents got home . . .

Therapist: Where were they?

Patient: They would be out at work or at my grandmother's and they would leave him to babysit. I'd tell them but they wouldn't believe me. He was the beloved son who could do no wrong, and was an angel for babysitting me.

Therapist: Even though he was torturing you.

Patient: One time he tied me to a tree. The neighbors found me and brought me home. When I told my parents that my brother did it, they said, "What did you do? You antagonize him."

Therapist: So there was no one there to protect you. You must have lots of feelings toward your parents too.

Portrait of the Impulse

Patient: I hate my brother. I really do.

Therapist: And since no one else would take him on, you are aware of a murderous rage toward him. How would you kill him yourself?

Patient: I remember washing the dishes and how this cast iron skillet was so heavy I had to use two hands to hold it. I would sneak up on him when he's watching TV in the living room, and just bash his head in with the skillet.

Therapist: How do you see that?

Patient: Smash his head on the top and the side. His head is caved in and he's dead. It's a bloody mess, with the side of his head caved in.

Therapist: What does he look like?

Patient: I just see a form, not his face.

Therapist: But if you look at his face?

Patient: He was a handsome guy—kind of like Elvis or Ricky Nelson. I must say, it feels OK to see him down—I have no remorse.

Therapist: But now you seem detached.

Patient: I am detached. I would have a lot of explaining to do to my parents. I killed the Prodigal Son. There would be no explanation good enough. It wouldn't matter that he was trying to kill me. I would be completely ostracized. You know, I hate to say this, but I get great satisfaction out of the fact that he is such a fuck up. He has so many problems. It's like revenge. At the same time, I have been successful.

Link Between Brother and Therapist—Consolidation of Insight

Therapist: But you're not allowing yourself to enjoy your success and are getting into battles with people at work. What we have seen today is that there is some link between me and your brother. This pent up rage toward him was being directed at me, as a member of this class of people who you see as having some power over you.

Patient: Now I don't feel any anger toward you. I like you and want to open up so you can help me.

Therapist: It's really important that this all came out so clearly here, because we could see that the suppressed anger was going into opposition— that you, in a sense, would want to . . .

Patient: Oh—I wouldn't want you to succeed—to give you the satisfaction! Now I see it. Actually, I really do want you to succeed in helping me.

Therapist: And by putting down your guard and opening up about these feelings here toward me, we gained access to these important memories, so we can help you resolve these conflicts rather than just playing them out.

In this case, the defenses interfering with open engagement and cooperation were a specific manifestation of transference resistance. Initially, the therapist thought that she was dealing with character resistance. However, closer examination revealed that the patient did not have problems with intimacy and closeness with friends and loved ones, but only with those in authority. Consequently, a head-on collision with the resistance was not indicated. Instead, by exploring her feelings in the transference, the resistance broke down, feelings broke through, and the unconscious source of her conflict was exposed, worked through, and resolved. Unconscious guilt about murderous impulses—and sadistic satisfaction about same—has been operating in such a way that would have resulted in therapeutic failure. Following the breakthrough of feelings in the transference, with a link to the past, the patient gained insight into the unconscious need to defeat the therapist as a way of both exacting revenge and simultaneously punishing herself for her murderous impulses. Instead of simply repeating this unconscious pattern of reactivity with the therapist, the defensive enactment was blocked, allowing her to face and resolve the emotional conflicts that had been wreaking havoc in her life.

The Therapeutic Effect of Defense Work

When we help a patient relinquish defenses and experience his true feelings, several therapeutic goals are accomplished. In the process of facing feelings, without undue anxiety or resorting to defensive avoidance, the patient increases his ego adaptive capacity. Additionally, the experience of one's true feelings is an experience of "emotional truth" and authenticity, and leads to the consolidation of a solid sense of self (Coughlin Della Selva, 1992). It also constitutes a kind of internal corrective emotional experience, so central to deep and lasting change. It's an experience of getting on friendly terms with feelings that had generated anxiety in the past. This is often a revelation to patients. Following the direct, visceral experience of previously avoided affect, there is often a clear and unmistakable de-repression of memories, dreams, and associations, shedding light on the origin of the patient's conflicts. In this way the past is present, and available for reworking. This process helps the patient to integrate head and heart; to understand the mechanisms responsible for his suffering; to liberate himself from self-destructive habits; and to achieve emotional freedom. The recent data on memory retrieval and reconsolidation (Ecker, Ticic, & Hulley, 2012) provides empirical support for this clinical finding.

Summary

Put very simply, most of our patients' symptoms and suffering are the inevitable (though unintended) result of excessive reliance on defenses against painful and anxiety-provoking feelings and impulses. Patients tend to think of their defenses as allies. Typically, they are aware of their benefits, but blind to their substantial cost. Therefore, it is incumbent upon the therapist to help the patient see that her reliance on defenses against feeling and connecting are responsible for her symptoms and suffering. In so doing, motivation to approach, rather than avoid, one's own emotional truth is enhanced. Effective defense work includes a process of identification and clarification. With relatively healthy and highly motivated patients this process is usually sufficient to render them dystonic. Previously avoided feelings are activated, experienced, and freely shared in the process.

In contrast, defenses that are tightly held and ego-syntonic require a phase of challenge, along with a process of identification and clarification. In addition to causing the patient's internal difficulties, when knit together these defenses create a resistance that prevents genuine connection with others, including the therapist. If the patient is resisting emotional involvement with the therapist, this resistance will undermine all her efforts unless removed. While it is the therapist's job to identify and challenge the continued use of these resistances, the ultimate decision about whether to abandon them in order to engage actively in the process is always up to the patient. That said, if a patient declares he is not willing to open up and engage with the therapist in a collaborative effort, the treatment is destined to fail and must be discontinued. This confrontation with reality constitutes a "head-on collision" with the resistance (Davanloo, 1990). When therapists avoid this confrontation and continue to see a patient who is not authentically engaged in the process, they inadvertently co-create a collusive alliance.

Assessing the types and tenacity of defenses used by the patient is vital for developing a therapeutic strategy designed to overcome these obstacles in the way of development. The more we can help patients relinquish these avoidant strategies, in favor of facing their emotional truth, the further they will be from suffering. Not only will patients be relieved from the suffering their defenses entail, but will have free access to the energy and information contained in the feelings that are now accessible to them. Once defenses have broken down, and feelings have broken through the repressive barrier, patients are empowered and have a choice about who, when, where, and with whom they might express these feelings. Developing skill in the area of defense work will pave the way to the kind of emotional activation and engagement required for deep and sustained therapeutic change to take place.

Chapter Five
A Focus on Feelings: Facilitating the Experience of Emotion

Human beings are wired for emotion and emotional connection with others (Damasio, 1994, 2000; Gross, 1998; LeDoux, 1998). Having free and unfettered access to our deepest feelings, fears, and longings helps us to develop a sense of self, direct our behavior, attach to others, facilitate decision making, motivate us to attain desired goals, and navigate the interpersonal field. Emotions constitute a primary signaling system that activates action tendencies and facilitates meaning making. Emotions tell us what is important and aid us in decision making (Greenberg, 2002). Without clear and unencumbered access to our emotions, we are sailing through life without a rudder.

Now, "after three decades of the dominance of cognitive approaches, motivational and emotional processes have roared back into the limelight" (Shore, 2007, p. 1). In particular, we are in the midst of a paradigm shift into the unconscious affective-relational functions of the right brain, requiring clinicians to understand these mechanisms and use them to promote deep and lasting change in the patients they treat. Of late, there has been a growing consensus that deficits in emotional awareness and regulation are a core feature of many, if not most, psychiatric disorders (Barlow et al., 2011). Increased attention to emotional activation and regulation in treatment is consistent with the emerging data on the nature of the underlying factors responsible for our patients' suffering (Barlow et al., 2011).

As Wachtel (1993) has suggested:

The patient's problems are understood as deriving most fundamentally from his having learned early in life to be afraid of his feelings, thoughts, and inclinations, and the effort to help him overcome his problems is focused very largely on helping him re-appropriate those feelings and incorporate them into a fuller and richer sense of self and of life's possibilities.

(p. 32)

The question is how to accomplish this goal in a consistently effective manner. Since many of our patients' difficulties are the result of early, implicit emotional learning that remains unconscious and embedded in procedural memory, the successful therapist must become adept at identifying these emotional conflicts as they become apparent in the therapeutic interaction. In order to achieve these ends, therapists must learn to watch their patients as well as listen to them, carefully attending to nonverbal cues alerting us to the patient's areas of sensitivity.

The data are clear—those who are aware of their feelings, experience them freely, reflect upon them consciously, and express them constructively, are happier, healthier, and more successful than those who lack such abilities (Peterson, 2006). Longitudinal research supports the notion that even the most intellectually gifted fail both occupationally and socially, if they do not possess these crucial emotional skills (Bond & Vaillant, 1986; Goleman, 1995, 2007; Pennebaker, 1990; Vaillant, 2015). Given this, the effective therapist must develop specific skills and interventions designed to help patients identify their emotions, activate the multilayered experience of these emotions in session, and support new emotional learning within the context of a therapeutic relationship. It seems increasingly clear that psychotherapy helps people heal in large part by (1) helping patients become aware of their feelings; (2) increasing their ability to tolerate, reflect upon, and integrate these feelings; while (3) learning to express these feelings constructively (Greenberg, 2008).

Identifying Emotions

"An emotion is a complex psychological state that involves three distinct components: a subjective experience, a physiological experience and behavioral or expressive response" (Hockenbury & Hockenbury, 2007). It is generally agreed that human beings have six basic emotions: happiness/joy, sadness, fear, anger, surprise, and disgust (Ekman & Davidson, 1994). While our ability to be aware of, tolerate, integrate, regulate, and express our emotions vary widely from person to person, the pattern of physiological activation characteristic of our most basic emotions appears to be universal (Nummenmaa, Glerean, Hari, & Hietanen, 2013). Similarly, the facial expressions that accompany emotional states also appear to be universally understood (Ekman, 2007). It has been suggested that this universality binds us together and allows us to be understood by all human beings, regardless of race, religion, or verbal language (Eckman & Friesen, 1975).

Davanloo (1990) has developed a concrete and operational definition that is helpful here. He suggested that, to be considered "in touch with feelings," three essential components must be in evidence: (1) a cognitive label for the feeling or emotion in question, (2) physiological activation in the body, and (3) mobilization of impulses. Therapists must be familiar with these basic emotions and their physiological pattern of activation, in order to ensure effective and therapeutic processing of the patient's core feelings. We will begin with an examination of the emotions central to attachment—anger, pain and grief, love and joy, and guilt.

Anger

Anger is a built-in response to unfairness, violation, and trespass. The experience of anger in the body is one of heat and energy, emanating from the center of the body and extending outward. In particular, the jaw, neck, shoulders, and arms become mobilized, activating behaviors that enable us to stand up for ourselves, protect ourselves and others, and fight off attackers, if need be. Those who repress anger cannot defend themselves physically or emotionally. Conversely, those who can access anger without undue anxiety or defensiveness can use this energy and information to assert themselves in a constructive manner.

Pain and Grief

Pain and grief are typically experienced as a heaviness or pain in the chest/heart, along with a lump in the throat. Grief is the natural, built-in response to loss. The impulse associated with grief is to cry, and express this emotional pain and sadness in order to elicit support from others. There is often a felt desire to be reunited with the lost love, with wandering and searching prominent following a loss. Reviewing memories, and a preoccupation with the lost love, is also common. This process is necessary in order to come to terms with the loss. Without support through the grieving process, including the experience of all the mixed feelings toward the loved one who has been lost, defensive operations come into play that can derail the grieving process and result in symptomatic suffering.

Love and Joy

Love and joy are also experienced in the chest; typically described as a sensation of openness, lightness, and expansiveness. The impulse associated with love is to reach out and connect with others in an affectionate manner. When love is experienced toward an actual or potential partner, sexual feelings and impulses can also be activated.

Guilt

Guilt, an exquisitely painful and often misunderstood emotion, is often described as gut wrenching. To face one's own destructiveness, and the pain of having harmed someone we love, is a highly aversive state. It is not uncommon to hear people say, "I feel sick about it. I can't believe I did that." Guilt is tied to love, and prompts us to want to re-engage and repair broken relationships. Defenses against guilt, ranging from self- punishment to denial and justification, damage both the individual who perpetuated harm, and the victim of his cruelty. All too often therapists encourage patients to avoid guilt, and to justify their own poor choices. This does no one any favors. Being able to have a long, hard look at the impact of our behavior on others, including facing our pettiness and vindictiveness, is essential to growth and maturity. Without this, patients become perpetual victims or remain self-absorbed. As Winnicott (1963) has reminded us, guilt is connected to concern and is a healthy, mature affect that motivates repair attempts. As such, the ability to experience genuine guilt is considered a developmental achievement.

Understanding the Role of Emotion in Development

Feelings have been built in over the course of evolution, and are an invaluable aid to survival and adaptation. Our basic emotions are potent sources of both energy/fuel (the "juice") and information. Additionally, feelings and emotions function as a kind of glue and conduit for attachment. As such, our most basic feelings constitute a kind of internal guidance system, helping us adapt and maneuver in an interpersonal world. Our ability to be aware of, and reflect upon our feelings, so that we can use the information and energy contained therein to express ourselves, connect with others, and attain goals, constitutes what has been referred to as "emotional intelligence" (Goleman, 1995; Mayer & Salovey, 1995). This type of reflection upon felt experience is central to the task of meaning making, so vital to human beings, and constitutes a vital component of what is referred to as "working through" in psychotherapy (Wachtel, 1993, 1997).

"A picture has emerged of a set of pervasive, adaptive, sophisticated mental processes that occur largely out of view" (Wilson, 2002, p. 5). Some have gone so far as to suggest that this sort of automatic, implicit processing that takes place in the unconscious mind does nearly all the work (Wilson, 2002). Because the conscious mind (neo-cortex) is slow and limited in its capacity, there is only so much information it can process. It appears that:

> the mind operates most efficiently by relegating a good deal of high-level, sophisticated thinking to the unconscious, just as a modern jumbo jet-liner is able to fly on automatic pilot with little or no input from the human, "conscious" pilot.
>
> (Wilson, 2002, p. 6)

As such, this automatic processing is viewed as adaptive, and not merely the result of repression due to anxiety, as Freud proposed.

However adaptive this automaticity may be in some instances, a lack of emotional awareness can also prevent necessary reassessment and alteration of faulty, outmoded, or dysfunctional emotional learning. This is the concern for most psychotherapists. Some have suggested (Ecker, Ticic, & Hulley, 2012) that implicit emotional learning regarding "attachment patterns, family of origin rules and roles, unresolved emotional themes, traumatic memory, and compulsive behaviors" (p. 15) are tenacious and require very specific interventions to bring to consciousness, in order to be deleted or revised. Since the "emotional learnings maintaining the clients' symptoms are complex and are areas of deep vulnerability that consist of implicit memory and implicit knowledge" (Ecker, Ticic, & Hulley, 2012, p. 28), they are not conscious or available when the patient enters therapy. It is up to the therapist to initiate a process that will lead to an unlocking of the unconscious emotional system, where the source of the patient's conflict originated and is being maintained.

Understanding Emotional Problems

While many, if not most, of our patients come for help because of emotional distress, I want to suggest that emotions are rarely the problem. Emotions have been selected for by evolutionary processes designed to help us function in an optimal manner. Rather, it is high levels of anxiety, and reliance on defenses against the experience of feelings, that cause most of the problems our patients are struggling to resolve. This is a key distinction required to intervene specifically and effectively. We want to regulate anxiety and block defenses so that the direct, visceral experience of the avoided feelings can be facilitated in a safe and tolerable manner. Then the energy and information contained in these feelings can be utilized for constructive action.

Furthermore, the visceral experience of anxiety-laden feelings triggers an opening of the unconscious, accompanied by the downloading of memories associated with these feelings (Davanloo, 1980). In this way, we discover the source of the patient's distress and understand how his anxiety about feelings makes all kinds of sense—or at least DID make sense in the past. This understanding promotes integration and coherence and solidifies the process of change (Ecker, Ticic, & Hulley, 2012). The need to understand what has been emotionally experienced must not be overlooked or given short shrift. The cathartic discharge of emotion is of little lasting value. Instead, the deep understanding of self and other that follows the experience of previously avoided feelings seems to be required for sustained change to take place (Pennebaker, 1997).

Emotional Awareness

Whether we are aware of our feelings or not, there is a good deal of data to suggest that our behavior and decisions are profoundly influenced by our emotions (Damasio, 1994, 2000). In other words, unconscious feelings exert a significant influence on behavior, despite our lack of awareness of these feelings (Neisser, 2006; Ryan, 2007; Shore, 2007). Damasio (1994) contends that we can't make the simplest of decisions without access to our emotions, which imbue our choices with valence. Emotions prioritize. Without conscious awareness of our feelings, we are "driving blind," and are not in a position to choose how to handle our feelings.

Helping patients become curious about and connect with the internal experience of their feelings and emotions is often a first step in the process. Without knowing what we feel and what drives us, we are strangers to ourselves. Such emotional awareness is a boon to physical as well as emotional health (Pennebaker, 1997). We experience feelings in the body. Consequently, the habitual suppression of feelings and emotions has demonstrably adverse effects upon physical health and well-being (Mate, 2003; Pennebaker, 1997). Chronic pain and unexplained medical symptoms have often been found to arise from an emotional, rather than organic, cause (Abbass et al., 2010; Abbass, Kisely, & Kroenke, 2009; Abbass, Lovas, & Purdy, 2008; Sarno, 1999, 2006; Schubiner, 2011). The routine repression of feelings has also been associated with suppressed immune function, increasing susceptibility to illness and infection (Coughlin, 2009; Pennebaker, 1997). A recent study is pertinent here. While 80% of "non-stressed" adults who received a flu vaccine developed immunity to the virus, only 20% of those caring for a loved one with Alzheimer's disease were able to do so (Malarkey, 2001). Often caretakers suppress their own needs and feelings in order to care for others. Clearly, doing so can take a physical, as well as emotional, toll on caretakers.

Clinical Strategies

Working With the Implicit, Unconscious Emotional System

Findings from affective neuroscience, and the development of therapeutic strategies that incorporate these findings, are enhancing our clinical effectiveness (Abbass, 2015; Abbass, Town, & Driessen, 2012; Greenberg, 2008). It is only in the last decade that we have discovered that early implicit emotional learning can be completely rewritten (Ecker, 2015; Ecker, Ticic, & Hulley, 2012). Prior to this, it was generally agreed that well-established emotional learning was indelible and unalterable. We thought that "learnings formed in the presence of intense emotion, such as core beliefs and constructs formed in childhood, are locked into the brain by extraordinarily durable synapses, and it seems as though the brain threw away the key" (Ecker, Ticic & Hulley, 2012, p. 3). Given this assumption, the best we could do was help patients learn to suppress or override, rather than eliminate, early and dysfunctional patterns of emotional learning altogether.

This tenacity of early emotional learning has been an ongoing challenge for therapists of every orientation. Yet, the latest research findings suggest that our brains are far more plastic than previously believed. In fact, it seems as though our brains were designed to update and rewire itself through new experience (Doidge, 2007). These new experiences can be imaginal as well as actual, as the emotional subcortical structures of the brain make no distinction between what happens internally and externally. This is a most important finding, suggesting that working with the activation of emotion in session, when the patient is imagining or remembering past incidents, can, in fact, change the brain.

Nadar (2003) and others (Przybyslawski & Sara, 1997; Schiller et al., 2010) have confirmed the hypothesis that "reactivation of a consolidated memory can return it to a labile, sensitive state—in which it can be modified, strengthened, changed or even erased!" (Nadar, 2003, p. 65). The ability to erase old, dysfunctional emotional learning ("I am just too much to handle and have to disappear into the woodwork") results in transformational change, in which the patient's whole sense of self is liberated from pathological and limiting beliefs. "The prison of emotional memory, built over the eons by evolution, comes with a key, and that key has now been found. Synapses can be unlocked. The limbic life sentence can be commuted" (Ecker, Ticic, & Hulley, 2012, p. 20). This has profound implications for our work. In order to achieve these ends, very specific therapeutic interventions designed to reactivate and then fundamentally alter emotional response patterns must be employed. These include (1) targeting the symptom/presenting problem, (2) reactivating in conscious awareness the emotionally charged schema (mental model or set of core beliefs) that underlies and generates the target symptom, (3) providing contradictory experience or corrective emotional experience that disconfirms the symptom-generating schema, and (4) repeating that new experiential learning several times (Ecker, Ticic, & Hulley, 2012; Schiller et al., 2010). Each step of this process will be elaborated upon and illustrated with clinical vignettes.

Identification and Clarification

We must be able to recognize and label feelings accurately, as well as detect whether the patient is actually in touch with the feeling he has identified, in order to facilitate the therapeutic process. Patients are often anxious about their feelings and impulses, and defend against them. Remember, anxiety is a signal that conflict is present. In this way, it is an invaluable aid in assessment and tracking. If we follow the anxiety, we are likely to discover the underlying cause of the patient's suffering. However, the very defenses that help to reduce anxiety come at a cost—the very symptoms and problems that cause suffering. It is essential that patients are helped to distinguish these three aspects of their emotional conflicts (feeling, anxiety, and defense), and how they have worked together to create and perpetuate their suffering.

Patients often enter therapy with what we might call a circle of conflict, in which feelings, anxiety, and defense are all mixed up. It is a great service to patients to help them sort out and understand their core conflicts—for example, that when he begins to feel anger, he gets anxious instead, and starts to berate himself (a defense against this anxiety-provoking emotion). Patients often find such clarifications remarkably helpful. Human beings seem to have a need to understand themselves and make sense of their experiences. Helping patients gain clarity about what has actually happened to them, how they really felt about it, and how the ways in which they have been dealing with or avoiding feelings about how these life events have affected them, is highly therapeutic. In addition, such clarity regarding previously unconscious and automatic reactivity puts the patient at choice—to face and experience, rather than avoid, anxiety-provoking feelings and impulses, for example. We begin our exploration of feeling and emotions by identifying the feelings evoked in the areas of difficulty in the patient's life. Keeping our eye on signal anxiety helps us reliably identify the emotional conflicts responsible for the patient's symptoms and distress.

Woman With a Cough

The opening sequence of the session with this patient (detailed in Chapter 3) demonstrated the ways in which her body provided vital information regarding the nature of her disturbance—information that her conscious mind had no access to. As I inquired about her mother's death, she began to cough. Knowing that the body is often the repository of unconscious emotions, I asked how her mother had died. "Lung cancer" was her response. As soon as she made that connection, she began to cry.

The following vignette provides vital information, helping us to understand the factors contributing to her symptoms and a pathological grief reaction.

Therapist: How did she get the cancer?
Patient: She has been smoking all her life.
Therapist: So this complicates the picture.
Patient: Yes, it does.
Therapist: She killed herself, in a way.
Patient: Yes, and she had a warning 14 years ago. She had cancer in another part of her body. At that time she was told to stop smoking, but she didn't (points to her own chest).
Therapist: It's interesting because you point to your chest when you talk about it. There are lots of feelings here—not just grief stricken, but she did this to herself in a number of ways. She smoked and, even after she got sick the first time, she kept on smoking. Many steps along the way. So it's not just sad, like she got cancer out of nowhere.
Patient: No, I am so convinced that it is not out of nowhere. It was obvious . . . so obvious!
Therapist: Now we can see and hear that you are really angry.

Patient: Absolutely. As we talk about it, there is another body feeling, a warm, kind of—that way.

Therapist: Rush of warm feeling? And your face is really red, so you can feel this anger coming up, but right away, you cry. So it's hard to face your anger toward her.

Patient: Yes, because at the same time, it was, I had to take care of her and she was so poor. Of course I couldn't be angry with her. She was so ill.

Therapist: But you were.

Patient: Sure.

Therapist: Then what happens to your anger?

Patient: I did not allow it to be there. I really did not allow it to be there. I just focused on letting her have a good ending of her life, and as good as it could be, have, make it the best for my father too. He suffered too.

Therapist: So, there is obviously an anger there. And telling yourself she couldn't stop and so on, doesn't help the feeling.

Patient: No.

Therapist: So that's one way to avoid your anger, by rationalizing and taking her off the hook.

Patient: Yes.

The patient was helped to understand the ways she has been avoiding the experience of anger toward her mother, and the price she has paid for this evasion. It was important to consolidate these insights before moving on to the step of pressuring the patient to connect with and experience the feeling she has been avoiding.

Therapist: It's hard to feel it. You love her but you are angry.

Patient: Yes, but you have to be an adult and you have to understand.

Therapist: What's to understand about destroying yourself?

Patient: It's so awful.

Therapist: Was it evident in other ways? Just smoking or . . . ?

Patient: She was, in many ways, tough to herself in many ways. She never let herself relax. There was always more to be done. Anyway, you know the house had to be perfect. Everything had to be clean. She—only the best was good enough.

Therapist: So she was demanding even before she got ill! She, all her life, she was very demanding.

Originally the patient said that her mother only became demanding when she became ill and was no longer "herself." As the patient's defenses were relinquished, and she got in touch with her mixed feelings toward her mother, the picture changed. In fact, her mother had always been highly demanding. In addition, it became increasingly clear that the patient had internalized these demands, treating herself the way she had been treated by her mother.

Therapist: Originally you said it wasn't like her and she got demanding at the end—get me this and that. But now you are saying she was always demanding and, only the best will do. Just for her or for you too? You had to be the best?

Patient: Yes, sure. The best in class, the best . . . Of course, that also means I am very demanding for myself. I discussed it with myself even before coming here. I am ill and I said to myself, "Why do you have to go if you are ill?" Of course, I convinced myself that I had to go because it was so interesting and I want to learn and to meet you, but it's so typical for me that I never let myself go.

Therapist: You don't let yourself relax either.

Patient: No.

Therapist: Like today, you would have liked to stay home and get in bed and take care of yourself, but insisted that you push yourself to go to work. So this is really, really important. It's almost like you take your Mommy and you swallow her whole.

Patient: I do not want that. I do not want that (crying). I want to feel the life—to have the space to live a happy life with my husband and my kids. I want space for myself. That's another thing I've been thinking about since I lost her. These, I, of course I learned a lot from her, good and bad. And I can also be a very busy person, doing the best I can for my kids and my husband and my job. Yeah. And in some way, sometimes it seems, if there is time, then there is something for me. That's what I have been thinking since I lost her, I must take some time to put me first because if I don't, there will never be time.

The patient was able to see the mechanism of identification in operation, as well as the enormous cost it had exacted in her life. As she felt the pain and grief associated with these defenses, her will to put a stop to it increased. Then she went a step further, declaring a determination to achieve emotional freedom and authenticity.

Therapist: You don't smoke, but you could wear yourself out and that's no good. So you could learn a good lesson from your mother—not by repeating it, but by being kind to yourself and take time and let go—let go and let yourself feel instead of keeping everything under management. Because how does it feel just to let yourself feel this pain and sorrow and anger?

Patient: It feels good.

Therapist: That's a way to be good to you.

Patient: I feel a relief in some . . . I feel a kind of calmness.

Therapist: So you chest isn't all constricted?
Patient: No, in fact, you can hear that. I am not coughing anymore.

As the patient was supported to identify, experience, and express her mixed feelings toward her mother, a sense of peace and calm emerged. Her cough dissipated in the process. This provided support for the hypothesis that her cough was the result of defensive avoidance of strong feelings. When these defenses were relinquished in favor of the direct experience of her true feelings, her symptomatic coughing ceased. In addition to symptomatic relief, the patient developed a whole new perspective on her experience.

Patient: I saw everything. I saw everything. We live in the same town, and I had the opportunity to see her every day, and I saw every single step of her being worse and worse and worse. That part was kind of OK, because I thought that being so close to death would be much worse than it was in reality. I was there and I saw it and I was near to her and I'm very grateful that we had some time, and that I had my Daddy and my sister and we talked over again and again. Everything that needed to be said was said. Now I have had a chance to feel the feelings I couldn't quite allow during that time. It is a huge relief and I feel really good, strangely enough, now that I've been through it all. Funny how I was so afraid of that anger!

The patient was supported to experience previously buried feelings toward her mother, as well as gaining insight into the mechanisms responsible for her symptoms. In the process, she understood how she had long identified with her mother in ways that undermined her happiness. Further work on integration and consolidation of these insights, required to prevent relapses in the future, will be detailed in the final chapter.

Diagnostic Significance of Emotional Activation

All three levels of feeling—cognitive, physiological, and motoric—need to be present for the full and direct access to feelings to be achieved. It is important to assess which aspects of feeling are in place, as well as the particular aspect(s) of feeling the patient is avoiding. For example, histrionic patients often experience a good deal of physiological activation of emotion, along with a tendency to act on these feelings, without a clear cognitive awareness of what they are feeling toward whom. Given this, helping such patients identify their feelings consciously is indicated. "Name it to tame it" (Seigel, 2010) is particularly useful in such cases. In contrast, intellectualizing and obsessive patients might be able to label their feelings, and even talk freely about how they might want to express or act on them, while being completely detached from the inner experience of their feelings. Suppression of the visceral experience of emotions leads to symptoms of depression, fatigue, and "emptiness." In extreme cases, patients can have tears in their eyes but deny feeling sad (Pennebaker, 1997). In such cases, interventions targeted at the physiological experience of feelings, while working to turn the patient against his defenses against the same, are required.

Finally, we need to help patients connect with the impulses that are mobilized when feelings are activated. If feelings are activated in session, but not viscerally experienced and expressed in some fashion, they will have nowhere to go but back into defense and symptom formation. Facing the impulses that accompany feelings is often the most difficult aspect of the process for patients and therapists alike. Most therapies neglect this aspect of feeling. They help patients talk *about* their feelings without necessarily feeling them viscerally. Yet, it is the visceral experience of emotion that activates the impulse to express it. Since acting on feelings, especially angry and sexual feelings, can have very negative consequences, and suppressing them exacerbates the patient's suffering, we need to help create a safe and therapeutic space in which the experience and expression of intense feelings and impulses can be facilitated.

In order to complete our assessment of the patient's emotional capacity, it is essential to evaluate which feelings are freely experienced, and which are avoided. This detailed information has diagnostic significance and provides guidance for treatment efforts. Some patients have free and ready access to their own inner feelings of longing and sadness, but avoid and even deny feelings of anger toward others who thwart and deprive them of their needs and longings. This is common among depressives. Conversely, more narcissistic patients have easy access to admiration of and rage toward others, but are often completely out of touch with their longings for closeness and tenderness or pain regarding loss. This kind of assessment allows us to both diagnose the exact emotional problem underlying the patient's difficulties, and employ specific interventions to address these problems in an intentional and systematic fashion. While the depressive needs help to access, experience, and face his repressed anger, such a focus would be ill considered with a narcissist, who can easily face anger toward others for whom he has contempt.

The Anxious Meditator

The initial evaluation of this patient was discussed in Chapter 3. Inquiry revealed that anxiety was being channeled into both striated and smooth muscles, as well as affecting her cognitive-perceptual system. Initially the patient got glassy-eyed and "spacey" when I asked her about her feelings toward me. Several rounds of clarification were necessary to increase her capacity to tolerate feelings, without undue anxiety. Once the patient returned to striated muscle activation and redirected our attention to feelings toward the therapist, pressure to those feelings could safely be resumed.

Patient: You know, like I knew I was coming, so I was talking to you in my head. I realized that, sometimes when I'm in class, I'm either really enthusiastic or kind of annoying. Sometimes I feel guilty, like am I being too assertive, because no one is really responding. They are really timid so I think I'll do it—I'll answer.

Therapist: So all that was going on, even before you met me. You realize, and even said to your husband, you were already creating this scenario in your mind, that it was your responsibility to make sure I—

Patient: I realized I did that. I went to see another therapist and I intuitively felt—like I was just smiling and nodding, but I already knew everything she was saying to me.

Therapist: So it was a cover-up. This people pleasing is a big cover-up, because you are saying she wasn't telling you anything you didn't know. What kind of feeling do you have toward her?

Patient: Kind of disappointed and, um, I just feel disappointed and . . . I guess I felt aggressive, like "I'm smarter than you" and I felt guilty about feeling that.

Therapist: But the feeling toward her?

Therapist: Well, I feel like that's getting stirred up a lot right now, like with my supervisor, uh, I don't know, I do a lot of smiling and listening, but I feel like she's not listening and we are not connecting. I knew when I met her that we weren't going to be a good match, but I also knew I needed to be there. And I also knew that my faculty field advisor, who I really respect, I wanted to impress him with my flexibility, you know. I told him what my concerns were and he said, "Do you think you can make it work?" and I said, "OK, I can make it work." Then I feel disappointed in myself, like I should have told him this probably won't work.

Careful inquiry and tracking of the process provided very important information about the nature of the conflicts giving rise to the patient's symptoms, i.e., intensely mixed feeling toward authority figures at work, and with the therapist. The fact that the patient spontaneously reported these feelings, while striated muscle anxiety could be observed, suggested that a focus on these feelings was indicated. The focus on feelings prompted defenses of rationalization and explanation. Acquainting her with these defenses and their cost was required to help restructure these defenses and build her capacity to tolerate these feelings without undue anxiety or defensive avoidance.

Therapist: But let's forget about this rationalization and just focus on your emotional life and what goes on within you, we see already this pattern of anxiety about your angry feelings, right?

Patient: Yeah.

Therapist: And the tendency is to smile and cover it up with people pleasing, which is taking kind of a powerless position and doesn't serve you very well. Or, even worse, and maybe with someone you care about, you internalize it and start to attack yourself—"now I'm mad at me"—not you're mad at the other person for disappointing you.

Patient: Yeah.

Therapist: There is a feeling coming up, if you make room for it.

Patient: Um, I guess it's just sadness, you know. Trying to be good and do a good job.

Therapist: As we look at it, you feel sad about that—that you treat yourself that way.

Patient: Yeah, I mean, I feel that, but then I think, "What does she know? She doesn't know me!"

This response clearly indicated a rise of feeling toward the therapist. Now the therapist can press for feelings, and simply block defenses that may appear.

Therapist: Let's look at what happened there. There is some feeling coming up toward me and then wanting to distance. So what is the feeling?

Patient: Well, like levels, like definitely, physically, I feel it here—like a little more open and tender—and then some excitement, like I wanted to explore that, and then some aggression toward you, like I don't want you . . .

Therapist: So there are mixed feelings—tenderness but then aggression. Right? You can just feel that. So we have an opportunity. We can look at that, right? Or cover it up and smile and be nice.

Patient: Yeah, we better look at it.

Therapist: How do you experience that anger?

Patient: That's much harder to feel. I feel it in my jaw—I've had that since I was a kid. There is so much tension there.

Therapist: Yes, you are tensing up around the anger. Everywhere you have tension, chronically, is where we experience anger. So you can feel it here, and where else?

Patient: That is something I get jealous about. It seems men can easily feel angry around each other—it's just part of the interaction—and I feel like, when I'm angry it creates all this—I'm working with all these women—you can't just be angry, like this isn't working for me.

Therapist: But you are angry.

Patient: I AM angry!

Therapist: So you would like to be able to connect with your anger without all this anxiety, tension, and pain. So let's do that, because you're aware there is anger and aggression here that you feel, so if you don't clamp down on it and turn it into anxiety, how do you feel that anger?

Patient: I guess it just feels like a lot of tension and tingling.

Therapist: I notice your fists—can you feel that? So it really is this whole area. So if you let yourself have that anger and mobilization of aggression and don't clamp down and direct it at you but face it toward me? If it came out toward me with those fists and your jaw?

Patient: Well I'm not that angry with your right now, but if I were angry, I sometimes have a fantasy of taking people down.

Therapist: And here toward me?

Patient: Yeah, like pound you—pound your face and like, uh, yah.

Therapist: Right in the face. What else, if you release all this rage you've been keeping inside?

Patient: Most of my fantasies I have them on the ground and am pounding their head into the ground. I am standing up. I am towering over them.

Therapist: Is it just focused on the head? Is it all out or is there more?

Patient: Um, I don't know—like I am just pounding somebody.

Therapist: Who comes to mind?

Patient: The way I just imagine pinning you down and punching you in the face. That is what my brothers did to me.

Therapist: Your brothers would hold you down and overpower you?

Patient: Oh, yeah. I mean, in my family history, my Dad was very violent, very anxious. Even now, to be around him, is like . . . this is my life story.

Therapist: Maybe what we are uncovering now, which you may not have been as aware of, is your own retaliatory rage. I mean, somebody does that to you, boy, you want to do it back.

Patient: Yeah, but I feel like this rage—I always need something from these people, so I can't be retaliatory. I need my supervisor to evaluate me.

Therapist: Right, so you can get bollixed up and anxious about being so angry with the same people that you need.

By facilitating the experience of mixed feelings toward the therapist, from tenderness to rage, the unconscious attachment system was activated and brought to consciousness. The impulse to punch and "take down" the therapist was linked with memories of her brothers and father, all of whom abused her in childhood. She was able to understand the origin of her anxiety regarding anger and aggression, as well as the current trigger to her symptoms—working with violent youth (like her brothers and father) and dealing with difficult and unresponsive supervisors (like her mother). By helping the patient access her retaliatory rage, without undue anxiety or resorting to defenses, her capacity to tolerate the intense mixed feelings, without resorting to symptoms, was increased.

Changing Implicit Emotional Learning

Patients cannot tell us about the unconscious source of their suffering. We must discover this through the use of effective strategies for activating the unconscious attachment system. Feelings mobilized in the transference are a particularly potent vehicle for facilitating rapid unlocking of the unconscious. This process was illustrated in the previous case of "The Anxious Meditator."

In the following case, referred to as "The Woman Heading for a Heart Attack," previously referred to in Chapter 4, work on the cost of her defenses resulted in the experience of deep grief over self-imposed suffering. Following our initial evaluation, there was a two-week wait for a follow-up session, as the therapist was traveling and unavailable. The patient entered the session with anxiety and resistance, indicating that strong feelings toward the therapist were just beneath the surface. It is important to remember that an increase in resistance is a good sign, suggesting that strong and conflict-laden feelings have been activated and are present in the here and now. The patient often tries to protect the therapist from her frightening feelings and impulses, while taking the hit herself. The therapist must convey confidence and determination in the quest for emotional truth, and be willing to be the target of the patient's rage, pain, and thwarted desires for love.

Woman Heading for a Heart Attack

Patient: It's been really rough the last few weeks. It's good to see you but I'm not sure if I want to get into it.

Therapist: Clearly you are in conflict. A part of you excited to be here and wanting to get to work, but another part shut down and hiding behind a wall. Which part of you would you say is stronger right now?

Patient: The wall.

Therapist: The wall. So, you can feel that? There must be a lot of feelings behind that wall, including feelings toward me, because you come in saying I've been away. We are stirring up this stuff, then you are left alone with it. Right?

Patient: Not that I'm aware of—but actually, I was going to call and say, "I'm not feeling very well this morning, I'm not coming in." (This comment suggests the unconscious alliance is gaining strength.)

Therapist: OK, so what does that make you aware of? In a sense the wall is getting higher and thicker. That just means that the fortification is against even stronger feelings.

Patient: Right, yes.

Therapist: Including here toward me. So we have an opportunity, we could have an honest look at those or leave them behind the wall and then what's going to happen to our relationship and your goals?

Patient: Right.
Therapist: So, you really want to look at that.
Patient: I do.

Now that the patient had declared her will to put down the wall, a shift in focus to the experience of the previously avoided feelings was required. It must be the patient's choice, and not that of the therapist, that determines this shift. If the therapist is too demanding and controlling, she will inadvertently encourage compliance or defiance. This is a very difficult intervention to master. It is easy to get into a battle of wills with the patient, rather than helping to intensify the patient's internal struggle. In this case, a tight intrapsychic focus, with sustained emphasis on the patient's choice, circumvented any such interpersonal battle.

Therapist: So what's the feeling toward me behind the wall?
Patient: I guess anger (hands go up into fists).
Therapist: You say I guess and then something came up in your body. If you pay attention . . . did you feel that for a sec?
Patient: Yeah, it was a shooting something.
Therapist: Some kind of energy.
Patient: Not like lightening or anything, but then it went down.
Therapist: So let's see what you want to do about this constriction and keeping it down inside you.
Patient: Well I can say it, but I won't feel it.
Therapist: Right, so that's what we want, the feeling, which is driving this whole thing.
Patient: Exactly.

In this case, the patient was able to label the emotion of anger, and even acknowledge that some impulse was being mobilized, while still repressing the actual physiological experience of the anger. This is very common in depressives and patients with pain syndromes. This patient suffered from a myriad of physical complaints, as well as lifelong depression. Consequently it was essential to remove the barriers to the internal experience of this rage, lest she continue to be tired and depressed.

Therapist: You can say you are angry, but the visceral experience of the anger, that's what's getting turned into anxiety and depression and so on.
Patient: It's so silly for me to be angry with you—which is something that I say (patient catching her own defenses as they emerge, and casting doubt on them).
Therapist: How does that help?
Patient: No, it doesn't.
Therapist: So again, let's pay attention to what is happening in your hands. Do you feel something getting mobilized in your hands?

Patient: Yeah.

Therapist: Terrific, so let yourself stay with that and feel that anger inside. What does it feel like in your hands and in your arms?

Patient: Um, um! (Patient has a great deal of energy in her voice and has her hands in fists).

Therapist: You feel that inside. And when you feel that anger inside, what happens to the anxiety?

Patient: It is gone.

It was of crucial importance that this new experience of feeling her anger without anxiety be underscored and explored.

Therapist: Fantastic. So you can see how one replaces the other. So we can have a look at this feeling of anger that gets mobilized in your hands, your arms, your jaw. And if that anger comes up and out toward me, what does your body want to do? In your imagination?

Patient: Punch you.

Therapist: Where?

Patient: In your face.

Therapist: And what else, if all that anger came out at me?

Patient: It would be a real rage.

Therapist: Yes, it is. So, in your imagination, if that rage came out of you onto me, what do you see yourself doing?

Patient: Punch the hell out of you—I mean all over. Kick. And my whole body would be reacting.

Therapist: Absolutely. So you are activated head to foot.

Patient: I feel full. That's how it feels—I feel full, full. Yeah, and . . . strong!

Therapist: Really embodying that and not shrinking down—full, strong. Is that a good feeling?

Patient: Yeah, absolutely.

Therapist: A strong, powerful feeling.

Patient: It makes me feel alive!

This is a very important moment in the process. Perhaps for the first time in her life, this woman has allowed herself to feel the heat and energy of anger, without doing anything to suppress it. In so doing, she reported feeling strong, powerful, and alive. For someone who has spent most of her life killing off her own aliveness, this constituted a profoundly corrective experience.

Patient: Feels good, not to punch you but . . .

Therapist: But it feels good, and the cost of putting the kibosh on that is to feel empty, dragged out, small. So when you are fully alive, embodying this feeling, a rage comes out at me—what ends up happening to me? I mean, in your imagination—kicking and punching . . .

Patient: Well, you'd be a bloody mess and begging . . . oh, begging for forgiveness.

Therapist: What came just now, you had a smile?

Patient: Well, I started to say forgiveness because I meant to say something else, but that's what came up (unconscious alliance).

Therapist: That's right. So what comes to your mind?

Patient: My Mom and, my father, actually, now that I think about it. I've been aware, a little bit, of the thoughts, "How could you leave me?"

Therapist: Now we can see the link, this rage toward me, which got triggered by my leaving, and your mother comes to mind, and then your father.

Patient: With my mother, I mean, I have always been rageful, but my Dad, I have always had him on a pedestal. So that's new.

Therapist: That awareness, yes. So when you saw I would be a bloody mess, in what position?

Patient: Down, down on the floor.

Therapist: And I'm still alive and begging for forgiveness. What else?

Patient: Crying, sobbing, basically, scrunched up. "Please don't hurt me." "What do I need to do to stop you from attacking me?" What's filtering in now is that it's me on the floor too—begging (more images emerging from the unconscious, which is in an open and fluid state).

Therapist: Yeah, a huh. So just let yourself feel this, because you have been anesthetizing yourself, and not letting yourself feel how painful this is—how you have been hurting yourself. It's almost like you've internalized this struggle, which used to be between you and your parents. Now, you are saying to that sadistic part of you, "Stop, don't hurt me anymore."

Patient: Also, on the way in today and within the last day or so, I felt like crying that I haven't taken care of myself.

Therapist: Right, right. Just really let yourself feel that because that is tied to love because you feel grief stricken that you haven't taken care of yourself. Yeah. Just let that come.

Nearly all her life, this patient had been anxious about her anger and avoided it in ways that created and maintained enormous suffering on many levels—physical, emotional, and interpersonal. In this session, the patient was encouraged to face, rather than avoid, these anxiety-provoking feelings and impulses. In so doing, the therapist was urging the healthy part of the patient to stand up to internal forces responsible for the perpetuation of her suffering. Once the resistance was overcome, and previously buried feelings were experienced, healing could take place. Further, the direct, visceral experience of the violent impulses accompanying her rage operated as a kind of trigger, unlocking unconscious memories that were made available for reworking.

While she had been aware of rage toward her mother nearly all her life, she had never gotten close to anger toward her father for dying. It was only through the experience of rage toward the therapist, triggered by being away for two weeks, that unconscious feelings of rage toward her beloved father for leaving her, were brought into conscious awareness and directly experienced.

Patient: Initially if it's you, my mother, or father, it's, "Suffer, you bastards."

Therapist: Right, so let's really get that out. It's like, not so fast. So initially when I'm begging, you are not feeling too sorry for me. So, OK, there is still anger there. So what is the response that you have?

Patient: Laugh. I would just laugh at you.

Therapist: Sadistic, you mean.

Patient: Sadistic, exactly.

Therapist: Some pleasure in my suffering. So how do you torture me then—let me keep suffering?

Patient: I would continue, but I wouldn't kill you, because I want you to suffer more.

Once defenses are out of operation, and the patient is deeply in touch with feelings and impulses, we must make room for the unconscious to speak. Here, the patient made it clear she wanted to torture the therapist and not let her die, as if that would be letting her off too easy. This impulse was linked to torturous rage toward her mother. These impulses were distinguished from those toward her father. In both cases, the impulses were very specific and revealing.

Therapist: So how do you keep that suffering going?

Patient: I would start screaming, screaming words like, "You fucking asshole. I don't deserve this. I didn't deserve it. You screwed me up. I didn't deserve this. I didn't deserve this. You have no right to treat me this way—to ignore me, to ignore me."

As she grabbed hold of her rage, the patient's tendency toward self-punishment disappeared, and was replaced with healthy self-assertion. She declared that she did not deserve to be ignored. This was a clear indication of the patient's healthy ego standing up to the superego's demands for a life of suffering.

Therapist: So who are you talking to?

Patient: Mom. Dad, it would be for leaving—for abandoning me—I am so furious about that. How could you do that? I can feel my shoulders and everything. I would like, I want to, I guess, to beat him up but I also want to say, "I'm sorry Daddy, I'm sorry."

On the morning that turned out to be his last, the patient's father became angry with her for spilling milk. He yelled at her and stormed out of the house, never to return. He had a massive heart attack and died later that day. This complicated the grieving process significantly. She was angry with him before he left the house, wishing that he would disappear and never come home. In her child's mind, she got her wish. The ensuing guilt regarding this wish was clearly unbearable and was rendered unconscious, particularly because she had no one to help her process these feelings at the time. Now that these feelings and memories had resurfaced, they were available for reworking and resolution.

Therapist: Much more mixed feelings toward him. But he had really read you the riot act and humiliated you before leaving, so it's not just leaving you, but humiliating you, walking off and never seeing you again.

Patient: Right. I could scream at him, "You left me with all this unresolved stuff. I had no place to go with it." I tried, in my own, young child way, I did try—I became encopretic.

Therapist: This is new. Tell me what happened there.

Patient: Well, I mean. I can remember just holding it in and then it would just come and then I would hide it.

Therapist: Of course, so that was all very symbolic—what you were holding inside, that then came out and you had to hide and cover up is what, that we are starting to look at now. Is all this rage at him?

Patient: Right. Definitely rage.

Therapist: What you are most enraged with him about?

Patent: Dying and leaving me with my mother—completely alone.

Therapist: And unprotected. And can you feel that in your arms?

Patient: Definitely.

Therapist: So what wants to come out at him if you let it come up and out?

Patient: Stab him, right in the heart. Over and over and over and over. (Patient is full activated and making a stabbing motion with her dominant hand.) I'm seeing him on the floor and me whack, whack, whack. Him I want to kill. My Mom, I want to suffer. Him, I just want to kill him.

Therapist: You can really feel that, with a knife, over and over again, into his heart. Does it feel like it's all out or . . .

Patient: No.

Therapist: OK, so if it all came out?

Patient: Just stab him, stab him, stab him. Just his heart. Just his heart, and to break it like mine was broken. (Now grief starts to break through.)

Therapist: Underneath this rage is enormous pain—a heartbreak. Once the rage is out, and he is dead, this grief comes out. What do you want to do?

Patient: Sit down and cry—just wail.

Therapist: Next to him or . . . ?

Patient: By myself.

To allow the patient to stay alone with her grief would only perpetuate her suffering. Instead of allowing this self-punitive mechanism to re-emerge, it was vital to activate the direct and visceral experience of guilt over her rage, so that it could be directed at healing. As Carveth (2006) has reminded us, self-punishment is a defense against the experience of guilt. Only the direct experience of guilt will eradicate the defense against it. In addition, the experience of guilt is tied to love and activates attempts at forgiveness and reparation.

Therapist: Yeah, isn't that the problem? You have isolated and punished yourself rather than feeling your grief and guilt—because you say you are heartbroken and his body is lying there.

Patient: I want to say "Oh, how heartbroken I am."

Therapist: What do you want to say if you open your heart to him and don't keep it inside? Because you have kept your heart locked up—not to let any man in.

Patient: Right.

Therapist: If you cracked open?

Patient: I see him there, and me laying next to him, right next to him, sobbing.

Therapist: You have your arms around him?

Patient: No, actually his arm is out and I am snuggled under there (starting to cry).

Therapist: If you don't choke it down and let yourself have this, it is gut wrenching because you loved him so. (There was just a pause, while the patient cried, then I asked:) Did you kill your father?

Patient: No.

Therapist: Do you continue to need to suffer in solitary confinement for a crime you never committed?

Patient: Absolutely not.

In the process of overcoming defense and resistance to the experience of mixed feelings toward the therapist, deeply buried memories from the past became available for reworking. Intellectual insight alone was not sufficient for change to take place in this case. The patient had to approach, and viscerally experience, the feelings she had avoided all her life, in order to get to the original source of her suffering—the guilt regarding the belief that her rage had killed her father. This experience proved to be transformational. She felt completely different than she had all her life—strong and capable, instead of helpless and depressed; deserving of love, instead of perpetual neglect; and calm, instead of anxious. These changes were profound and sustained, generalizing spontaneously to her life outside of therapy. She started to use her anger constructively, by asserting herself, and was neither anxious nor guilty about doing so. Instead, she felt proud of herself!

Integrating Mixed Feelings

Many therapies focus on some aspect of feeling—perhaps the ability to talk "about" feelings (CBT or mentalization), a focus on the somatic, visceral experience of feelings (somatic experiencing), or on the ability to communicate feelings to a valued other (EFT for couples). However, since emotional health and well-being (Coughlin, 2009) require the integration of all these levels of awareness, a therapy that can systematically assess capacity, or lack thereof, in each area should be both more comprehensive and applicable over a wide range of emotional disorders. When we are talking about helping patients achieve deep and lasting transformational change, activating and integrating all aspects of feeling seems to be most effective. Fosha (2002) has asserted that "accelerated change results from the deep and rapid transformations that occurs in the wake of affective breakthroughs, and the full processing of viscerally experienced emotion" (p. 5). In order to achieve this, therapists have to be skilled and knowledgeable in this particular area of human functioning. They also need to be in touch with, and comfortable with, their own feelings and emotions.

We often seem to forget that our emotions toward others are almost always complex and multifaceted. If we only focus on one emotion—say love or anger—we may be missing the mark. It is relatively easy to simply feel anger toward someone we find irksome, or to have positive feelings toward a loved one. The closer we become to a valued other, the more mixed our feelings toward them inevitably become. In fact, no one can hurt us more deeply, or provoke more intense retaliatory rage, than someone we love and depend upon. Often patients have feelings that are not only mixed but contradictory and incompatible—"I love you and need you, but am so angry I want to kill you." No wonder such strong mixed feelings evoke anxiety and tend to get avoided!

The ability to acknowledge and integrate these mixed feelings is of the utmost importance for our own health and that of our relationships. If we deny anger toward a loved one, the anger will operate outside awareness. Our perception of the other will likely become distorted. Especially in intimate relationships, anger seems to serve a vital function, helping us deal with the inevitable conflicts that arise when living in close proximity to another. When anger and conflict are avoided, the relationship suffers and growth is stunted (Schnarch, 2009; Tatkin, 2012). On the other hand, when long repressed anger surfaces, the love that has been trapped beneath is released, and the relationship can come back to life.

Love, pain, and rage are all connected. The more strongly we love someone, the more intense the pain of loss or betrayal, and the deeper the anger about the pain being caused. Furthermore, if we create distance in order to avoid our pain and rage, genuine feelings of love and a desire for closeness will go with it. This is the therapeutic task in many, if not most, instances—to encourage the direct experience of complex mixed feelings toward others in an effort to come to terms with them. In this way we can help to facilitate healing and restore the patient's ability to love and be loved.

Under-Regulation of Emotion

Barlow and his colleagues (2011) have suggested that nearly all psychiatric disorders are essentially disorders of emotional awareness and regulation. Put very simply, most of our patients suffer the effects of either over- or under-regulating their feelings and emotions. In the following case, a 55-year-old woman reported a lifelong pattern of under-controlled emotions, resulting in impulse control difficulties. Her tolerance for the internal experience of anxiety and emotional activation proved quite limited. She relied on the defenses of acting out and discharging emotions, which only exacerbated her problems. Specific interventions were employed in an effort to help her gain awareness of anxiety and the strong mixed feelings that lay beneath, so that she could be helped to tolerate, experience, and integrate these feelings without acting on them.

The Impulse-Ridden Woman

Therapist: Why don't you start by telling me what your concerns are, what you'd like help with?

Patient: I'm over 18 years sober and have been working with AA and therapy. I'm 55 and I've been in therapy since I was 19. I have had a very challenging two years. I lived in Minneapolis for 30 years, got a divorce, moved to Delaware, and was transferred by the company. I started a relationship with a married man at the same time, while I was still in the Twin Cities. He lives up here, which is a lot of the reason I'm here—not only, but a lot.

In the patient's opening statement she revealed a long history of substance abuse and interpersonal turmoil. Despite 35 years of therapy and self-help groups, she seemed to be stuck on a path of self-destruction. The first question was used to assess the syntonicity of this pattern of acting out.

Examining the Cost of Acting Out Feelings

Therapist: To be with a married man?

Patient: (Laughs.) At this point he has separated and is filing for divorce. That was always imminent, though it was never going as fast as I wanted it to. My MO in relationships is, "If you're not doing it fast enough, I will push you to do it quicker." That's my MO all my life.

Therapist: How is that working?

Patient: Clearly not. The anger and rage comes out in all my relationships and I have seen it at a level this year that frightens me. In fact, I actually got fired for mouthing off at an employee. I've been afraid before but never at this level.

Therapist: So what happened that really frightened you?

Patient: The most recent one was with my boyfriend and a simple statement he made. He made a comment about having fun with his brother and sister—that he hadn't had that much fun in a long time. It came out and I couldn't control it. I was hitting him and throwing shit at him. After that happened, I was looking for something because I knew I was in trouble. I was stone cold sober—no drugs, no alcohol, nothing to blame it on, except my own inner stuff and I'm scared. I felt completely gone and it's frightening to me because I don't want to behave that way, I don't know how not to behave that way (starting to cry).

Therapist: It causes you tremendous pain also.

Patient: Tremendous pain, tremendous pain.

The patient was clearly in crisis. The defense of acting out, in this case toward her boyfriend, had frightened her and propelled her into treatment yet again. As she relayed this information, painful feelings regarding the cost of these defenses emerged, suggesting that these defenses were becoming dystonic. This pain proved to be an ally in the process, providing motivation to abandon defenses that cause grief and destruction.

Assessing Anxiety

Therapist: Are you aware that you are anxious also?

Patient: Yeah.

Therapist: OK, let's look at that. How do you feel that anxiety right now?

Patient: Tingly in my arms. Sometimes it just surges through me.

Therapist: How do you feel it right now? You feel some tingling in your arms and hands?

Patient: Down my arms and into my feet.

Therapist: And then your gum chewing—is that a way to try to dissipate the anxiety?

Patient: Yeah.

The patient came into the initial session armed with supplies—coffee, water, and chewing gum—all used as external means for regulating her internal state. This provided more evidence that a discharge pattern of anxiety and emotion was the primary strategy used for self-regulation—a strategy that was causing great harm. As an alternative, it was suggested that patient and therapist attend to the patient's internal experience so it could be regulated carefully. After attending to and down-regulating her anxiety together, the patient spontaneously removed the gum, indicating she was able to self-regulate and no longer needed the external crutch.

In the next vignette, the therapist made an explicit link between the patient's tendency to ignore what is happening within, and deficits in regulating her internal state effectively. This led to agreement about the therapeutic task—to pay attention to the visceral experience of feelings in the body.

Therapist: If you're not aware of what you are feeling you're not going to be able to regulate it very well. It seems to come up suddenly but that's because you've been ignoring it. One of the things we're going to want to do differently is to keep you connected to what you are feeling in your body, not just your thoughts, but keep connected to the feelings within you.

Patient: OK. That makes sense, but I am really frightened of this anger.

Therapist: You can get yourself in a big old loop. You are anxious about your anger, and you ignore it, which makes it much more likely that, if someone looks at you funny, you're going to blow. So does it make sense to you that we are going to pay attention to that?

The patient went on to report that this tendency to act out anger started in early adolescence, in relation to her father. She continued to live her life focused upon, and in response to, men. While focusing on pleasing the men, her own needs, feelings, and impulses were mounting outside of awareness, making an explosion inevitable. We examined the precipitating incident in further detail in order to understand it.

Therapist: Let's look at the nature of the problems in your relationships— is it something that develops over time or are you concerned about your choices from the start?

Patient: (Makes a face.) I choose a man who is married. How available can he be? How available am I? Do I want someone who is available? If he said, "I am here, I am committed. Let's go," I would freak out. (All of this is said in an angry, sarcastic manner.)

Therapist: Terrified of intimacy and closeness.

Patient: Well it's never happened—starting with Dad.

Therapist: And at this point, starting with you. You don't have an intimate relationship with you. You are always acting and reacting—repeating destructive patterns—but without awareness.

Patient: I can feel stuff in my arms.

Therapist: What would you say that feeling is? You are having an emotional reaction here with me, as we go over these difficulties. What is your feeling toward me?

Patient: Oh, am I angry with you for pointing that out? Probably.

Therapist: Let's find out. Something is happening on a physical and emotional level. Are you aware of anger toward me? If you could feel the anger without all the anxiety and tension?

Patient: They come together.

The following vignette demonstrates the vital role of dealing with negative feelings in the transference in a calm and direct manner, as soon as they become apparent. When these negative feelings are present, but not taken up directly, they contribute to the resistance, as well as exacerbating the patient's difficulties. Most important among the common factors reported in the literature "is the therapist's ability to understand and respond empathically to negative affective arousal" (Markowitz & Milrod, 2011, p. 124). In fact, it has been suggested that the therapist's "ability to respond to a patient's negative affect without flinching, is a key aspect, sometimes *the* key aspect, of conducting successful psychotherapy, independent of modality" (A. Freud, 1979, p. 28). Despite its crucial importance, in my experience, this intervention is actually quite "uncommon." The good news is, this intervention that can be taught and learned. However, it requires courage, maturity, and a good deal of emotional awareness on the part of the therapist in order to implement effectively.

Focused attention on the internal, visceral experience of anger in the body is especially important in patients who have a tendency to discharge and act out. It is also essential that the patient's anxiety be in the striated muscle before pressure to feelings is attempted. Patients who lose control and act out their anger do so because of high and unregulated levels of anxiety that accompany their rage. Consequently, they "blank out" when discharging anger. Instead, we invite the patient to be fully present and connected to the visceral experience of anger, without doing anything to get rid of it. It is also vital that the patient be in direct eye contact with the therapist during this experience.

Therapist: How do you experience this anger in your body?
Patient: Energy does go through me.
Therapist: So if that came up and out at me? What's the impulse?
Patient: (Sigh.) Yell and scream.
Therapist: But it's a physical energy in your body.
Patient: I want to strangle you.
Therapist: You can feel that?
Patient: I could fly off this chair and put my hands around your neck and I shut you up! My body is really getting hot. (Clearly in a physiological state of activation with awareness, necessary to continue.)
Therapist: How does that go, if it all came out?
Patient: I would roar. I would (sigh) . . . A lot of power. I could fly over there and put my hands on your neck until you shut up—until you fucking shut up! (Sigh.)
Therapist: When would that be?
Patient: I would have to kill you.
Therapist: Are you in touch with that?

Patient: Oh yeah—yeah. My hands are on your neck. You are choking. I'm not stopping. I am choking you and choking you. Your eyes are watering. Your breath is gasping and you take that last breath (starts to cry, with head in her hands). I'm thrilled, and then I am devastated.

Therapist: At first there is triumph.

Patient: Victory and power, and then this horrible sadness (sigh). I still feel it but it's . . . and . . . now I feel guilty and ashamed.

Therapist: Guilt is connected to some positive feelings. What is the impulse that comes with the guilt and sorrow?

Patient: I want to die.

Therapist: That would be the punishment. But what's the feeling toward me now, and what do you want to do with the body?

This was a crucial juncture in the treatment. Having gotten in touch with murderous impulses toward the therapist, guilt regarding this rage was activated. At first, the full experience of guilt was derailed into a pattern of self-punishment ("I want to die"). She had, in fact, been hospitalized for suicidal impulses in the past. Now, we were uncovering the driving force to her destructiveness—guilt over rage. Self-punishment was blocked in order to facilitate the experience of guilt with a desire to repair the damage done.

Patient: I want to bring you back to life (crying). I would try mouth to mouth to get you to breathe (sigh).

Therapist: What do I look like?

Patient: Your eyes are open. I close them—can't stand to look at them.

Therapist: Let's see if we can sort this out and see what feeling there is if you look into my eyes.

Patient: (Sigh.) If they were opened I would see fear and panic. If there were closed, I wouldn't have to see that.

Therapist: What's the feeling when you see that last vestige of fear and panic?

Looking into the eyes of the slain is typically effective in evoking deep feelings of guilt. Guilt is ultimately a healing affect, so helping patients feel and bear their guilt, rather than continue to defend against it, is a compassionate act and one that facilitates therapeutic effects.

Transfer of Images

Patient: I caused that, and now I feel painful and guilty. I want to talk to you and tell you I'm sorry. I wish it hadn't gone that far (crying). I'd hold your hand and want to talk to you. Oh . . . (crying hard).

Therapist: What do you want me to know?

Patient: I didn't mean to do this. It was my anger—I shouldn't take it out on you.

Therapist: Who is it meant for? Who comes to mind?

Patient: My Dad is dead, but I feel it now toward my Mom.

Therapist: Can you remember a time when you felt that toward her?

Patient: I can't go see her because I'm angry that she is losing her mind and that she lived for my father and fucking neglected her children! She would wait for him to come home—wait and wait for him—and we were right there under her nose. If she didn't get what she wanted from him she would leave. She'd leave and go shopping and get out of the house and away from us. She was so angry that he was working and spending time with patients and his nurse rather than her. She could not, just could not, take care of us. That's why I'm so angry and living the life SHE did.

Therapist: So tell me about the links you are making—you mean the way you search so desperately for a man and his attention?

Patient: I have been waiting and sitting and waiting for any attention I can get.

Therapist: Do you see how you have been doing that to yourself? Ignoring your own needs and feelings, and focusing all your attention on the man. You are treating yourself the way she treated you.

Patient: Exactly!

Therapist: Shall we turn that around?

Patient: Absolutely.

By attending closely to the transference pattern of behavior, this patient's core conflicts were intensified and brought to consciousness, where they could be transformed. Rather than just talking about her difficulties, the patient was encouraged to viscerally experience the intense mixed feelings coming up toward the therapist. As long as her anxiety was in striated muscles, and she was in good contact with her own sensations, and with me, it was deemed safe to proceed to a breakthrough into the unconscious. In the past, her feelings were either acted out or internalized, with highly self-destructive results. This new experience with the therapist produced profound therapeutic effects in a very brief amount of time. In addition, we were able to uncover the engine to her suffering—punishment for her murderous feelings and wishes toward others. In this case, the link was between the therapist and her mother. Further, she could see the process by which she had identified with her mother and internalized this conflict, acting it out over and over again throughout life. This provided insight and motivation to turn the pattern around. In the next session, following a one-hour break for lunch, the patient reported on the immediate effects of the work achieved in the morning.

Therapeutic Effects

Therapist: What's been going on for you during the break? Thoughts, feelings, connections?

Patient: Well, honestly, I did feel peaceful. It felt relaxed. I got a text from my sister and sent one to David. He replied, she didn't, and it was OK. I sat in the sun, reading my Big Book and going through the steps in Al Anon.

Therapist: Before we go to the book, let's stay focused on you and that experience of being calm and peaceful inside, between you and you.

Patient: Yeah, and I was cold, so I went to get warm. I went to the sun and felt warm and good. I didn't feel desperate that I have to connect with someone or hear from someone.

Therapist: You could connect with you actually, and it felt good.

Patient: I felt I was able to take care of myself and to be good to myself and not need it from out there. I nourished my body with food. I was cold and got warm. It sounds simple but it's a place for me to start.

Therapist: Am I understanding you right, that you first had this feeling of calm connection and then you were able to take care of yourself with some sense of ease?

Patient: Exactly. It wasn't a big effort. It sounds really simple but it is huge for me.

Once again, this transcript demonstrates the fact that response to intervention, rather than DSM diagnoses or the patient's history, provides the most accurate information on the patient's current capacity to heal. This woman had a daunting psychiatric history, with very serious symptoms and character pathology. However, she was in a state of crisis, motivated to seek help, and proved highly responsive to intervention. She was able to turn against destructive defenses of acting out and internalization in favor of the direct experience of intense mixed feelings toward the therapist. Doing so resulted in a newfound experience of calm. No longer relying so heavily on external factors, including constant contact, approval and validation from others to soothe herself, she was content to be on her own. More importantly, the pattern of self-punishment was immediately replaced with self-care. She was able to respond to her own needs for warmth and nourishment in an appropriate and caring way. Vignettes from subsequent sessions in this nine-hour treatment will be included in the next two chapters of the book.

Over-Regulation of Emotion

This 47-year-old man came for help to understand and overcome internal obstacles to finalizing his divorce. Even though he had been very unhappy in his marriage and been separated for three years, he was not able to move forward with divorce or free himself to pursue a new relationship. Inquiry revealed a man detached from nearly all his feelings and desires. He was an engineer who lived as if life was a problem to be solved logically. In contrast to the previous patient, this man was clearly "over-controlled": isolating affect, and avoiding the experience or expression of all heartfelt emotions. It became evident early on that all the ways he avoided anxiety-provoking feelings and impulses interfered with his optimal functioning and with his relationships. The first four sessions were focused on helping the patient turn against defenses that kept him stuck in automatic functioning, created sterile relationships, and interfered with the closeness he desired. He responded well to this phase of the work, abandoning these defenses and beginning the process of allowing himself to feel the feelings he had been avoiding all his life. Anger toward his wife was paramount among the emotions to emerge. We begin at the start of his fifth session.

The Man Who Couldn't Get Divorced

Therapist: How are you feeling?

Patient: Oh, wiped out tired—and I have been angry lately.

Therapist: So you feel that right now?

Patient: Well, it's for a specific reason. Today, this morning, I've been working on some unfinished projects at the house that my wife and I own, trying to get it ready to put on the market and she has the day off, so she was around and I can just feel . . . just being around her sets me off.

Therapist: So where is it right now? Where do you feel it in your body when you think about your wife and seeing her today?

Patient: My body feels jumpy and on edge.

Therapist: Sounds like a mix. There is definitely anger and you are nervous about it.

Patient: We had a conversation about money. And I just got so mad with that. I found, in order to continue with what I was doing, I had to shut down and go flat emotionally. So, right now, I feel like I'm just recovering from the dead.

Therapist: OK, so let's look at what you are saying here because it is super important. You can feel anger come up and that mobilized impulses. You see fists come up—then you get afraid, what if you lose control—so you have a turnoff switch.

Patient: Yeah, I always turn off with her.

Therapist: Right, but then we have to see what happens to you, because you "kill off" all your own feelings and then end up dead. Isn't that what you said?

Patient: Yeah, but I was so pissed off.

Therapist: So, let's give you the opportunity to express and release this pent up rage. Every time it comes into your fist. What you are most livid about?

Patient: Just her existence on the planet.

Therapist: A part of you wants to kill her—wipe her out.

Patient: A lot of years when I thought it would be so much better if she was just dead.

Therapist: It's a murderous wish, any way you slice it.

Patient: I felt my pulse quickening and feel myself tense up inside. You know, this is a really hard one to pin down because I have been killing her for so long that this is really buried.

Therapist: It starts to come up with all that power and energy and then it comes into your hands and if you don't stop it, because it is an anger that wants to come up and out at her, right?

Patient: Yeah. Grab her and slam her against the wall.

Therapist: What else, if all of it came out? Where is the anger right now?

Patient: I'm still clamping it off.

Therapist: Yeah, who is getting it?

Patient: Me.

Therapist: Who is paralyzed?

Patient: Me.

Therapist: Do you see that mechanism? Because if this came out at her she would be the one paralyzed and not moving. You instantly do it to yourself. That's pretty self-destructive. Is that what you want to do, kill off your own liveliness, crippling yourself, putting yourself in a paralyzed state?

It is essential that the patient gain insight into the direct link between his suppressed murderous feelings toward his wife, and his own inner deadness. He has been doing to himself what he wanted to do to her. In so doing, he spared her and punished himself. This could make sense of his inability to "cut the cord" and free himself of his wife and this unwanted marriage. His punishment was to remain tied to the woman he wanted to be rid of. Further exploration was required to test out this hypothesis.

Therapist: So let's see if you'll let yourself feel this real, live feeling.

Patient: I really just want to beat her to a pulp to be honest with you. Just beat her to a pulp. I'd grab her bodily and slam her against the wall.

Therapist: What wall, where do you see it?

Patient: Some flat wall where I can smack her head against the wall. Just knock her senseless. And smash her head. Slamming her against the wall until she drops. Kind of like picking up a weight and throwing it away from me.

Therapist: So what just happened?

Patient: Oh, at some point she just goes limp and collapses on the floor. I'm done with her.

Therapist: How do you see her on the floor?

Patient: Just crumpled and lifeless.

Therapist: So she is dead? A head injury? What does her face look like? Her eyes?

Patient: Blank—nothing there. Kind of dilated—the remains of terror.

Therapist: Does it feel like the anger is out of you?

Patient: Yeah.

Therapist: It came out of you onto her and now she is dead and lifeless. And when you look at her, what is the feeling toward her now?

Patient: Well, that's the complicated part. That's what keeps me from doing it.

Therapist: In reality. That's good. We don't want you to do this in reality, because there will be no freedom for you! That's why it's important to face it and work it through emotionally so you can actually have your freedom. Because, in a sense, you have been punishing yourself and jailing yourself. You are still tied to this woman. You are not free. So there is some self-punitive mechanism here. For what?

Here, the therapist made it clear that the patient had been punishing himself for a wish. Since self-punishment is a defense against the experience of guilt, it was essential to facilitate the direct experience of this guilt regarding the impulses to kill the mother of his son in order for healing to take place. Details of the work on guilt and resolution are included in Chapter 8.

Working With Sexual Feelings and Conflicts

In the following case, conflicts regarding sexual feelings and desires, along with themes of competition with other men for the possession of a desired woman, figured prominently. By working to expose these feelings in the transference, we were able to quickly unearth the origin of these conflicts.

A Wolf in Sheep's Clothing

Therapist: How can I help you and what would you like to get out of our work together?

Patient: Main thing is that I want to get in touch with my mixed feelings toward others.

Therapist: What makes you think you're not connected as fully and deeply as you could be to your own true feelings? What gives you that impression? How do you know that?

Patient: I have a sense of some sort of veil over everything—a slight kind of depression that is always there. I have been to several therapists to address this, but we get stuck when it comes to my deep feelings, especially anger. I mentally know I'm angry, but don't actually feel it (isolation of affect).

Therapist: The result is that you are missing the energy in that feeling and end up a bit depressed.

Patient: I drop my feelings and go passive. That is a theme. I just withdraw and get depressed (looks sad). I never figured it out. When I was 21 and 22, I had two severe depressions, with severe self-attack. I wanted to kill myself but never found out why. I don't get that depressed anymore but I never understood why I got suicidal.

Therapist: What's the feeling right now?

Patient: Sad—that I did that and never got help with that.

Therapist: What about your feeling toward the therapists you went to for help?

Patient: My head says anger, but I don't feel it in the body.

This patient had relied on the defense of isolation of affect, especially regarding anger. He knew he was angry, but didn't feel it viscerally. Instead, he would tense up, clamp down, and contain the anger in such a way that his energy and vitality were depleted. Consequently, he had the sense of being slightly depressed all the time. Since he was able to see all this clearly, and we agreed that our goal was to help him abandon these defenses in favor of connecting to his true feelings, pressure was required to do just that.

Anger Toward the Therapist

Patient: I also feel it toward you right now. It seems like, when this deep feeling comes up, it's an energy in the body.

Therapist: So how do you feel that right now?

Patient: It's really strong—like heat and energy that just wants to come out.

Therapist: If that came out—this vicious, primitive rage came out toward me?

Patient: Yeah! It's really (sigh) deep and unconscious.

Therapist: If you pay attention to your body, what are the impulses coming up?

Patient: It's like I'm stopping myself.

Therapist: But it looked like you saw something there (could see his eyes moving).

Patient: Grabbing your ankles, for some reason.

Therapist: If you go with that . . .

Sexual Feelings and Impulses

Patient: Shoooo . . . sexual impulses are coming up—like spreading your legs. I feel that coming up—this urge to spread your legs, and I get this picture that you are lying back and we make love. There is a lot of love.

Therapist: How does it turn to that, because it started with an aggressive taking?

Patient: I don't know, it's just the picture. Actually, a couple of weeks ago, I had a dream that I stayed at your place rather than a hotel, and we were sleeping together—not sex or anything.

Therapist: But here it goes further, with us making love, and with you on top of me. You imagine it as mutual. What happens in the fantasy?

Patient: First I spread your legs forcefully, then you take me in and there is no rage anymore (starts to cry). Now I get a picture of my wife. She had some conflicts and it took a while, but recently she has said she is surrendering (cries deeply) . . she was totally opened—her legs out and no holding back (sobs).

Therapist: This is what you want, and there's a lot of pain and rage about being kept out, kept at a distance, kept waiting and the joy of being let in. Joy and pain come up when you get what you've so longed for.

Patient: The feeling of being rejected vs. let in and accepted. There is still energy inside.

Therapist: What do those hands want to do?

Patient: (Smiles.) I just see some breasts—wanting to hold some breasts.

Link to the Past

Therapist: Whose?

Patient: My Mom.

Therapist: What do they look like?

Patient: (Laughs.) Kind of . . . not . . . like sagging, hanging. I've seen them.

Therapist: When?

Patient: Lots of times

Therapist: So she exposed her body to you? (Nods.) And could you touch her?

Patient: No.

Therapist: So that would stir up lots of feelings—showing herself to you but keeping a distance, no touch.

Patient: I have sudden associations. I have seen her naked. Then, an association when she was pregnant with my little brother.

Therapist: How old were you?

Patient: Eight. There is a picture where she is naked with a big belly and I was holding it. I was trying to look joyful but I guess I was . . . But I didn't like her being pregnant.

Therapist: You were interested in those breasts.

Patient: There is another memory, from an earlier time, maybe I was five, and I asked her if we could go to bed and have sex together. I'm not sure I knew what it was, but I heard about it. She said no.

Therapist: So it's a bit of a tease—in your face—what they have that you can't have.

Patient: I don't remember being angry, just curious, but very insistent. I just wanted to separate them—move between them, and what comes to

my mind now (sigh) is that my father is very introverted and shy
and passive. My mother is more aggressive. He can't really stop her,
and in a way, he's very difficult—hard to be open.

Therapist: Lots of mixed feelings coming up.

Patient: I am furious! She just doesn't see me. It's the same thing with that
guy I was talking about at work. It's just like "Arg!" (Clenching his
jaw and growling.) I want her to see me but she can't and that's what
I'm so angry about. Mission Impossible.

Therapist: Yes, if your goal is to change her. All you can do is deal with your
own anger more effectively instead of detaching, going passive and
compliant, and getting depressed.

Patient: It's like the body wants to fight. Cover her mouth and hold her
down. I see my fist now—wanting to hit her in the face. I am holding it back.

Therapist: Who does that hurt?

Patient: Me. I am tensing up. Like there is this energy but then I freeze.

Therapist: Protecting her and keeping it all in. If you didn't do that and this all
came out?

Patient: It would be punching, also on her breast. There is more energy now.
It's difficult though. It's in my legs now too. Walking on her—on
her legs and stomach and sit on her breast and hold her down and
punching her. My jaw is really tight.

Therapist: What is the impulse in your jaw?

Patient: It's actually to—I get a picture of biting her breast—actually biting
it off. Oh! (Shivers.) I have the nipples in my mouth and it's—augh!
I want to spit it out and her breasts are bleeding. Whew! (Wracking
sobs.)

Sexual and aggressive feelings toward the therapist were linked with the same
feelings toward the patient's mother. Finally, deep waves of guilt over his violent impulses were experienced. Then the patient experienced a spontaneous impulse to repair the damage, and put her nipples back on her breasts.
Instead of needing to punish himself for these previously forbidden feelings
and impulses, he was able to embrace his desires for closeness. Additional layers
of feeling and memories will be outlined in Chapter 8.

Therapist Factor

Helping patients connect with and experience all of their strong feelings and
emotions is often necessary to activate the unconscious attachment system,
discover the source of the patient's suffering, and facilitate deep and lasting
change. Research suggests that the experience of these feelings in the transference is a particularly powerful and effective means for attaining deep and

lasting therapeutic change (Abbass & Town, 2013; Shedler, 2010). Yet, all too often, therapists avoid this kind of involvement with their patients and simply talk "about" feelings from a detached position, or focus exclusively on the patient's feeling toward others, while avoiding work in the transference. Since intensely emotional sessions are most often those referred to as "significant" (Castonguay, Goldfried, Wiser, Raue, & Hayes, 1996; Goldfried, Raue, & Castonguay, 1998; Harnett, O'Donovan, & Lambert, 2010), and seem to have the greatest impact on outcome, it would behoove us to develop very specific skills in this crucial arena.

In addition to education and training regarding the working of the emotional brain, therapists need to attend to their own inner lives, in order to ensure that they are emotionally present and available for connection with their patients. The more we can develop our technical skills, as well as our own ability to be open, available, and emotionally engaged, the better our results should be.

Summary

Most psychiatric patients suffer from disorders of emotional awareness and regulation (Barlow et al., 2011). In order to create the kind of emotionally charged atmosphere required to promote deep and lasting change, a number of interventions designed to activate and intensify emotional experiencing (cognitive, physiological, motoric, and interpersonal) were outlined and illustrated with a number of cases. Strategies for identifying and removing obstacles to emotional engagement with self and other were included. Doing so often creates the kind of corrective emotional experience vital in the process of transformation (Alexander & French, 1946; Fosha, 2007). In addition, the actual, visceral experience of previously avoided emotions appears to be the key that unlocks unconscious memories that become available for reworking. This process consistently leads to profound and enduring change.

Chapter Six
The Therapeutic Alliance:
Conscious and Unconscious

"The alliance refers to a positive, viable, and meaningful attachment between therapist and patient that . . . promotes an effective therapeutic process" (Binder & Beitan, 2013, p. 31). The therapeutic relationship is the vehicle for change, as well as the delivery system for the treatment itself (Barber, Connolly, Crits-Christoph, Gladis, & Sinqueland, 2000; Bordin, 1979, 1994; Castonguay, Constantino, & Holtforth, 2006; Horvath & Greenberg, 1994; Wampold, 2001). Therefore, technique and relationship factors are "actually inextricably intertwined" and can't be separated (Butler & Strupp, 1986; Elkin, 1995, 1999). In other words, therapists who have a method they believe in, and are skillful in applying, are more effective in creating strong alliances with their patients than their less enthusiastic and competent colleagues. Furthermore, a strong alliance promotes the kind of emotional bond required to build trust and facilitate a therapeutic process. The alliance and therapeutic progress go hand in hand, each influencing and potentiating the other.

Research findings make it increasingly clear that "therapist variability in the alliance appears to be more important than patient variability for improved outcome" (Del Re, Fluckinger, Horvath, Symonds, & Wampold, 2012, p. 642). This is particularly true when it comes to the ability to deftly handle challenging interactions with patients (Anderson, Ogles, Patterson, Lambert, & Vermeersch, 2009). In complex cases, a therapeutic alliance can be precluded or undermined by the patient's resistance and negative transference feelings. Given this, the ability to facilitate a working alliance, while addressing obstacles and barriers to engagement from the first moments of contact, may be the difference between effective and ineffective therapists (Abbass, 2015). As has been emphasized throughout this volume, it is both *what* the therapist does, and *who* he is, that matters.

In addition to elucidating the characteristics of a successful therapeutic alliance, the notion that there is an unconscious component to the alliance will also be emphasized. The new perspective on the unconscious, affective-regulating function of relationships, mediated by the right brain, "highlights the clinician's role as co-participant in the creation of the therapeutic alliance and as a regulator of the patient's dysregulated affective states" (Shore, 2007, p. 7). To this end, understanding the role of unconscious processes in creating and maintaining a vital emotional bond between therapist and patient will be underscored.

The relationship between alliance and outcome, alliance and improvement, and alliance and resistance will also be explored. In addition to outlining particular tasks and strategies designed to establish, maintain, and repair the alliance, a focus on the therapist's contribution to this crucial variable will be examined and illustrated.

Research

Despite its popularity as a research topic, all the data suggest that the alliance has only a modest impact on outcome. A meta-analysis by Horvath and Symonds (1991) found an average effect size of 0.26 between alliance and outcome. A more recent meta-analytic study (Martin, Garske, & Davis, 2000) computed an effect size of 0.22, accounting for no more than 10% of the variance in outcome (Horvath, Del Re, Fluckiger, & Symmonds, 2011). There is increasing consensus that a strong working alliance is an absolutely necessary, but woefully insufficient, factor to achieve therapeutic change (Weinberger, 1995).

The notion that a therapeutic alliance must be established prior to the actual work of therapy has been questioned of late. There is a growing body of evidence that therapeutic change contributes to alliance, just as much as alliance contributes to change (Barber, Connolly, Crits-Christoph, Gladis, & Sinqueland, 2000; Klein, Milrod, Busch, Levy, & Shapiro, 2003; Zilcha-Mano, Dinger, McCarthy, & Barber, 2014). More recently, "evidence for a reciprocal causal model, in which the alliance predicted subsequent change in symptoms while prior symptom change also affected alliance" (Falkenstrom, Granstrom, & Homquist, 2013, p. 317) has been advanced. These two factors seem to influence each other in a mutual and reciprocal fashion: "Thus, through development and maintenance of the alliance, the therapist can simultaneously attend to the context of the client's relationship difficulties and foster a process conducive to client change" (Horvath & Greenberg, 1994, p. 1). When examined over time (as opposed to early sessions alone), the alliance "significantly predicted subsequent change in depression when prior change in depression was partialed out" (Barber, Connolly, Crits-Christoph, Gladis, & Sinqueland, 2000, p. 1027).

The relationship between alliance and symptom change appears to be complex, and the understanding of how one affects the other is not completely clear. In cases where the patient enters treatment with negative transference feelings, exhibits high levels of resistance, and/or demonstrates a disturbed attachment pattern, therapeutic intervention is often required *in order to* develop an alliance (Frederickson, 2013; Polaschek & Ross, 2010; Saxon & Barkham, 2012). In contrast, healthier patients can, and may need to, establish an alliance before commencing the work of therapy per se. Even among psychotherapists seeking their own treatment, 21% of the sample studied had an experience in therapy that they considered harmful (Buckley, Karasu, & Charles, 1981). Clearly, the ability to create and maintain a viable alliance is not something we can take for granted, but requires specific training in order to achieve and maintain in a consistent fashion.

Therapist Contribution to the Alliance

Bordin (1979) has defined the therapeutic alliance as an agreement between patient and therapist on the nature of the problems to be addressed, the goals to be obtained, and the therapeutic tasks involved in the process of change (see also Bordin, 1994; Frederickson, 2013; Tyron & Winograd, 2011). In addition to these factors, the quality of the emotional bond between therapist and patient is understood as central. This bond is not just about sympathy, or a sense of liking the therapist, but the creation of an emotional connection between patient and therapist that involves trust, respect, and a joint commitment to the process and outcome of treatment (Bordin, 1994). In particular, a relationship based on "confidence and regard," involving both the patient's belief in the therapist's ability to help, and the therapist's confidence in the patient's capacity and resourcefulness, seem to be key (Bordin, 1979; Ardito & Rabellino, 2011). When therapists view their patients as pathological, failing to recognize their strengths, and underestimating their capacity, they unwittingly undermine the alliance (Duncan, 2010; Wampold, 2011, 2015; Wampold & Brown, 2005; Wampold & Budge, 2012). Other therapist characteristics associated with the development of poor alliances include passivity, rigidity, emotional detachment, and a domineering or authoritarian style of interaction (Ackerman & Hilsenroth, 2001; Lillengren, 2014; Wampold, 2011). In addition, the use of overly structured interventions, inappropriate self-disclosure, the excessive use of silence, and an "unyielding" use of transference interpretations are also associated with poor alliances (Ackerman & Hilsenroth, 2001). In other words, even if a therapist possesses highly refined skills and a method of proven efficacy, if he cannot engage the patient in a joint effort, his knowledge and skill will go to waste.

In contrast to their less effective colleagues, "therapists who demonstrated a mix of cognitive and emotional speech content, who conveyed warmth, and who were seen as actively listening to their clients, had a better overall connection with patients" (Sexton, Littauer, Sexton, & Tommeras, 2005, p. 110). The best therapists possess of number of seemingly contradictory qualities: they are confident but humble; lifelong learners with high levels of skill and expertise, who are simultaneously open to feedback; and are flexible but systematic in their approach (Wampold & Brown, 2005; Wampold & Budge, 2012). These therapists are masters at handling negative emotions and are courageous in handling conflict directly and non-defensively. Finally, they are ambitious and push themselves and their patients to work hard and endure discomfort in the pursuit of exceptional results. In other words, they are not content with mild or moderate improvement, but make an effort to obtain the best possible outcome for their patients (Gawande, 2004).

From the inception of treatment, the effective therapist is actively engaged, demonstrating skill and competence by employing specific interventions designed to develop a joint understanding of the nature, severity, and duration of the presenting problems (Sherer & Rogers, 1980; Wampold & Budge, 2012). "Therapists who conduct longer, more involved and more in-depth initial sessions, sustain active attention and concentration on areas of difficulty, and topics pertinent to understanding these problems, explored the therapeutic process in session, were emotionally attuned and were able to pinpoint new issues for the client to understand and gain insight into" created strong alliances with their patients (Hillsenroth & Cromer, 2007). The fact that it takes time to achieve these initial therapeutic goals is a point well worth reiterating. Davanloo (1990) has advocated spending at least three hours conducting the initial assessment, or "trial therapy" as he calls it. The patient is rarely more acutely distressed and more motivated than when he first arrives for help. In order to provide him with a therapeutic experience, rather than a mere exploration of history, we must take the time to examine the patient's concerns in detail. In so doing, the whole therapy has a chance to get off to a strong start.

A study on the impact of the trial therapy on outcome demonstrated its effectiveness in achieving rapid and significant improvement, and underscores the need to take sufficient time to achieve these ends (Abbass, Joffres, & Ogrodniczuk, 2008). Thirty consecutively referred patients received a trial therapy, and no additional treatment for six weeks, at which time they were reevaluated. Therapists were rated as highly engaged, making approximately 165 interventions per hour. The most common intervention (58%) involved a focus on the patient's feelings and emotions in the situations that triggered anxiety and symptoms. The second most common intervention involved linking the patient's present patterns of emotional response to those from the past (linking the two triangles). At the six-week follow-up, one-third of these patients had fully recovered and required no additional treatment. All patients experienced a significant reduction in symptoms as evaluated by the Brief Symptom Inventory, 35% went off their medication, and two returned to work after a significant period of unemployment. It should be noted that this was a highly impaired "treatment resistant" population of patients who had tried but failed to achieve results in at least three previous therapies. Sixty-seven percent of the patients had been on medication for a substantial period of time, and 87% had an Axis II personality disorder in addition to Axis I symptomatic disturbances. The results of this study confirm the notion that taking time to intervene and providing a therapeutic interaction in the first meeting is associated with the development of both a strong alliance and positive outcome. The ability to develop a therapeutic alliance, while intervening rapidly and decisively in blocking the defenses and resistances that would otherwise undermine that alliance, appear to be key factors in achieving these results. It is important to remember that we may only have one chance to engage with and help a particular patient. By intervening actively from the start, and allowing time to process the patient's responses to our interventions, we should be able to solidify the alliance and achieve improved outcomes.

Clinical Strategies for Creating and Maintaining a Strong Alliance

Achieving Agreement About the Nature of the Problems to Be Addressed

Achieving agreement on the nature of the problems to be addressed in treatment is one of the first and most important tasks in the development of a working alliance. Patients are often aware of symptomatic disturbances and troubles in living, but have no clear idea about the underlying cause of these difficulties. Careful inquiry, with specific attention to the precipitants of the symptoms and problems to be addressed, is particularly important in achieving consensus on the underlying nature of the problems at hand. The more explicit and transparent the therapist is in sharing her understanding of what the patient is struggling with, the better. In ISTDP we do not keep our hypotheses to ourselves, but share them with the patient in order to test them out and refine them. If patient and therapist do not agree on the nature of the problems to be addressed, therapy cannot proceed. Consequently, we continue the process until there is a consensus on the problem, an integral step in the process of creating a strong collaborative alliance.

Phoenix Rising

This patient began our first session reporting that she had been depressed all her life. Despite many years of therapy, she still had no clear understanding of the internal factors contributing to her depression. She seemed to think that she was just "depressive by nature," or was inevitably so, given the way she was raised. Consequently, she was passive and resigned about her life and its possibilities. However, response to intervention began to alter this view of herself and her difficulties. In the following sequence, approximately 10 minutes into the first session, the patient revealed having developed a serious visual impairment as a side effect of medication she had been prescribed. She reported being depressed and hopeless as a result. Exploration of her feelings about what happened paved the way for a new view of the mechanisms responsible for her depression.

Therapist: So you have some serious vision impairment?

Patient: It's the result of medication I took for arthritis (lets out a big sigh).

Therapist: Did you notice you just had a big sigh? Some feelings are coming up as you talk about this.

Patient: Sometimes I'm very sad about this, and also scared. I don't feel well equipped to go through life with these physical problems—and to get to the heart of one of my issues—I am terrified of becoming dependent and helpless, because at the beginning of my life when I was helpless and dependent and . . .

Therapist: It didn't go very well?

Patient: So it has always been hard for me to imagine that people would want to take care of me when I need it, in the later part of my life (hands clenching into fists).

Therapist: You are aware of feeling sad and scared. I don't know if you were aware of it, but your hands just went into fists. (Attending to the nonverbal unconscious signaling of emotion.) Where is your anger about this? This condition is the result of medication side effects? Are you aware that you are angry too?

Patient: Yes.

Therapist: OK, so how do you feel the anger, because that's not so obvious?

Patient: Well, muscle tension, constricted breathing . . .

Therapist: Is that anxiety or anger?

Patient: Anxiety and tension.

Therapist: This is interesting, because you get tense and anxious, but don't mention anger. You go quite readily to sadness, anxiety, and fear. Is anger harder for you to access and use in your own behalf?

Patient: Oh, yeah.

Therapist: So is that one of the things you want help with?

Patient: Yes, please.

While initially viewing her circumstances as the source of her depression, careful inquiry revealed that anxiety about, and avoidance of, anger was a significant contributing factor to her depression. By agreeing on the underlying nature of the problems to be addressed, and the tasks involved in the process, the alliance was strengthened. In this case the task involved facing and experiencing feelings of anger she had habitually repressed. Joint work on this task strengthened the alliance and led to immediate changes. In the very next session, the patient reported having asserted herself with her husband, something quite new. However, she soon deflated, saying she "did not prevail." This ushered in a much needed conversation about the nature of the patient's therapeutic goals.

Agreement About Goals

The therapeutic alliance is strengthened when patient and therapist agree about both the problems to be addressed and the goals to be achieved. Then the tasks involved in getting from the problem to the goal also become clear. Often patients view their problems, and the solutions to those problems, as external to them. Such was the case here. At first, the patient saw her husband and her circumstances as the problems. Given this, her solution was to fix or change these external factors. This left her in a helpless, frustrated position. In the following vignette, the nature of the problem and its solution were refined as the result of therapeutic exploration. The patient began by reporting a long withheld resentment toward her husband, regarding a gift he had lost years ago.

Patient: I spoke up, but I didn't prevail. He just argued with me. It reminds me of this endless conflict we have about the ways in which he has self-destructed at work.

Therapist: I think you give us a hint when you say, "I didn't prevail." That lets me know that you have a mind set to focus on winning. You want your partner not only to hear you, but to agree with you. This is very different than speaking up in order to be honest and self-expressed. Whether he agrees with you or not is a separate matter.

Patient: OK. Yeah, that, I think, makes it much more doable, because I have been taking the failure to change his mind as a failure.

Therapist: Exactly. And, also, it's an impossible task that you set yourself. So it sets you up for failure. You can't change him—that's up to him. Conversely, the only person you can change is yourself. That is where your power is (reestablishing an internal focus).

Patient: Yes. It sounds as if, no matter how much I speak up and speak my mind, I will still be angry that he torpedoed his own career.

Therapist: That's just what's so.

Patient: At least I don't have to have the struggle within myself about whether to express it or not.

Therapist: Right. And, in a funny way, interpersonally, it's just much more powerful to declare yourself and not to need—which is a big part of your vulnerability—to be approved of. If he doesn't validate you, you crumble or give it up. As you get more self-defined and stronger, and don't need his approval so much, it will shift the dynamic.

Patient: Yes.

Agreement on an Internal Goal

Therapist: That need for approval and recognition from others has made you very vulnerable. So does it make sense, then, that we will spend our time focusing on you—so you can stand with yourself, stick with yourself, care about and validate your own feelings? (Reestablishing our agreement on the therapeutic goal and task.)

Patient: Yes (smiling and sitting up in her chair).

Therapist: What is happening inside? It seems like there is a shift.

Patient: Yes there is. That is a very powerful paradigm shift. I am excited about it and am reminding myself, "Hold onto this."

Therapist: And hold onto *you*, instead of dropping you and siding with others, as you've had a tendency to do in the past.

The patient's initial goal—to get her husband to understand and agree with her—actually set her up for failure, and fed into her sense of hopelessness and futility. By reassessing her goals, and reestablishing an internal focus, therapeutic progress was made and the alliance was fortified. In fact, this therapeutic intervention resulted in what the patient referred to as a "powerful paradigm shift," in which her sense of personal agency was greatly enhanced.

Agreeing on the Therapeutic Task

Once the problems and goals have been elucidated, the tasks involved in the process must be made clear. As demonstrated in the preceding example, when the patient understands that avoidance and repression of feelings is the primary mechanism responsible for creating her symptoms, then approaching and experiencing these feelings becomes the obvious task. Creating and sustaining an internal focus is both a task and a goal for treatment. Both augment the alliance and provide fuel for the work ahead.

The Man With Self-Loathing

A patient with a pervasive sense of self-loathing came to therapy for help with anxiety and depression. Neither could be effectively treated without addressing his habitual tendency to put himself down, criticize himself, and blame himself for any and all ills befalling those around him. At first I focused on the harmful way he treated himself, with little effect. Over a number of sessions, it became clear that his relationship to this "introject" was operating as a barrier to genuine contact between us. In a sense, his "critical self" stood between his "true self" and me, preventing any real connection. I began to point this out to him.

Patient: I'm just such a loser.

Therapist: Do you see how this self-attack gets in the way here, between you and me? It's like you have this primary relationship with the voice in your head and you're not really present here with me.

Patient: I never saw it that way before, but you're right. It's a real turnoff to people when I start criticizing myself.

Therapist: Are you willing to put that aside so that we can connect here, and see how you really feel in this situation?

Patient: That sounds good.

Therapist: So, if you remove that barrier between us, what feelings do you notice coming up within you?

Patient: Oh my God, it's anger!

Therapist: How do you feel that anger inside?

Patient: It's really strong—heat and energy moving up.

Therapist: Who comes to your mind—who is all this anger toward?

Patient: My ex-wife!

Therapist: So if we direct that anger at her, where it belongs, instead of back at you, with all this criticism and self-attack, how would that come out?

Patient: I can't do that. That's not right.

Therapist: I am not suggesting you act on these feelings and impulses, but just face them honestly here with me. The fact is, you have a massive reservoir of rage toward your ex-wife. The only question is how that is going to get dealt with. When you keep it inside, you are filled with anxiety and self-doubt. You can attack yourself and put yourself down. The alternative is to face the anger honestly, toward her. Would it make sense to you if we created a space here to examine these feelings honestly—to use your imagination to release them— where nobody gets hurt?

Patient: That really makes sense. I never understood that before. My other therapist kept urging me to imagine hitting my wife. I just couldn't do it. Now I see what you mean—I can just imagine it without doing it!

In this vignette, clarity and specificity proved essential for the facilitation of a joint understanding of the therapeutic task. The steps involved in the process must be elucidated. For example, opening up is a necessary prerequisite for receiving help. In this example, the patient was helped to see how his attachment to the "voice" inside his head undermined treatment. When he dropped the defense, he was surprised to find anger rising within him, something he had previously denied experiencing. Once anger emerged, the therapist clarified the therapeutic task—to *experience* the feeling and face the impulse in fantasy (where no one gets hurt), rather than criticize himself for this feeling. In fact, multiple tasks were identified and clarified along the way: (1) to abandon destructive defenses, (2) experience his true feelings and impulses, and (3) reveal them to the therapist, without acting on them or suppressing them. Previous therapeutic attempts had failed, in large part, because the patient had no clear idea what therapeutic steps were required to obtain desired change. Again, this phase of consensus building is essential in order to solidify our alliance and achieve therapeutic progress, both of which are highly associated with outcome.

Relationship Between Alliance and Resistance

Since defense and resistance undermine the development of the alliance neces-sary for therapeutic effectiveness, assessing and regulating the balance between these two forces is essential work (Abbass, 2015; Binder & Beitan, 2013; Freder-ickson, 2013; Polaschek & Ross, 2010). Initially, Freud (1914/1962) took a fairly active stance in this regard, suggesting that removal of the resistance was the primary therapeutic task. However, he became increasingly passive and pes-simistic over time, suggesting we would have to "bow to the superiority of the forces to which we see our efforts come to nothing" (Freud, 1979). Davanloo (1990) turned this notion on its head, asserting that the resistance is to be wel-comed as an indicator that painful conflicts are not merely being approached but can be brought to the surface and resolved. Each time the resistance is penetrated, there is a marked and unmistakable increase in the strength of the therapeutic alliance. He found that this shift was particularly dramatic when the resistance in the transference was overcome. Following the breakdown of resistance, and breakthrough of feelings and impulses into consciousness, there was often a sudden and dramatic download of memories, dreams and associa-tions shedding light on the origin of the patient's conflicts.

In particular, Davanloo (1990, 2000) observed a phenomenon he referred to as "a transfer of images," in which images of a past figure would suddenly and unmistakably become superimposed on the face of the therapist. This literal transfer of imagines from the therapist to a key genetic figure makes the link between past and present explicit. Once the feelings and memories about the past are revealed and processed, the need to defend against them by distorting the present is no longer necessary. Consequently, the *real* relationship between therapist and patient, marked by a strong alliance, takes increasing precedence over one distorted by transferential phenomenon.

It should be emphasized that it is not sufficient for the patient to drop her avoidant strategies, but to declare a willingness to approach the feelings and expe-riences she has been avoiding instead. This requires skills aimed at bolstering desire and motivation, as well as overcome resistance. Randeau and Wampold (1991) analyzed the verbal exchanges between patients and their therapists in treatments rated as both high- and low-level alliance. Their findings support the notion that the therapist's focus on the patient's conflictual pattern in the here and now improved the alliance, while those avoiding this challenge contributed to poor alliances. This kind of "one-two punch," in which the therapist calls defense and avoidance into question, while focusing directly on the patient's emotional conflict, seems particularly effective at getting stalled treatments moving.

Working With the Twin Factors of Alliance and Resistance

To my knowledge, Malan (1979) and Davanloo (1990, 2000) are the only clinicians who speak directly of the existence of an unconscious therapeutic alliance operating as a guide to the underlying areas of disturbance responsible for the patient's symptoms and suffering. This unconscious alliance is viewed as separate and distinct from positive transference feelings, and constitutes a powerful source of healing that can speed and deepen the therapeutic process. While a positive transference, based on an association between the therapist and benevolent figures from the past, can distort the alliance and promote regression, the unconscious therapeutic alliance is a growth-promoting force from within, like an emotional immune system (Coughlin, 2009).

Davanloo (1990) has suggested that resistance and alliance exist in inverse proportion to one another. This idea was presented in my first book (Coughlin Della Selva, 1996/2004) 20 years ago. In the ensuing years, my experience suggests these two forces are intertwined, but not always in such a direct and straightforward manner. In fact, patients can exhibit high levels of both alliance and resistance (when the conflict about opening up and getting help is very intense), or low levels of both (when the patient has no real interest in the process). In any case, the ability to help the patient drop the resistance in order to face what he has been avoiding boosts the collaborative alliance and is a key task in the therapeutic process.

In the following case, work on the resistance was effective in activating both a conscious and unconscious alliance, necessary to move the therapy forward. This patient had tried but failed to get help in the past with therapies of various stripes, as well as a number of self-help groups. Without careful attention to the twin factors of resistance and alliance, this therapy would end as the others had—in failure.

The Man Addicted to Pornography

Therapist: Tell me what brings you and how I can help.

Patient: What started it was—my wife was concerned about the Percocet (pain killer prescribed by his physician for a back injury), but then what really got me into hot water was, I have had a fixation for years, since age 11, on pornography, which started to focus on fetish photos of ladies in boots and all the BDSM kind of photography. And, in later years, it's just been a fetish of, hum, a, uh, though there were times years ago—we've been married for 24 years—but there was a period a few years ago, between 10 and 5 years ago, a little bit of dabbling near the fringe with ladies— I am not proud, but . . . .

This patient entered therapy in a state of considerable conflict. He began the session by articulating his *wife's* concerns. His focus was external, and he had come for therapy in order to appease others. At the same time, he was quite open about his own behavior, and provided important and specific information, suggesting the presence of at least some unconscious desire to cooperate in the process. Still, it is critical for patients to make a conscious decision about entering treatment, rather disowning that desire, and attributing it to someone else. In this case, if the patient came to therapy in order to satisfy or mollify his wife, the therapist would become an unwitting proxy for her, rather than an ally of the patient in his quest for healing. Instead of creating a therapeutic alliance, a collusive alliance would be established.

Blocking Externalization and Pressing for the Patient's Will

Therapist: So these are her concerns, but what is your concern about it?
Patient: Just that this is serious stuff for me. She is a serious issue for me.
Therapist: In other words . . .
Patient: I'm not anguished over it.
Therapist: It doesn't concern you?
Patient: Only insofar as, I am not going to let this take my wife.

His responses revealed a habitual tendency to take a passive, subservient, and even beaten position in relation to others. His focus was also external. Given this, his only motivation was to keep his wife from leaving him. Maintaining such a powerless position in the therapy would undermine the development of a therapeutic alliance and prevent growth. Therefore, the initial task involved the creation of an internal focus.

Creating an Internal Focus

Developing and maintaining a therapeutic focus on the inner life of the patient is one of the first and most central tasks of any psychotherapy. Focused therapies tend to be more effective than those lacking focus (Hartman & Levenson, 1995; Hubble, Duncan, & Miller, 1999; Luborsky, McLellan, Woody, O'Brien, & Auerbach, 1985). In fact, a failure to achieve a therapeutic focus is consistently associated with negative outcome in psychotherapy (Mohr, 1995). Research suggests that those who have an internal focus and locus of control are healthier, happier, and more successful in life than those with an external focus (Dweck, 2007; Pink, 2009). Similarly, those who focus on intrinsic sources of motivation are more effective, productive, and satisfied than those who focus on external rewards (Pink, 2009). Therefore, helping patients develop an internal focus, fueled by curiosity and a desire for autonomy and self-direction, is a prerequisite for deep and lasting change.

Therapist: So this behavior is very destructive. It could destroy your relationship with your wife. But it sounds like you don't see that it is destructive to you.

Patient: Well, the doctor said . . .

Therapist: I'm asking you, not the doctor, not your wife, not this one and that one. I am asking you: Is this a fine way to treat yourself?

Patient: No, there is a lot of guilt involved, but I've been doing it for so long.

The therapist's persistent focus on the patient's internal life started to have an impact. For the first time, he began to experience some sense of inner conflict regarding his behavior, as well as the guilt he lives with as a result.

Therapist: So the issue is, do you want to get to the bottom of this, to what is driving this self-destructive behavior that could destroy a very good marriage of 24 years?

Patient: Yeah, I think I should. I'll tell you why.

Therapist: Not should, is that what you want?

Patient: Yeah, because here is my thinking, doc. I went for a period of about three months when I wasn't doing it. Then I backslid, for no reason.

Therapist: Well, obviously there is a reason.

Patient: Maybe there is a related issue. I have always been with this—on the one hand, this obsessive sex drive, but on the other hand, almost squeamish about having sex and it disturbs me because I am married to a girl who is cute as a button. She is 55 years old and probably the cutest 55-year-old in the world, and sometimes I find—and she feels I'm cold sometimes, and I am—I know I am, and it bugs me, and I think its related.

Therapist: Totally related. You can relate to a fantasy, but to have a real relationship and to get close to another human being . . . you are aware you have trouble with that.

Patient: Right.

Therapist: To feel a real connection with a real person. And this is undermining you because you want to stay married.

Patient: Absolutely.

Persistent focus on the patient's internal concerns and personal goals resulted in the declaration of a desire to resolve conflicts regarding sexuality. Once the problem of "squeamishness" was identified, we shifted our attention to the desired goal of initiating sex and having a closer relationship with his wife and overcoming the obstacles in the way of that goal. This enabled us to move forward toward his goals, as opposed to his initial motivation to simply avoid unwanted behavior.

Therapist: You want to get close, but do you notice that you avoid my eyes, tend to go passive and to remain somewhat vague?

Patient: Yes, I know that. I need to look away to think.

Therapist: And obviously, it's not just here. Even in your marriage you want to get close, but you get anxious and keep a distance. So would you say this is a primary conflict in your life?

Patient: Yes, that is a conflict in my life. I think a lot of people have this conflict I have. They have difficulty . . .

Therapist: To want intimacy but be afraid of it.

Patient: That's exactly the conflict I have—exactly what is hanging me up in my life, and hangs me up with interactions with other people. I have tremendous self-doubt.

The patient had become increasingly engaged in the therapeutic process and revealed a pattern of interpersonal distancing in all his relationships, including the one with the therapist. Now the patient had a choice—to continue to avoid closeness and to suffer alone, or to open up and get help. When resistance is overcome, both the conscious and unconscious alliance increase markedly.

Therapist: If we stay focused on what is going on here, we see that the very same thing is going on—same conflict you have with other people—is alive here between you and me. That is the good news, because now we can deal with it live, not just in the third person. You seem to have some idea that underneath this anxiety are all kinds of strong mixed feelings toward other people. And you are saying, even here, you know you are having reactions to my approach, about being direct, interested in you and getting to know you in a deep and intimate way.

Patient: I'm not having any negative feelings about it, but I am intimidated.

Therapist: Even though you say, "I don't have negative feelings," obviously that comes to your mind. So what kind of negative feelings are you aware of?

Patient: What kind of negative feelings am I aware of in myself—not necessarily toward you? Um, a real problem I have, negative feelings wise, is what goes along with what we've been talking about, this lack of confidence in myself—inability to see my own skills, powers, competencies. I have had other lawyers, guys of note, say "You underestimate your abilities constantly."

Therapist: OK. So let's look at what just happened here—it is very important. You begin to indicate, which is great, because you are being honest—that you are anxious because you have some mixed feelings about being here, and mixed feelings about getting close and letting me see what's behind the wall. You want to, but you don't want to. And you have mixed feelings toward me. Some positive, but also some negative feelings from the part of you that wants to keep me out. Right? So, what happens when we go to look at that is, you say, "Oh, no, I don't have any negative feelings toward you, I have negative feelings toward me." We could see that, in a split second, you protect the other person, "Oh, you're just great" and you turn your angry, negative feelings back on yourself—turn on yourself, undermine yourself, kill off your confidence. Do you see that?

Patient: You mean in my relationships in general or in my reaction to you? No, I don't think I was trying to mask negative feelings toward you. I don't have negative feelings about this approach you're taking. Honest, I'm not. Actually, as we talk, I'm very impressed and I think this is really weird because it's different and I went to a therapist for seven years and heard less from her in seven years than I've heard from you in 17 minutes. Not that he wasn't a fine individual.

Therapist: There it is again. Let's slow this down. So you can really get some insight into things. You went to see someone for seven years, to get help, but you say she said less in seven years than I've said in 17 minutes.

Patient: Right.

Therapist: You've got to have feelings toward her if you don't protect her.

Patient: Oh, but doc, I have explosive anger. I really have to mind how I deal with that.

Therapist: OK, let's look at this because if you are ignoring and denying your anger—it's there, building up, and then, suddenly, you will explode? What is an example of that?

Patient: I was a mediator in a court proceeding two days ago. Without getting into details there was this very young, aggressive lawyer for the injured party and my job was to recommend a settlement figure. I thought, given this extent of the complaints, that I bent over backwards to give him a fair shake, even though I thought he woefully failed to document his claims about what she would have been worth to a jury and when I explained how I evaluated it, the guy kept going, "You obviously, because my client is a paranoid schizophrenic, you probably can't deal with that." And he went on and on. I was ready to smack this motherfucker.

Therapist: I bet. You have a lot of anger inside right now.

Patient: I don't know what to do with it.

Therapist: Do you need some help with this?

Patient: Oh yeah. Every time I get angry I end up in one of these "Oh, now I have to apologize."

Therapist: So that whole pattern, of suppressing emotion, then acting on it, then getting in trouble for it, feeling bad—that's a negative, destructive pattern. And you get other people also to punish and chastise you. So, for us to turn that around, you need to become aware of, interested in, and paying attention to what is going on inside, before it gets to the point where you are ready to blow.

Patient: As far as experiencing the anger, it's probably what you say—either masking it or going ballistic.

Therapist: So, is that healthy—to swallow your anger or spit it out?

Patient: I have no notion of anything in the middle.

Therapist: So, again, is this something you need help with?

Patient: For sure.

Through a process of clarification, we have achieved agreement about the underlying nature of this man's problems—his intense conflicts over strong mixed feelings toward others. In particular, his anxiety over rage toward those who have failed or thwarted him was being defended against with passivity, subservience, and emotional distance. In the end, this strategy only increased his feelings of impotent rage. Occasionally this pent up rage would explode in a verbal tirade, which triggered guilt, more repression, and renewed self-punishment. Consequently, the therapeutic task involved approaching, rather than avoiding these feelings, so that he could use his feelings to assert himself constructively and attain desired goals, while discovering the source of these conflicts.

Maintaining a Strong Alliance Over Time—Dealing With Ruptures

While establishing a strong alliance at the start of therapy is necessary to prepare a foundation for the work, it must also be maintained over time. Failure to attend to the quality of the therapeutic relationship can lead to stagnation or deterioration. Svartsberg, Stiles, and Seltzer (2004) studied the process of alliance growth and variation over time in the short-term (18 sessions) therapy of depressed patients. In some cases, the alliance was strong and steady. In others it deteriorated over time and, in still others, there was an erratic pattern. Cases characterized by a rupture to the alliance, followed by repair, were associated with positive outcomes. In the case being presented here, defense and resistance were weakened in the first session but resurfaced in the second session. Exploration was required to understand this and reverse it.

Therapist: Do you want to get to bottom of your current problem?

Patient: I definitely want to get to the bottom of it.

Therapist: Do you just want to manage your symptoms, or do you want to get to the engine of this thing?

Patient: I do, yes. I do want to get to the bottom of it.

Therapist: You want to free yourself of that and live a happy life?

Patient: Absolutely.

Therapist: Do you see then, that it's of crucial importance that we do this process differently, that you pay attention to yourself and instead of avoiding, we focus on you, your feelings, your desires, what you want for yourself. Does that make sense?

Patient: That's a big concept for me to understand. I certainly want to change. Now what you are saying is, by focusing on the feelings, is the first step in moving away from that behavior. What I'm wondering is, well, if focusing on the feelings—I know the feeling that goes with the pornography is almost recreation.

Therapist: Let's slow down. You saw yourself that these behaviors are distractions—ways to avoid you. You are running from yourself and your inner life by getting involved in these outer things. Does that make sense, because I don't just want you going along with me? Our task, to get you to your goal, is to approach and face, rather than to avoid and distract.

Patient: OK.

Therapist: So if we look in this moment, how you are aware of feeling inside right now? And pay attention to what you feel in your body.

Patient: Well, I'm nervous, I'm distracted.

Therapist: Where do you notice it—in your stomach or . . . ?

Patient: It's in my chest. The thing is, the physical feeling is just sort of a heightened sort of excitement. This is what I function by.

Therapist: You have a chronic level of anxiety you mean?

Patient: I always think—all my life—I sympathize with people who are going to be executed because every time I am about to engage in some activity where I am going to be up to public display, it is like an execution.

Therapist: Wow—this is really important. You are letting us know that, for some reason—you get really scared, like deathly afraid.

Patient: The anxiety is the anxiety I feel on a daily basis—it's mostly about my professional activities. That's where I feel a tremendous inadequacy. After I stopped drinking, a guy I worked with got extremely well connected, and every once in a while they bring me along to an affair like this, and my wife tells me I do well, but I think it's unbelievable and frightening.

Therapist: This is very important. You have this free floating anxiety that comes to a peak when you are with people, especially when you are with people who you consider powerful, successful, smart, whatever it might be, and in the face of your anxiety, you add insult to injury by putting yourself down. So you are already anxious, and then you tell yourself you are no good, you are inadequate.

Patient: I don't even have to say it to myself, I already know it.

Therapist: That's part of the self-destructive system—putting yourself down and then acting in ways that support that—that you are no good and so on.

Patient: You know, I had a breakthrough the other night. I got on the elevator, and there was a guy who I recognized from the newspaper and he had a case that was related to a case I had, and it was just a big thing for me to say, "Are you Richard? My name is Joe. I was wondering, I had a case like yours." It is absolutely something I would not have done years ago.

Therapist: Wow.

Patient: I did it because the curiosity I had about the case overcame my fear.

Therapist: So the healthy part of you—the part that wants to connect, that wants to learn from him—was greater than your fear, so you actually approached him and initiated a conversation and felt good about yourself instead of bad.

Patient: Absolutely! I was really happy that I was able to do that.

Therapist: So how do you feel that happy, proud feeling inside right now?

Patient: I feel stronger.

Therapist: So the anxiety goes down and then . . .

Patient: Yes. I feel bigger. Oh yes, it's a physical feeling—instead of being hunched over, I am being erect (a communication from the unconscious about the link to his sexual feelings and behavior).

Therapist: That's also a very interesting word you use—that even sexually you have been limp, and something has gotten in the way of being strong and erect. So you can have, for brief moments, had the experience of being healthy, strong, initiating contact, feeling good about yourself and you want that to expand and be your baseline.

The work designed to overcome resistance and strengthen his healthy strivings simultaneously strengthened the alliance, and yielded further fruit. He went on to initiate a discussion of our relationship, which he had previously avoided.

Feelings Toward the Therapist Regarding the Rupture

Patient: Absolutely. It has everything to do with the feelings. There was a certain anxiety about our relationship. When you said at the end of the last meeting, you have to decide whether you want to look at this or not. I didn't want—I'm not saying it to please you—but I didn't want to walk away from here saying, "Oh well, you don't have enough commitment to benefit from this process." Then I would be striking out.

Therapist: So it wasn't accurate to say you don't have the will and determination. You're saying you have a lot of motivation actually.

The therapist acknowledged that her challenge to the patient at the end of the previous session was both inaccurate and ill timed. Following this acknowledgment, the therapist encouraged him to experience and express his feelings about this directly.

Patient: I do have a lot of motivation. You talked about my age, and it may seem like if a person reaches the age of 63 and they haven't changed, if you were a betting man you might bet against them, but . . .

Therapist: So let's look at the feelings that you are having toward me, because you were hearing me challenging you, and even being pessimistic in some way, or doubting that could change, by asking if you had the will to change—were too old, or something like that. Right?

Patient: Right.

Therapist: That would definitely stir up feelings. What is the feeling toward me?

Patient: The first meeting was wow—great—she got me to want to face these feelings, but then I felt resentment, where does she get off?

Therapist: So you had mixed feelings toward me—positive feelings and negative feelings—that are generating anxiety. So how do you experience in your body this anger inside?

Patient: I felt comfortable just sharing the things that were causing me anger, and the fact that you didn't react in any way—that's all I needed to hear—I feel I'm alright. As far as reaching my feeling, that is my intent, I will do that.

Therapist: You're saying that the fact that you could get in touch with your anger and express it directly, and that I could just listen to you, not get defensive or issue ultimatums, was new. For you to say it, is that right, it felt new? Like talking to the guy in the elevator?

It is important to give the patient credit for the efforts he makes to change. He reported a "breakthrough" during the past week, which became evident in the assertive way he related to the therapist. He acknowledged angry feelings regarding comments made at the end of the first session. By abandoning defenses of compliance and expressing his feelings toward the therapist, the ruptured alliance was repaired and the work deepened. In fact, this interaction seemed to provide the patient with a corrective emotional experience.

Patient: The fact that you listened and didn't take offense, that's all I need. I feel like, what you are doing is—you're saying we are going to make a bond and work on understanding the world together—and understanding me together. And it's an extraordinary—unusual and striking and extraordinary—and I didn't expect that. I didn't know you were going to do that. I'm not at all put off by it.

Processing Positive Feelings

Therapist: What are the feelings about what we have been able to do together?

Patient: It's a great thing—that you would try to be my partner in doing this is, I'm thrilled (patient is getting choked up, with tears in his eyes).

Therapist: It looks like you are moved on some level.

Patient: It is extraordinary. It takes, I guess, you know, I guess I do it in my life with people. I didn't think, in my experience with other folks who do what you do that we'd be doing that, but it does make sense.

Therapist: And you can feel, there is something very powerful and extraordinary happening here, if you and I both devote ourselves and give 100% of our effort to you and your emotional life so you can get your freedom.

Patient: Absolutely.

The patient communicated a great depth of feeling about what we had been able to do together. Having taken the risk to reveal, rather than conceal, his mixed feelings toward me, and having these feelings explored in an open and non-defensive manner, allowed the alliance to deepen considerably. Prior to this corrective experience, all relationships, including those with previous therapists, had been characterized by a pattern of dominance and submission. The experience of the therapeutic relationship as mutually respectful and collaborative was something new and "extraordinary" in some way. This experience was therapeutic and speaks to the reciprocal nature of alliance and therapeutic progress. In other words, the development of the alliance was a result of the work we had completed. Further, the strengthening of the bond allowed for deeper levels of change to take place. His sense of self was profoundly altered—from impotent to courageous.

Therapist: How do you feel about being open, honest, and direct, with yourself and me?

Patient: Yeah, I really haven't held anything back.

Therapist: So that takes courage. You set yourself a goal and you did—you have been direct and honest in your own behalf. Can you acknowledge that you are already doing it and let yourself feel some sense of pride?

Patient: I'm thrilled.

Since an enhanced sense of mastery and competence is a vital factor in healing, as well as in preventing relapse (Weinberger, 1995), attending to the patient's expanding sense of self must be included in our repertoire. In this case, the patient was able to express appreciation to the therapist for her help, while also experiencing pride in his own efforts to overcome long-standing difficulties. His long held view of himself as incompetent and fatally flawed was replaced with an increased sense of himself as solid and capable. At the same time, this experience strengthened the alliance and promoted further growth.

Overcoming Resistance

In the following case, a 69-year-old woman with a history of failed treatments entered therapy reluctantly, with signs of extremely high resistance, preventing the development of an alliance. Therapeutic intervention was required in order to penetrate the resistance and make contact with the suffering woman beneath, in order to establish a therapeutic alliance.

Intensely negative affect was close to the surface from the start of the interview. While it might be tempting to want to "down-regulate" these emotions with cognitive techniques, such an approach is unlikely to help her in life, where her strong feelings were easily triggered (Raio, Oredery, Palazzolo, Schurick, & Phelps, 2013). Instead, these feelings were greeted openly, as the vehicle for overcoming resistance and gaining rapid access to the unconscious source of her suffering. Such an approach has been viewed as especially significant with difficult and "highly resistant" patients (Butler & Strupp, 1986; Kernberg et al., 1972). Kernberg et al. (1972) reported that "low ego strength patients were significantly more likely to improve with therapists who were highly skilled, where 'skill' refers largely to interpreting (rather than ignoring or reciprocating) the strong, negative transference dispositions that interfere with a cooperative, supportive relationship" (Butler & Strupp, 1986, p. 36). Since for a "sizable group of people whose chronic mistrust, hostility, and negativism (that is, 'characterological' problems) seem to preclude . . . a constructive, collaborative relationship with a potential helper" (Butler & Strupp, 1986, p. 36), a direct approach to these pervasive and preexisting feelings must be taken. Once the feelings are experienced directly and then linked to early attachment figures, the therapist can been seen more accurately—as someone there to help.

The Woman Who Thought It Was Too Late

Therapist: Why don't you start by telling me what brings you and what kind of help you are looking for?

Patient: I don't know. I think I have to decide. This is the problem—and I do have a close friend I talk to about this. I may be—uh—I have sat— uh—all my life and because of anxiety—she feels—and I asked her because she knows me since graduate school—a lack of self-esteem, anxiety, inability to make a decision. I just sit and I really haven't gotten any . . . I think it's too late to get where I want to get at 69, so I go through a little anger about this nastiness about being an old maid.

Therapist: So, let's just slow down and look at what you're saying so far. You are aware that you have quite a lot of anxiety and you can get paralyzed in the face of it, so that you are not able to make decisions that are in your own best interest, and then you can begin to give up on yourself, with "It's too late, I'm 69." So, here you are, for a two-hour session, but a part of you is already saying, "It's no use."

Patient: Because what I want you're not—I'm not going to be able to get.

Therapist: Which is what, if you don't . . .

Patient: I would like a better partner. I would like more money.

Therapist: If we stay with you, Eleanor, because these are external things. So let's start with how you are experiencing your anxiety.

Patient: I am starting to—I'm sorry—I didn't mean to interrupt—I am very, my mind . . . I may be ADD. I hope I am going to remember this.

The patient's disorganized opening statement, obstinate attitude, resignation, and focus on external sources of satisfaction were all factors contributing to her current misery. If neglected, "such resistances form a ballast which is difficult, if not impossible, to remove" (Reich, 1980, p. 51). In the preceding vignette, the therapist's efforts to interrupt this resistance yielded a positive response. The patient started to shift her attention internally. In so doing, she alerting the therapist to the fact that anxiety was already over threshold and too high to facilitate effective engagement.

Therapist: So, again, in the face of anxiety you can have difficulty focusing, being clear in your thoughts. I'm glad you let me know that. Let's slow down so we can really look at how you are experiencing this anxiety in your body. What is happening inside that lets you know you are anxious?

Patient: Everything starts going around like this (hand swirling around her head).

Therapist: Does it actually affect your visual field, like do you get blurred vision?

Patient: No. If I'm furious, I can lose.

Therapist: You can get so anxious you can't see straight?

Patient: No, that's fury.

While this response lets us know that fury is beneath the anxiety, the patient's anxiety is still too high to safely investigate feelings of rage. Until the patient's anxiety is in striated muscles and her thinking is clear, an examination of her underlying feelings would be both premature and possibly damaging.

Therapist: And fuzziness in your thinking.

Patient: Yeah.

Therapist: And what in your body, if you come down a bit? What is actually happening in your body that lets you know you are anxious, nervous?

Patient: It's just spinning up there.

Therapist: So you don't allow yourself to experience the anxiety in a bodily way—it goes up into your head and your thoughts.

Patient: Maybe I do because one of my major problems is back pain. I get so tight.

Therapist: OK, so are you willing to actually pay attention to yourself and to focus—do a body scan here—to see if you have tension in your body, and if so, where? Do you feel any up here? Let's just scan your body and see.

Patient: See this is a test and I'm going to fail it.

Therapist: Again, are you interested in looking at the way you relate to yourself?

Patient: Um hum.

Therapist: A part of you comes here to look at some debilitating difficulties but this other part of you is mean, and telling you, "Don't bother. You can't succeed anyway." This is a mean, nasty way of treating yourself, hum? Do you see that? Can we put that critical voice . . .

Patient: I have been working on myself, plus everybody else.

Therapist: But do you see that, the way you are relating to yourself? And then also, in a sense, from the very beginning, how you are inviting me to treat you?

Patient: I don't know.

Therapist: Well, let's look at that, because we are having a conversation, but you are wanting to turn it into a test that you are going to fail. What kind of way is that to treat you and what does that set me up as, from the get-go?

Patient: Because I really can't do it.

Therapist: If you could, you wouldn't be here, right?

Patient: I can't do anything.

Therapist: Let's not exaggerate. You got yourself here. So, let's slow down and see what's happening inside. You've got a lot of anxiety and it's almost like you are afraid to even hope that you might be able to get some help. You have this tendency to put yourself down and go hopeless. What kind of way is that to live? You must get depressed.

Patient: (Big sigh.)

Therapist: What are you feeling right now? This is good, it's getting in your body more. Do you feel those sighs?

Patient: All of the sudden I felt this whole area (motioning to the center of her body).

Focused attention on the experience of anxiety, in order to down-regulate it and keep it in an optimal zone, was called for in this case. At the same time, regressive defenses of helplessness and projection were blocked. In addition to blocking unhealthy ways in which the patient was relating to herself and the therapist, attention to her strengths, will, and determination were identified and reinforced. These interventions were effective in increasing the patient's capacity and mobilizing her core conflict. Her thinking cleared up and she started to sigh, indicating that anxiety was being channeled into the striated muscles. This was another positive sign, and paved the way for examining the feelings that were generating her anxiety and driving regressive defenses.

Feelings Toward the Therapist

Therapist: What do you feel there?

Patient: Just a weight or something. I am just aware of it. I am tight up here.

Therapist: There is this tightness and anxiety and a lot of feelings underneath. Right, you said, "There is fury." It's like, right under this anxiety, there is a lot of anger that starts to come up. Yes?

Patient: Yes.

Therapist: So if that anger came up and out, here, against me. What do you see, what do you want to do?

Patient: Start hollering at you.

Therapist: Holler what?

Patient: Like, "Why am I here and you can't help me. Why am I here and what is, why are you here? You don't get it. You don't get it."

Therapist: So the words don't quite make it. There is this vicious anger inside you.

Patient: Yeah, I can get very angry (big sigh).

Therapist: And if that got let loose, this animal part of you came out at me. No words, right? What is in your body that wants to come out with this pent up rage?

Patient: I don't understand. You mean what would I physically do?

Therapist: Right. In your imagination if you lost control and all this tremendous rage came out toward me?

Patient: I'd probably flip you over. Maybe slam some lamps around.

Therapist: But it would be slam me around—the lamps didn't . . .

Patient: Right, yes.

Therapist: So there is this vicious rage with the impulse to slam me around and push me over—how?

Patient: I would just take your legs and just bash you into the wall with your legs.

Therapist: What else?

Patient: Stomp on your head. I don't know.

Therapist: Stomp, yes, because there is something in your feet and you can feel that.

Patient: Yes. I stomp on your torso.

Therapist: What else, if all this came out?

Patient: Bite you.

Therapist: Where?

Patient: In your face. Rip your arms out. Smack you. Kick you.

Therapist: Where do you kick?

Patient: Anywhere on your torso.

Therapist: So it is biting, kicking, smashing me—a massive attack, on me, on my head, on my torso. Anything else in you that wants to come out at me?

Patient: No, that's the problem. I think. I was biting in the third or fourth grade.

Therapist: So you have had this rage almost all your life right?

Patient: Yes.

Therapist: So in your imagination, when all that rage is out, my head is smashed, you bite my face, you have kicked me, stomped me, what do I look like? What is the picture?

Patient: You're broken. You are lying there. You are not moving. You are not talking, thank God. And I leave you.

Therapist: OK, but before you do that?

Patient: You are not moving.

Therapist: So, I am dead?

Patient: Maybe.

Therapist: You smashed my head.

Patient: Yeah!

Therapist: So, if you look at my face.

Patient: You can't bother me anymore.

Therapist: What do you see?

Patient: I just see you lying on the floor. Your head is down.

Therapist: But if you rolled me over and look into my face?

Patient: You are just—your eyes are rolled up into your head, like dead people.

Therapist: So I'm dead.

Patient: Your mouth would fall open and maybe I'd just step on you a couple more times.

Therapist: So there is more anger?

Patient: 'Cause I can't have you to beat anymore. It's not fun to kick a dead body.

Therapist: Kind of futile, huh? So then what is the feeling after all this rage is out? What is the feeling toward me now?

Patient: I guess I'm leaving but I don't know where I'm going.

Therapist: But what is the feeling, before you leave?

Patient: Well, I got the rage out, so I am quiet for a while. I don't care about you.

Therapist: But you have killed and destroyed another person.

Defenses Against Grief and Guilt

Patient: Why should I care about you? Why, when no one cares about me or ever has? (Starts to cry.) I've cared—see, that is the problem. I have cared too fucking much about people and I always get left in the lurch.

Therapist: So you have had a lot of pain and a lot of rage and you don't want to let anybody get close to you. You'd rather be the one to destroy them. Where does that leave you then? You destroy me and there is no possibility. And then you leave—by yourself again. And, even though you try to convince yourself that you don't care, what we see underneath is a lot of pain. A lot of grief. You actually do care.

Patient: I don't care. Finally, this is the first time that I just care about myself! The first time.

Cost of Defenses

Therapist: What's it like to live only caring for yourself? What kind of life is that?

Patient: Lately I've been living—it's brittle and dry.

Therapist: Not much of a solution huh?

Patient: No.

Link to the Past

Therapist: So when you said, "I don't want to care about you. Nobody cared about me," who were you talking to? Who are you so angry with, who hurt you so badly that you just want to kill them, stomp on them?

Patient: I don't know that she hurt me, but I just absolutely adored my mother and she was always so fucking busy and she was so nervous. People would never know this. Everyone loved my mother. Loved her.

Transfer of Images: The Unconscious Opens

When the unconscious alliance gains precedence over the resistance, there is often a transfer of images from the therapist to important figures from the past, accompanied by clear memories of traumatic events, which become available for reworking. In this case, the patient's primitive defenses formed a resistance that had prevented her from getting help in the past. In fact, she had frightened and alienated almost everyone she encountered. Decades of pent up pain and rage were barely concealed behind a snarling exterior. Terrified of facing these feelings within her, yet unable to completely mask them, she was left alone in a state of torment and isolation.

Left unattended, her defenses against these feelings, and resistance against closeness, would have undermined all efforts to establish an alliance and work therapeutically. Many interlocking interventions were required to forge an alliance. These included interventions designed to regulate anxiety, turn the patient against defenses, and facilitate the experience of intensely mixed feelings in the transference. This work solidified the alliance and created an opening that allowed us to understand the origin of her suffering. The conflicts regarding closeness, and the intensely mixed feelings that closeness engendered, were clearly tied to unresolved feelings regarding the patient's mother, who was neglectful and preoccupied throughout her childhood. This experience helped her to understand the underlying cause of lifelong difficulties that had been confusing, as well as distressing. After this first two-hour interview, the referring physician called to say, "I don't know what you did, but I had the first coherent conversation we've ever had. She was calm and cooperative. Now I can work with her."

After three additional sessions, the patient reported having ended two highly destructive relationships with "friends," going to New York City on her own to visit museums (something she greatly enjoyed but had never considered an option before), and starting to work as a docent at a local museum.

Summary

An effective therapeutic alliance is one based on collaboration, respect, and trust, as well as agreement about the problems to be addressed, goals to be achieved, and tasks required. The working relationship between therapist and patient is the very vehicle for change. The stronger it is, the more likely a positive outcome. Research suggests that the therapist variable is the most significant factor in creating this type of alliance. In other words, the most effective therapists are interpersonal masters who are able to forge a relationship for change even with patients with complex and long-standing difficulties (Frederickson, 2013). They do so by managing negative feelings in the transference, helping the patient relinquish defenses, and actively encouraging him to engage in a collaborative effort. By making this kind of therapeutic progress, the alliance is strengthened. In turn, the strong alliances promote therapeutic change. There is a mutual and reciprocal interaction between these two key variables.

The therapeutic alliance has both conscious and unconscious elements. The conscious alliance is created by an explicit agreement about problems, goals, and tasks. The unconscious alliance is fueled by the patient's innate desire to heal and grow, to become who he really is, and to form a secure attachment to others. Since these innate capacities are often blocked by defenses against anxiety-provoking feelings and resistance against closeness with others, these obstacles must be removed for development to resume. By helping patients overcome resistance and abandon defenses, feelings become accessible. The experience of previously avoided feelings activates unconscious memories and associations that help therapist and patient understand the origins of the patient's suffering and, in so doing, fortify both the conscious and unconscious alliance.

The alliance is a dynamic variable and shifts from moment to moment, and session to session. Relationships are not static, but change over time and are rarely smooth. Effective therapists keep their eye on the health and vitality of the alliance throughout the course of the relationship. It is absolutely vital to construct a collaborative relationship at the inception of treatment. Then, in order to facilitate working through, the alliance must be maintained and fortified over time. Again, the more progress is made, the stronger the alliance. If and when the alliance gets off track, repair to the alliance is indicated, lest the therapy stall. Therapist errors and avoided feelings toward the therapist are common factors increasing resistance and undermining the alliance. The more the therapist invites the patient to face and share his feelings toward him, the stronger the alliance he will form with the patient.

Chapter Seven
Intimacy With Self and Other: Facilitating Profound Moments of Meeting

The innate drives to be a separate self and to connect deeply and lovingly with others define our dual nature (Blatt & Fonagy, 2008). In other words, the more securely attached we are to others, the freer we are to be autonomous, self-directed, and self-defined. In turn, the more clearly defined we are as a separate self, the more we have to offer to others. However, achieving and maintaining a balance between these two motivational drives is a lifelong task, and often involves struggle.

The triangle of conflict depicts the patient's internal struggle with his own anxiety-provoking thoughts and feelings. The way a patient deals with or avoids his own urges and desires reflects the patient's relationship with himself. He is either aware of and connected with his inner being, or neglectful and detached from his own essence. He might even be his own worst enemy, punishing himself for his own feelings, wishes, and desires, often without any conscious awareness that such processes are at work. In any case, the triangle of conflict helps us understand, track, and heal divisions within the self. Conversely, integration within leads to harmony and health (Siegel, 2010). In addition, the ways in which the patient relates to his own needs, wishes, feelings, and desires dramatically impact his ability to establish and maintain healthy relationships with others. The triangle of person depicts the ways in which the patient plays out his inner conflicts in the interpersonal field, as well as revealing their origins in the past. So, in a way, the two triangles provide another way to depict the patient's relationship to "self" and "other," as well as linking the two. In this way we can monitor and modify what happens both within the patient and between the patient and others.

The two triangles provide a visual tool for mapping out what Wachtel (1993) has referred to as "cyclical psychodynamics," in which intrapsychic and interpersonal patterns of behavior interact, affecting and reinforcing each other in a mutual and reciprocal fashion. The effective therapist is adept at identifying and tracking these patterns of interaction so that old, dysfunctional ways of relating are replaced with healthy alternatives. Patients often sacrifice one these primary needs for another. In other words, they either abandon themselves in an attempt to hold onto others, or forgo relationships in an effort to hold onto themselves. Evaluating the balance, or lack thereof, between the patient's need for autonomy and attachment needs to be in the forefront of the therapist's mind in order to facilitate the kind of integration required to achieve health and well-being.

We map each other's minds and change each other's brains through close and emotionally meaningful interactions (Schnarch, 2009; Schore, 2001). Learning how to harness this power in order to promote "profound moments of meeting," enhancing the patient's ability to tolerate intimacy and closeness, is one of the most important skills for the effective therapist to master. ISTDP is a model of treatment that promotes the development of intimacy with self and other quite explicitly. In addition to listening to the content of the patient's message, we observe his nonverbal behavior and pay special attention to the pattern of interpersonal relatedness. In particular, we encourage direct eye contact and open sharing of all the patient's complex emotions toward us, as well as others. In this way, we can assess, track, and modify neglected areas of development in order to facilitate growth. Only if the therapist is available for intimacy will this kind of deep change within the patient be achieved.

Transcripts from treatments illustrating a therapeutic process within which intimacy with self and other is developed and strengthened will be highlighted throughout this chapter.

Our Dual Nature

We begin life as totally dependent creatures, designed to attach to caretakers. Much early, implicit, emotional learning takes place nonverbally in the first years of life. In particular, the ways in which the child's attachment figures have responded to the dual drives to be separate and to attach closely to others has a significant impact on development. In many cases, our patients have learned, or somehow concluded from their experience, that they would have to sacrifice one of these innate needs for another. Many sacrifice self in order to maintain their attachments. In other cases, the child gives up on relationships and decides, "I just gotta be me." Giving up one need for another leads to distortion of our true nature. The narcissist renounces his desire for connection, and denies feelings of longing, pain, and loneliness. Not only does this choice undermine his ability to have healthy relationships with others, it grossly undermines his personal development as well. Similarly, dependent patients who abandon self for relationship undermine both aspects of development. In a sense, these patients don't have a solid and robust self to offer others, but are "shell figures" who create relationships designed to focus exclusively on the needs and feelings of the other.

Assessment and treatment of the patient's character disturbances is greatly enhanced by identifying and fortifying the primary need that has been relinquished in an attempt to preserve the other. Then treatment can be tailored to fit the particular needs of the patient. This assessment will largely determine how we go about responding to patients. We might take a "you can do it" stand with a dependent and subservient patient who has a shaky sense of autonomy and confidence, but would suggest more of a "would you let me help you out here" approach with an avoidant character who denies the need for attachment. Since a failure to develop one of these essential capacities always affects both polarities of experience, monitoring both autonomous functioning and attachment patterns should enhance therapeutic outcome (Blatt & Ford, 1994; Blatt, Sanislow, Zuroff, & Pilkonis, 1996).

The dual needs to be self-defined, and to attach and relate closely to others, are not opposites or mutually exclusive, though it can seem that way to many of our patients. In fact, these are two intertwined drives in all human beings (Blatt & Fonagy, 2008). Getting them into balance is an adult developmental achievement. In a sense, it is only when we can stand on our own two feet, soothing our own anxieties and revealing ourselves authentically, that we are truly available for intimacy and closeness with others. The more we invite patients to face their own truth—both about what has happened in their lives, and how they really feel about it—the more available they will become for authentic connection with others. When this happens, and the patient lifts the shades, allowing us to really see him in an unguarded way, there is a profound moment of meeting. Whether this takes place three hours into an initial consultation, or three months into a treatment, I am often moved to say, "It's nice to meet you!"

In order to facilitate profound moments of meeting, the therapist must possess a fairly high level of emotional maturity. Research suggests that therapists who over identify with patients are at risk for burn out (Siegel, 2010). Only if we can soothe and regulate our own feelings and anxiety while in close contact with another will we be able to truly help our patients. This involves the ability to be receptive rather than reactive. Just such an experience of being a true self in close contact with another was facilitated in the following case. Specific interventions designed to remove defense and resistance were required in order to create an opening for genuine feelings and relatedness to be freely experienced.

"Like Watching a Play From Beginning to End"

Patients who have had traumatic histories and chaotic attachments develop self-protective strategies to keep others at a "safe" distance. This was certainly true in the case of the "Broken Bird" (the opening phase of this case is recounted on pages 62–66), a Chinese immigrant who had experienced a great deal of childhood trauma; including repeated threats of abandonment by her mother, her mother's refusal to feed her, being accused of wanting to sleep with her father, hearing her parents' plot to kill her brother, and being sexually abused by that same brother. In order to survive, she had adopted a tough, self-sufficient attitude that amounted to "I don't need anyone." However, these self-protective measures cost her dearly in life. Not only was she unable to let others close, she remained a stranger to herself. She knew there was "something wrong with my heart," but had no idea what. She had strong emotional reactions that she found perplexing.

The Broken Bird

Distinguishing Feelings From Defenses

Patient: I feel so angry at Joe. I think if I lash out I would take the phone or book and throw it at him and hit him. I would hit him and hit him and say, "You don't deny it. I hate you." (Hands are in fists.)

Therapist: Where do your fists want to go?

Patient: On his chest (but she pounds her own chest very hard at the same time).

Therapist: On his chest, not yours (blocking the instantaneous turning of the impulse back on herself). Do you see what happens in a split second?

Patient: I am pounding on myself (starts to cry—a good sign that she is turning against the defense). I would hit him! I would let it out. I would hit him. Let it out on him until I calm down.

Therapist: Until it's all out. When would that be? What else wants to come out, if you release it all?

Patient: I don't really see myself hitting him and hitting him.

Therapist: You just did, though. What's happening—you are collapsing? He's the one who would be collapsing, not you. Do you see this—how you internalize this? It's really important. First you start to pound on his chest, then you flatten yourself instead of facing that it's him who would be flattened by this attack.

Patient: What? Why am I doing this?

Therapist: Good question. You protect him and you from facing this vicious part of you?

Patient: I want to get to that place so I can get to the rage and deal with it. I want to go there but somehow I can't find it and latch on and I am so exhausted.

Therapist: But how did you suddenly get so exhausted? Where did it go? What is exhausting is all the energy it takes to keep it contained.

Patient: Now I'm laughing. I laugh when I am nervous. Why is it funny? I don't know why.

Therapist: It makes you nervous and you make it a joke. First you want to cry over it and wash it away, or laugh it off. There is something really scary—anxiety underneath the laughing.

Her rather hysterical laughing suddenly gave way to sobbing and moaning. After allowing the pain to flow through her, she suddenly sat up and forward, revealing the images and memories that followed the breakdown of her defenses and breakthrough of her feelings. This material proved highly significant and shed light on the origin of her conflicts around anger and closeness.

Link to the Past

Patient: Something comes to me—an experience—at 13 or 14 when I start to rebel against my mother. She would yell at everybody in the household. She would yell at my father, and I started taking my father's side. I started to stand up to her and to—I rebelled against her. I stand up for my father and my mother is furious and she started to come hit me and I was—not afraid, I know I would not hit her but I could have hit her—I protect myself and I could hit her if I have to. She backed down and was really angry and she said, "OK you are big now you want to hit me, so you want to go sleep with your father? You want to go together? You want to take over the household?" She was vicious. She said those terrible things (crying). She was so angry. And I think that has something to do with it. That I stood up to her and fight her and challenge her and from then on, I was not the same, because I'm not a little girl anymore, and I start to have this role and I fight with her for the rest of my life until she died.

As the patient revealed the memory of this horrendous conflict with her mother, her arms made the very same movement she made when talking about the anger she felt toward her partner. Clearly anger was terrifying, because it had been associated with violence and counterattack. She had completely avoided any expression of anger with her partner in order to protect him from this violent rage. However, the result was a distant and lifeless relationship that had withered over the years. She was able to see how she had linked her partner with her mother in her unconscious mind. Now her conscious, adult mind could reevaluate this from a new perspective. Her partner was actually a kind and understanding man—nothing like her mother. She found a new determination to open up and be honest with him to see what they could create together.

In this next session it was apparent that the patient was still keeping a certain kind of emotional distance from me. The patient spontaneously related this pattern of wanting but avoiding closeness with me, to what happens with her partner. Clearly this was about more than just avoiding anger. Closeness itself seemed to be experienced as threatening.

Patient: We haven't had sex for a long time.
Therapist: How long—a month or a year?
Patient: Two years. I think I just shut down.

Therapist: This is your pattern. Do you see? Longing, pain, anger—shut down—withdrawal. But who is being deprived?

Patient: And I resent that. I sacrifice myself. Why I do that? I say, "It's a nice time we have."

Therapist: Yeah, but more like brother and sister than lovers.

Patient: I can't believe it. I want to give it to myself but have been fighting around it. It's like I'm holding the rose, but looking around the garden, where is it? But it's right here! I always hold back. Toughness is always comes out to play games. (Pause.) It's strange that you said, "You are more like brother and sister than lovers." I was molested by my brother—I never told you. I think that has something to do with it.

Therapist: I am sure it does. Do you think it would be helpful for us to look at what happened and how you felt about it so it doesn't end up interfering in your relationship with Joe?

Patient: Yes I do. This session was the best!

As we examined the patient's pattern of relatedness with the therapist, a new link to a pattern of distancing with her partner emerged. In addition, this tendency to shut down, withdraw (and withhold), and create emotional distance in her current life was related to past trauma, not only with her mother, but also with her brother. New memories of sexual abuse surfaced, helping us to understand the source of this adaptation gone awry.

Patient: Since I left you two weeks ago I have this real contained anger and hostility toward Joe since we talked about the sexuality because, all the time I say, "It's OK that we don't have sex because everything else is OK." But part of me is very deprived and I never really—I shoved it under the rug. So that come out and I—but I didn't know how to say it to him, so I noticed that I cannot cook for him—dinner—it took something out of me because I don't want to cook. I'm not interested in doing those kinds of things. "Why do I want to make your life better?"

Therapist: That's a conscious rationalization, but what we know is that that is an old way you have of dealing with your anger.

Patient: I see the pattern.

Therapist: So should we deal directly with this anger toward him regarding the deprivation around sex and physical love instead?

Patient: Actually, last night I sat down to talk to him, real calmly and talk about that. I told him. I said I feel very neglected and deprived and it is an issue. I think I recognize when it started. That process starts subtly and I didn't even recognize that. But we talked about it and I said I don't really know what to do. He says he's aware of it but didn't say much.

Therapist: No?

Patient: He is passive by nature—his whole family is. So, we'll see.

Therapist: So you are in touch with the longing for closeness, the pain and disappointment around the lack of closeness, and the anger about it. So you sat with that and thought about it and brought it up in a very calm and reasonable way—not the old way of yell and attack or shut down and withdraw. That whole cycle—no—you sat down and talked to him directly.

Patient: Yeah—it was OK. But what came up about my brother. I never dealt with that.

Therapist: We had better go to this, because this got messed up. Brothers and sisters don't become lovers, and lovers don't act like brother and sister. Then the last time it came out that you had a brother that molested you.

Patient: I never deal with it. But one day, after the session, I was thinking about it. I was thinking—what was it like? Do I feel it in my body? I was so young (age 5 or 6). How my body feels? Then I realized, when I was a little older, like 10 or 12 years old, I was scared that I would get pregnant. Even though it happened years ago, but suddenly I realized that sex was sex and you could get pregnant and I realized something was wrong with me.

Therapist: Wrong with you—or something wrong with your brother?

Patient: With me, that I had sex. This was when I was 10 to 12. I remembered I was holding my stomach in for years—afraid I was pregnant. I was holding my stomach all those years. For years and years I was afraid, if I didn't hold in my stomach, it would get bigger and bigger.

Therapist: And everyone would know.

Patient: Then they would realize I had sex.

Therapist: With your brother.

Patient: Yeah, that came out after that session two weeks ago. I don't remember the physical part. I just remembered the sex and intimidation when I was growing up.

Therapist: So this is extremely important.

Patient: Yes.

Therapist: That it came up first of all as we were looking at what was getting in the way of you having close contact with me. When you make a choice to tolerate the anxiety and stay with it, what came up was that closeness was experienced as dangerous because either you would be attacked, like by your mother, or your brother, in a sexual way. So you were avoiding all that by not getting close to anybody, and you have paid a huge price. So, what happened with your brother? How old were you when he approached you sexually?

Patient: He was about 10 years older than me. I was about 5 so he was 15 or 16, something like that. He's 16 or 17 maybe. He is rambunctious, the black sheep, the one . . .

Therapist: He is the one they tried to kill? (When she was a young teen, she heard her parents plotting her brother's murder. He had brought shame on the family with his misbehavior, her mother decided to kill him. When he came home, the father grabbed her brother, tied him in a chair, and started to beat him. The patient intervened, screaming and physically coming between her parents and her brother. The murder was averted.)

Patient: Yeah. The troublemaker. He said, "Would you let me put it in?"

Therapist: So, literally, to penetrate you? Because you said "molest."

Patient: Oh no, he said, "Will you let me put it in?" and I said, "No"—I don't know what I said, but he said, "I will give you five dollars," and I thought it was interesting. I think I was so loving, that I thought if he want it, I give it. I think that played a role in my relationships later on. If a man wanted to have sex, I would just give it to him, even if I had no feelings for him.

Therapist: And you wouldn't let yourself feel what you felt about it—what you wanted.

Patient: That only happened once, that I remember I was very aware of it. Nobody knows in my household, and I would pretend it never happened, and I actually could cover it up, and love him. That incident happened afterwards.

Therapist: What incident?

Patient: That he got beat up by my parents.

Therapist: Right. Well you have to have very mixed feelings about that and toward him.

Patient: At the time, I don't have rage—I didn't know anything—until later. But now I realize that he took advantage of me and I basically, it's a form of rape.

Therapist: What's the impact it's had on you? You tortured yourself for years with the idea you would get pregnant and, even to this day, won't allow yourself to have a good sexual relationship. This is punishment—you blame yourself, rather than face all the feelings you have toward him. Do you see this?

Patient: My stomach hurts. God it's so—I never know it's there. I put it so far away down—put it away. Nobody know. I thought, if you just don't look at it, it would not be there. I actually thought it was not there, it was past. I'm very surprised.

Therapist: And as long as you've had to keep those feelings down, you've had to keep a distance, an emotional distance from others—you couldn't get close to your partner, or here with me, so it's having the closeness that brings up all these unresolved feelings from the past and it gives us an opportunity to heal that now, so you don't have to continue to deprive yourself and attach with depriving people.

Patient: Oh, how can we act up in life? We love each other, we love and provide, but meanwhile, but this thing in front of you, you don't look at. How amazing.

Therapist: In this part of your life sexually, and in relationship to men, you get frozen.

Patient: But I forgive him at the same time.

Therapist: Too fast you forgive him, before you have faced all your feelings toward him, right? That might be fine in the end, but you use it now to jump over all your feelings of rage, and also to have him be accountable.

In the following sequence we used the "little girl," who had been appearing to her in dreams, as a metaphor for the feelings that were deeply buried at the time of this highly traumatic incident. When she denied and dismissed her feelings about what happened she was, in essence, abandoning herself in the process. Instead, I encouraged the adult patient to face these feelings, and invited her to share them with me, so that they could become integrated instead of repressed and denied.

Patient: I have to go so far back to that little girl.

Therapist: Yeah—who you keep abandoning. See?

Patient: That I keep abandoning, right. That I abandon (crying).

Therapist: OK. So if you reconnect with that little girl.

Patient: Before the forgiveness comes. Before the love and all that bullshit. Goes right to when I was 5 to 6 years old. How do I feel? I got a secret. I got a secret . . . (Crying.)

Therapist: Yes. Just let yourself have that pain. Because if you love her, you will be heartbroken that this happened. Can you let yourself feel that? What do you want to do for that little girl?

Patient: What I want to do is go to school—go to her and hug her and hug her so much. She would come into me and we would become one— that is what I want. (Patient is crying, bending over in her chair, with her arms wrapped around herself in an enormous hug.)

Therapist: So what does she feel in that embrace?

Patient: She would just let me—she is so quiet. She would, so willingly, walk into my arms and we would be together again. Oh, I can't believe it! (Sobbing.)

Therapist: So that feels good, huh?

Patient: My whole body is so numb, except here. My feet are numb and cold. Toes are very cold (now sitting up straight).

Therapist: What do you think about that?

Patient: I think—I hope—I think—I hope—I think—I hope it's defrosting.

Therapist: So if you completely defrosted?

Patient: My body must get warm. It's got to get warm and the fluids so I can do what I have to do, because so far, I've been saying I'm frozen.

Therapist: But haven't you had enough of this? How many years and decades? Never letting yourself have sex within a loving relationship that will be ongoing. You kind of chopped yourself into pieces—giving a piece of yourself here and there but . . .

As the patient approached the intensely mixed feelings toward her brother, the need to defend against them by shutting down lifted. These defenses had created a resistance against closeness—the problem with her heart that brought her to treatment—as well as making her a stranger to her deepest self. In addition, reliance on these defenses, including denial and rationalization, had also distorted reality, viewing sexual abuse as a manifestation of love. Her vision cleared both literally and symbolically, as she faced the fact she had been raped. Furthermore, making this distinction between love and abuse led to a clear distinction between her partner and her brother. Her desire to love and be loved was unleashed and deeply felt.

Patient: Oh, wow—I just had a vision that I would make love with Joe and so lovingly—like never before. That's interesting.

Therapist: Open hearted and tender. How do you imagine that?

Patient: It just come to me. When I was waiting for my body to defrost and I hear you say, "How long you are going to hold onto this?" That's right, how long I'm going to hold on to this?

Therapist: So what was the vision?

Patient: I see very loving image of Joe. It is so dear, so loving, but scary.

Therapist: Is he a safe person?

Patient: He is safe.

Therapist: You don't have to keep up your guard? Just let yourself feel that. It's so sad—how your heart has been locked up. Now you feel safe enough—that you are there with you.

Patient: You know what, Patricia? I'm hot right now. My whole body is hot. It comes up from here and my hands are hot. My legs are hot. And I can see!

Therapist: Coming alive again. You are a red blooded, hot woman. You can let yourself feel that?

Patient: Wow. And it doesn't take time! Like my belief is it has to take time, you know? And you say, "How long are you going to take?" and then the heat just come right up—overtaking. OK, that's it. Defrosted.

Therapist: So what does that feel like, to feel that heat?

Patient: The hot and cold in there, but the hot is going to wash out the frozen, so my body and blood can circulate again. So I will just let it be. I see you so clear, physically. Because all the time I am here, I see you, but not so clear. My vision was vague, but now it's clear.

Therapist: Now you can be fully embodied and present and be able to see.

Patient: Oh, God, this is amazing, like watching a play from beginning to end.

The patient was able to see that she had been repeating a dysfunctional pattern of distancing throughout her life, instead of remembering past trauma and experiencing all of her feelings about destructive family relationships. Prior to this, letting anyone close to her was viewed as dangerous. In this case, she opened up to the therapist and had a deeply corrective experience that was spontaneously generalized to other "safe" people in her life.

Generalization of Change

Patient: It was interesting, last Sunday, a week ago. I was taking a shower and I all of the sudden I thought, "Joe and I should get married." It come to me and I said, "That is interesting. I am thinking about it."

Therapist: Am I getting it right—you weren't actually consciously thinking about it, but it just came up spontaneously?

Patient: It was a feeling, a feeling—a wonderful, warm feeling that just come up and then I said, "It's silly we're not married."

Therapist: Yes it came up and you can feel it? You say it was a wonderful feeling.

Patient: It was a really warm, wonderful feeling. I was very aware of that. And the next day I told my girlfriend and then on Sunday night I told Joe. He was lying there reading and I went there but when I went to tell him I felt scared. I felt fear—this emotion come up. It's almost like, it's very scary and reluctant and yet, it feel very good. So it is very interesting this come up.

Therapist: What did he say?

Therapist: He jumped on it. He's ready. He jump right on it, but I feel that I hold back after I stepped forward. I got scared.

It was clear that the patient was in a state of intense conflict. The strong desire for sexual and emotional closeness that had been activated during the previous session was still triggering anxiety, along with an impulse to flee and avoid commitment to her partner. This very same conflict was being played out in the transference. In order to facilitate an intimate connection, remaining barriers to closeness between us had to be removed. The patient was speaking in a rapid fashion, with little room for interaction or dialog. She would ask, and then answer, her own questions. In a very real sense she was keeping me out with a wall of words.

Removing Remaining Defenses Against Closeness

Therapist: It's almost as if you are playing both roles here. Are you willing to let me do my job and help you with this?

Patient: Yes, of course. I am running my mouth!

Therapist: If you stay, right here, right now. You are doing the same thing here with me that you describe with your partner, keeping a certain distance with me behind a glass wall.

Patient: Right. It's a moss—like a dew, or the morning mist that keep things from being sharp—keeps things elusive. However, it is there.

Therapist: Do you want to keep it there or do you want to remove it?

Patient: Of course I want to remove it. You point out that is very important—I have never seen that before. Like this dew in the morning but it's over everything (laughs).

Therapist: So what happens in this moment?

Patient: It feels good inside—that's why I laugh. I hate to use your word, but you use the word joy.

Therapist: You can feel that come up inside you—that joy in connection—being unguarded?

Patient: That it is possible, it will disappear, lift, dissipate, just disappear. What even is it? I don't even know.

Therapist: But if you don't start to immediately go to your thinking about it.

Patient: The brain wants to know what it is so I can remove it, but . . .

Therapist: But the heart knows what the mind knows nothing of.

Patient: The heart knows. All together—I feel the lightness, the joy, the possibility—that the film can be lifted and it doesn't take much hard work to do—and at the same time, I also feel scared in my body, right about there.

Therapist: OK, why don't you practice choosing then?

Patient: OK. I practice choosing with you. There is no reason that I would choose otherwise.

Therapist: Let's just see if you can let yourself have the experience and just watch and pay attention as you choose to be present and connected. If you can trust yourself enough not to shut down but to be present and connected.

Patient: I am a little nervous. I am very comfortable with you. I am surprised there is still a layer that is so stubborn.

Therapist: Let's stay with this so you can be free to make the choice and not just automatically withdraw or distance.

Patient: Just to be quiet—not to say anything and run my mouth.

We just sat quietly, softly gazing at one another in relaxed silence for several minutes. Tears ran down her face and started to fill my eyes. At the end of the hour she just said, "Wow—that was really amazing." In the next session the patient revealed what this intimate connection had meant to her, as well as the changes that it inspired.

Next Session

Therapist: How are you?

Patient: Good. I was looking forward to seeing you and being together, without planning what I'm going to say or having any agenda. A good sign—a very good sign.

Therapist: When you say I feel good, what does it feel like inside?

Patient: Free of stress—relaxed. I'm surprised—it's rare.

Therapist: Last time we were looking at how you can use the talking and being busy as a way to detach, and interrupting that and letting yourself just be present and connected. Because all that talking and "working on things" was interfering with a certain kind of intimacy with yourself and others if you can't just be quiet. So something has really shifted.

Patient: That was very interesting and I was very aware of that when it happened. I told Joe and another friend about that and I says, when Patricia tells me to shut up, basically, I actually stayed there and I didn't say anything and she didn't say anything either and we sat there looking at each other. I was actually thinking about that and I realized, which I never realized before, that there is love between us—for sure, I can speak for myself. I thought it was a professional relationship and I thought love did not enter the picture, ever, but when we were doing that quiet thing, the feeling came up and then I thought, how could it not be—you open up to someone so completely and feel that deep emotion, but it was never addressed. Isn't that wonderful!

Therapist: Very.

Patient: I really feel the power of not saying anything.

Therapist: Right. That's what allows you to be present to that feeling of love and being loved. Feeling that connection.

Patient: So that was really powerful and actually, we had dinner with another couple the other night. We talk about love and the two guys get really uncomfortable. At first Joe is defending himself and I say he is getting to his mouth, trying to analyze and explain it. Bill was getting all worked up, so they had to jump up and take the tray into the kitchen. We started to laugh. It was so obvious and so funny. They are so uncomfortable. So I said, "OK, let's not say anything. Let's hold hands." So we all four of us hold hands and look in each other's eyes, because I learned it here, and it was fresh. Everyone held hands and didn't say anything and that was just wonderful!

The patient's newfound ability to drop her defenses against closeness and allow herself the experience of loving and being loved, first in the therapeutic relationship, and then with friends and her partner, affected her profoundly. This was also a deeply moving experience for me as the therapist. Without question, when patients like this really let us in, there is love between us. Having that loving connection was deeply healing. Then she was able to take her healing presence into the world and connect with others in a new way. Just as abuse affects all who are involved, so too are the effects of profound emotional healing felt by all who experience it. The effects ripple out into the world in either case.

Impulse-Ridden Woman—Creating Intimacy With Self and Other

Unlike the previous patient, who was excessively self-reliant, this patient (previously mentioned on pages 132–138) viewed herself as utterly incapable of functioning without continual support from others. She habitually relied on external means of soothing her own anxiety, regulating her emotions, and maintaining her own shaky sense of self. In the past, she used drugs and alcohol, as well as the validation of others, to achieve these ends. Even though she'd been sober for 20 years, her dependence on others to regulate her own inner state continued, and even intensified over time. Since she was not able to tolerate being on her own, being with others was not a choice. Reaching outside of herself for connection was felt as a need, an obsession, and a compulsion. There was no choice or judgment involved—nearly anyone would do. She would not be able to have a healthy relationship with anyone else until she could develop one with herself.

While focusing excessively on others, the patient tended to ignore her own inner feelings and desires. Consequently, feelings would build without awareness until she blew up and exploded. This pattern was highly destructive and had resulted in her getting fired from jobs, as well as relationships. In order to reverse this pattern, we agreed to focus on and track her feelings, so that she could experience, tolerate, and integrate them into a manageable and understandable process.

In what became the pivotal third session, she acknowledged feeling angry toward me for being away and delaying this session by three weeks. At the same time, she resisted pursuing these feelings, as we had in the first two sessions. She was adamant that she did not want to go through another portrait of rage toward me, despite the fact that this had been very helpful to her in the past two sessions. At first I regarded this as mere resistance. It took some time to sort out just what was transpiring between us. Finally I began to realize that the patient was trying to express something new and emergent, though she was struggling to do so in a clear and coherent fashion.

Therapist: So how do you experience this anger toward me?
Patient: Oh God. It's in me and wants to come out. I don't know what to do with it and how to stop it (crying).

Therapist: It's just a feeling, so if you don't fill yourself with anxiety but feel it and face it, there is also pain underneath.

Patient: (Big sigh.) It seems like a vicious cycle. You push me to get this out and there is this. I don't know how this helps me.

Therapist: Let's see if it does. That's the question. It looks like whenever someone tries to get close in a deep and intimate way—to see what is inside you—this rage comes up.

Patient: I feel like you incite that. It doesn't feel like you are trying to get to know me or be intimate or honest.

Therapist: I have no interest in inciting or pushing you. It's up to you if you want to face these feelings inside.

Patient: It feels very real, but doesn't feel appropriate to the situation. I don't like this. I can see how it progresses. I feel this—I feel this pain but it feels like work.

Therapist: Of course it is work.

Patient: It doesn't feel like a relationship, but what I'm supposed to do. It feels manufactured. Not that the feelings aren't there, but I don't know how killing you will help. How is that an intimate relationship?

Therapist: These feelings are a reaction to your needs and desires for closeness being frustrated. When someone you want to connect with doesn't respond in the way you want them to, it triggers this rage—whether it's me or your boyfriend.

Patient: Or my sister or my boss . . . When I don't get connection in the way I want, I say what I want isn't right and that I want too much.

Understanding the Resistance

This was all very new and rather contradictory material. She had found the two previous sessions extremely helpful and our alliance was very strong. Clearly something else was happening here. After trying to fit the interaction into my preconceived notion of increased resistance against increasingly strong feelings toward me, I went in a different direction. I wondered if a continued focus on her *reactive* feelings of anger and pain was no longer what she needed. Instead, I wondered if she was trying to connect with, and give voice to, her innate needs and desires. In other words, instead of just focusing on the pain and anger regarding thwarted needs, perhaps we needed to focus on helping her speak up and get her needs met in the first place. This shift proved pivotal and turned the whole treatment around.

Therapist: Turning on yourself instead. "I shouldn't be angry. There is something wrong with me." But I wonder if what you are saying is that just dealing with the anger and pain about not getting your needs met isn't enough. You want to connect with those needs and desires so you can get them met directly, instead of staying deprived. Let's look at that. What do you need and want to feel connected here?

Patient: That's a big problem. I don't know what I want. No one ever asked me that! Wow—this is big. No one has ever asked me that.

Therapist: OK. Would you like to know?

Patient: Now I can feel it—that is what I want to get to—that is what I want to get to here. I don't know that the rage toward you gets me to this, though clearly it has.

Therapist: This is where you want to be, and where you want to come from—your own desires. Let's stay with that and get acquainted with you.

Patient: It's good! (Hands on her solar plexus and belly. Laughs.) It feels good! I know I've been looking for this. Can I stay here?

Therapist: Let's see if you can stay here with me while connected to you.

Patient: (Joyful tears and laughter.) It's always there, and THAT I have felt for the first time. That this is always there and I can get there.

Therapist: No wonder you were so frantic, if you couldn't connect with something solid in yourself.

Patient: Yeah—it almost feels like being pregnant or something.

Therapist: It's as if you're giving birth to . . .

Patient: Myself!

Therapist: It's as if you really are covered up by your reactions to others.

Patient: Yes, but I am always reacting, always reacting.

Therapist: Perhaps you haven't felt safe and relaxed enough to connect with you. You have been constantly afraid and hyper vigilant.

Patient: Yeah, it feels good. I know I've been looking for this. It feels good to be here and not in all that constriction. How do I develop that? Can I stay here?

Therapist: Let's see if you can stay here with me, while connected to you. How wonderful to know you can be connected to this calm at the center of you.

Patient: Wow—this is intimacy!

The entire atmosphere in the room changed markedly as we shifted from a focus on reactive feelings of rage toward others, to her inner needs and desires.

She remained calmly connected to herself and to the therapist throughout the rest of the session, even when distressing feelings and memories arose. It was as if she could experience all her feelings and deal with painful memories without getting consumed by them. She was able to observe and experience at the same time.

The patient had been hospitalized a couple of times in her early 20s, for both substance abuse and suicidal impulses. Given this symptom profile, her previous therapist had assumed she had been sexually abused by her father. This all happened in the 1980s. So, while she had no memory of sexual abuse by her father, she was haunted by the notion she had somehow repressed it. In this session, new memories of her father's drinking buddy sitting on her and putting his hand over her mouth to "shut her up" came to consciousness. Now that she could remember what happened and deal with her true feelings about it, the need to continue to repeat it was eliminated. Remembering and reprocessing toward a new and healthy end was facilitated instead.

Last Session

The patient entered the session with a big smile on her face, reporting that she had continued to feel calm, clear, present, and alive since our last session. She then went on to reveal that she was nervous about telling me that she had decided to stop treatment. This decision was based both on financial and personal concerns. The expense involved in treatment had been considerable (she paid out of pocket), and she wanted to get her financial house in order (something completely new and quite healthy). She had achieved more than she ever dared hope in our nine hours together. We begin by examining her newfound sense of self.

Therapist: That's a nice, big smile.

Patient: I know. It feels good! It does. I was thinking about that. I feel this sense of joy and excitement. Fear—I still feel some fear and my back went squish when I was leaving the hotel. It was like, "It's OK." What's cool is that I can recognize I feel both.

Therapist: And are they even connected?

Patient: Honestly, I think it's the first time I have really—I can say I know it up here, but to really feel it in my body and to recognize, "It's fear. It's joy. I can do both." It's walking through that fear and not letting the fear drive me, but this instead.

Therapist: The desire, the joy, what is in you—instead of just reacting. Wow—so, have you stayed, somehow, connected to this since last time?

Patient: What I notice is when I'm not connected, and I'm full of fear and starting to get driven by that panic. I can say, "Take some time to get back to that." I know now, at the center of my being that I am whole and good at my core. And THAT, that is where I go to. I don't have to go to my boyfriend, or my job or any of that. I can go right here. It feels good! I was like, I was getting afraid of coming here and then I thought, "No, go to that spot—go to that spot. It's OK to be afraid."

Therapist: But it's not going to rule.

Patient: Let this rule. The closer I got to here, the bigger this got. That was so new!

Therapist: Wow! That's so nice and it's palpable. You are just shining.

Patient: The thing that I am both excited and a bit nervous about telling you is that I've decided to stop therapy—at least for now. I am really determined to get my financial house in order. As you know, I have always had a problem with spending. If I had a dollar, I would spend a dollar-fifty. I paid for this therapy out of pocket and am glad I did, but now I have a budget and am going to get out of debt. I feel really good about it. In the past, when that fear ruled, I wouldn't have even come back. Financially, I can't do this right now and I knew I had to tell you. What I would do in the past is just send an email and not come back.

Therapist: So it takes a lot of courage. You said, "I'm not going to do that."

Patient: I can get full of fear but then say, "No, because of what I do and especially in a relationship that is with a doctor. OK—she said we are partners." The closer I got the bigger this got. I didn't even have to concentrate on it.

The patient has made an enormous shift, from excessive reliance on external validation and support, to an inner focus on her own capacity to monitor and respond to her own needs and feelings. From this new sense of self, she was testing out her ability to be autonomous and self-expressed within the confines of a close relationship. In a very real way, the patient was testing out whether the therapist really meant it about being equal partners. Would I honor her autonomy and choice to end treatment at this time or have my own agenda?

Decision to End Treatment

Patient: So, I have decided to end for now. I have gotten a financial plan in order for the first time in my life. I am trimming expenses and getting out of debt. I will also be moving to a less expensive apartment. In my life, if I had a dollar, I would spend a dollar-ten. Now I am doing it differently and it feels good.

Therapist: That's great. First of all, you've already gotten so much benefit.

Patient: More than I ever imagined. And the last time, like I said, the knee jerk is the fear, but this kind of felt like the knee jerk. Like you said, that's a big smile.

Therapist: This is your true nature.

Patient: I love that—oh my God! (Spontaneously embraces herself.)

Therapist: And all the rest was reaction.

Patient: All of it. All of it. Being served up. When I got to be an adult and didn't have the parents, I served myself up, you know. Now that is a question I ask myself everyday. "Is this what I want or am I serving myself up?"

Therapist: What enabled you to make these changes?

Patient: I knew that AA and 12 Step couldn't do what we've done here. I've been in and out of therapy during 12 Step and that modality wasn't doing it either, you know. I saw a transformation in my sister, who hasn't gone to 12 Step. I saw it in her.

Therapist: And you wanted some of that.

Patient: Yeah, and when I first started, Dr. Coughlin, I was so afraid that I was so broken down, I thought I'd have to go to the hospital. I thought, "How could I do this and work?" Then it was like, "How could I not do this and work?" Then it was like, "OK, it started breaking down the stuff and breaking through the stuff." I did not expect to come in here beaming today. OK, I could have come in and cried and all that, but that's really not how I'm feeling.

It was surprising to learn that the patient was so overwrought when she first came to see me that she thought she would need to be hospitalized. This highlights the importance of prioritizing response to intervention over history and diagnosis in our assessment. If we focus exclusively on the patient's symptoms and disturbance, and focus too much on her past history (several hospitalizations, numerous failed treatments, a long history of impulsive acting out), we can get an overly pathological and pessimistic view of the patient's prognosis. However, by assessing the patient's current ability to make use of therapeutic intervention, we can engage with her at her highest level of capacity and in so doing, facilitate growth.

How is it that this woman, who had not responded to most treatment efforts for over 30 years, could heal in only nine hours of therapy? I would suggest that this result was obtained by a highly engaged therapist who employed very specific techniques to address particular problems, while also challenging and encouraging the patient to tolerate anxiety for growth, and take an active role in her own treatment. Of note, the patient was able to visit her mother, whom she had not seen for two years.

Generalization of Therapeutic Effects—Changes in Relationships

Patient: When I first started coming and uncovering all the family stuff, and even before, I had so much anger toward my Mom. It was really hard.

Therapist: You said you couldn't even see her.

Patient: Yeah, and she has Alzheimer's too, so it's really hard. My uncle died a couple weeks ago, and I took her, right after my last session here, to the calling hours. She got to see my aunt and cousins. She got to see her grandkids and some mutual friends. We are still talking about going to the calling hours. I went to see her again on Monday. We started talking about friends and the guy who I really think abused me. I said, "I hated him Mom and I still do." She said, "I know." She didn't try to change how I felt. She acknowledged it. We didn't need to say anymore. Now that—I get tingly. It was good.

Therapist: That was an authentic connection.

Patient: Very. And my sister said how her relationship has changed with Mom—I thought maybe I could get there at some point, but I sure didn't think it would be this quick! It was really good and I am glad we shared that. That time we had Monday night was very authentic. I felt like she heard me.

Therapist: And she acknowledged on some level what happened and how you felt about it.

Patient: No tears or any of that. And she said it like, "I know." It really was mine to say to her. It wasn't hers to say to me. It was for me to say. I needed to acknowledge it to me and to her. It was perfect.

Therapist: So there was something really healing about that. How did you feel toward her?

Patient: Incredibly close and loving.

Therapist: You were so angry with her you couldn't even see her in the last couple of years. How did you get here? What changed?

Patient: Clearly, I have changed. She hasn't!

Therapist: So how did that happen?

Patient: First of all seeing where that rage came from. I needed to know that. I really looked that in the eye, as I never had before (motioning arms toward me).

Therapist: And really experience it.

Patient: I felt it—was allowed to feel it! Allowed and encouraged, whereas, as kids, we were never encouraged to feel that. None of that was allowed.

Therapist: So where did it go?

Patient: Right in here (pointing inward).

Therapist: Into that path of self-destructiveness.

Patient: Wow—that was really big. That was huge.

It is of the utmost importance to ascertain specific information on the factors the patient views as therapeutic. Sometimes these are surprises, and other times they verify our own experience. In any case, in addition to examining the nature and extent of the therapeutic change obtained in the process, understanding the specific factors responsible for that change is essential for both the patient and therapist to understand. Here we see that the patient has a clear sense of what was causing her problems (internalizing her rage and pain) and what released her from it. In addition, she reveals that being encouraged to experience the rage directly toward me was a new and liberating experience. Anger had never been allowed in her family and had nowhere to go but into a self-destructive pattern of behavior—getting back at parents by hurting herself. She had adopted a highly dependent and subservient attitude toward others, while ignoring and neglecting her own needs. To become a true self in relation to others was a completely new experience. At first, her attempts at self-assertion came across as defiance. She reflected on what had transpired in the first part of the previous session.

Understanding the Process

Patient: I brought resistance in with me that day. I was like, "No, no, no," like a little kid saying, "You can't be the boss of me." I didn't want to be pushed. Then you asked, "What do you want?" That was the shift! I have asked myself that everyday since then. I finally felt myself rising up—OK—we really are in this together.

Therapist: So there was something healthy in that resistance—some attempt to be self-directed, but just resisting another isn't enough. Then there was the question, "What do you want?" It almost sounds like you had to have that experience here—test it out.

Patient: Absolutely. It was an experience I had to have. When you said, "What do you want?" That was a multilayered question. It was, "What do you want right now between you and me," but also in a broader sense. Now I ask myself, "Are you just serving yourself up or is this what you really want?"

Clearly these changes, many of which were the result of corrective emotional experiences between patient and therapist, had been internalized. The patient's relationship to herself, which had been characterized by neglect and punishment, was replaced with caring and respect. In the past she needed others like a drug, to regulate her internal states. Now that she was able to do that for herself, she could enter relationships out of fullness and desire, rather than desperate need. Additionally, having experienced deep guilt over rage toward loved ones, the unconscious need to punish herself was eliminated. She no longer needed to abuse herself, or be used and abused by others. This led to immediate changes in all of her significant relationships. After experiencing all her reactive feelings of rage, pain, and guilt, she was deeply connected to her desire to love and be loved. In the end, with her mother, what was left was love.

Experience of Intimacy and Closeness

Therapist: How does it feel to do that differently, here with me—that what is important is how you feel and what you need?

Patient: It feels wonderful, but I never would have done this, if it hadn't been for you constantly giving me the message of partnership, and that we're here together, we are doing this together, for my well-being. If you were pushing, it was for me. But I also think it's a way of not looking at the sadness. Because it is sad, but a good sad.

Therapist: Yes, there is something precious to lose—on one level you are losing, but on the other hand you always have you and what we have done together.

Patient: This is a very intimate—the most intimate experience I've ever had without having sex. And I just connected that.

Therapist: Tell me more about that, because in the last session you said, "I don't feel intimate." Then you it was, "Oh my God, this is intimate."

Patient: And seeing your face when I made that connection—and how happy you were made me feel very good (starts to cry). Like I said this is the most intimate relationship I've ever had and, what I really love is that I will be able to carry this and have this with people that are available to it.

Therapist: And you already have, starting with your mother.

Patient: And my sister and brother and boyfriend and good friends. Yeah.

Therapist: It's pretty amazing. Again, how did you get there?

Patient: It was that partnership and doing it together. I haven't experienced that a lot and certainly not in this kind of relationship—doctor and patient. And when I saw how happy you were that I was getting free—that was amazing! I saw tears of happiness in your eyes. Wow—that was something.

Transfer of Images With Positive Memories

Therapist: So tell me more—it stirs up a lot of feeling when you saw that look in my face. You allowed me the privilege of getting to know you in this way. It is a two-way street and it affects me too. It looks like something about that is moving or touching.

Patient: I was thinking about my Dad and remembering how he used to love just sitting back and listen and observe us kids as adults—and how we were interacting and laughing. That made him so happy, and I am so happy to have that memory of him. To see him light up. And that's another thing that was good to discover. Yes, there were no boundaries and emotional incest and bad things happened because my Dad couldn't protect us, but there was always this underlying fear that he violated me in some way. The violation was that he couldn't protect me and couldn't say no to his friends. Knowing that has enabled me to feel that love for him that I thought was gone.

Therapist: And to remember the love he had for you. Under it all, at the core, there is love.

Patient: If it is there for me, it has to be there for everyone else too. Thank you! I never thought I would be in this position in such a short time. I can always come back, but I never thought I would feel like this. I am sort of astounded and proud of myself. I have worked hard, but thank you. Thank you for pushing me the right way, and allowing all of it to come out.

The patient began by mentioning her reaction to a look of happiness on my face, in response to her growth. Prior to this, her only memories of her father were negative—either him being at work or with drinking buddies. She only remembered "getting an audience" with him when he called her into his medical office for a talking to. Now she had a memory of her father looking happy and proud of his children. Defenses against feelings create distortions in perception. Conversely, as her defenses broke down, and feelings broke through, new memories surfaced and perceptions expanded and sharpened. Being able to assess and tolerate mixed feelings toward loved ones results in a three-dimensional view. Her father had all kinds of problems, but could be loving too. Now she could see all the parts of him and remember the positive.

In addition to the removal of the patient's symptoms of anxiety, depression, and impulsive acting out, character change had been achieved. In other words, her old rigid, unconscious and automatic ways of responding had been profoundly altered. As a result, her sense of herself had also been profoundly transformed, from fatally flawed to whole. This newfound sense of self also resulted in dramatic changes in her ability to relate to others. She had not been able to visit her mother for two years prior to treatment, because she would get overwhelmed with rage. Having experienced and integrated all her mixed feelings toward her mother, she was able to visit her, and feel love and compassion for her. Reactivity was replaced with receptivity and responsiveness. These new ways of interacting further reinforced positive feelings about herself. Now she was experiencing an upward spiral of development, in which authentic connection to self and other were mutual and reciprocal, each potentiating the other.

The Therapist Variable

In order to create profound moments of meeting with patients, the therapist must be an emotionally engaged and available presence, capable of intimacy and closeness. Training that attends to both the therapist's skill acquisition and personal development is necessary to achieve these ends. The practice of ISTDP is quite demanding in many ways, as it involves exposing ourselves to our patient's intense feelings and often primitive unconscious material (not to mention our own!). We not only deal with a patient's feelings toward others, but encourage the patient to face, experience, and express his intense mixed feelings toward us directly. This requires a great deal of emotional stability on the therapist's part. The capacity to tolerate intimacy and closeness with another, while regulating our own emotions, is especially important here.

Supervision in ISTDP also involves the direct exposure of our work on videotape to others—a supervisor and, often, colleagues. In many ways, this is tantamount to exposing *ourselves*. It takes a great deal of courage and determination to tolerate this kind of anxiety for growth. However, trainees rarely see it this way at the start, and are often highly self-critical and self-doubting. In the last day of a recent training workshop, one of the participants, who had been struggling with excessive self-doubt, suddenly realized that he had been operating out of fear. The interventions he was using with patients were designed to *avoid* making mistakes, or offending the patient, as well as to "look good," rather than to *approach* anxiety-provoking topics out of a determination to expose and resolve the underlying source of the patient's suffering. In that very moment, I watched him grab a hold of himself, soothe his own anxiety, and move forward. He looked me right in the eye, without his usual guard in place. There was a profound and sustained "moment of meeting"—a genuine meeting of two hearts and minds. We could both feel this taking place. His ability to expose himself directly was an unmistakable experience of authentic relating. He had to change something within, in order to initiate that kind of contact with another. At the same time, the sustained contact, in which he was being met and truly seen, deepened and expanded the process of change. In order to facilitate this kind of profound meeting with patients, we must be able to tolerate the vulnerability entailed. We can't ask patients to do what we haven't done, and maintain our own integrity.

Instead, we need to help both trainees and patients shift from anxiety and avoidance of feared "mistakes," to activation of healthy desires for growth. Then, and only then, can the learning process support personal development. If we are going to *be* the change we hope to create, we must start with ourselves. Sadly, the personal development of the therapist is often neglected in the training process.

Summary

"It is an absolute certainty that no one can know his own beauty or perceive a sense of his own worth until it has been reflected back to him in the mirror of another loving, caring human being."

—John Joseph Powell

Many of our patients, certainly those like "The Broken Bird" and "The Impulse-Ridden Woman," had extremely damaged parents who were not able to see or reflect their children's inherent worth. The lack of such mirroring, along with abusive and neglectful treatment, created intense feelings of pain, rage, and guilt that overwhelmed the child. As a result, defenses against these feelings created symptomatic disturbances, lack of self-worth, and highly dysfunctional relationship patterns. A treatment that involved high levels of emotional closeness and attunement and deep levels of emotional experiencing, within the patient's optimal level of anxiety tolerance, was required to facilitate healthy growth.

This experience resulted in a solid, integrated sense of self, as well as the ability to hold onto herself in close relationship to others. In order to achieve such ends, the therapist must be highly skilled and emotionally present and available. Ongoing professional training and supervision, as well as personal growth and development, are required for therapists to enhance clinical effectiveness. The best therapists are lifelong learners who consider this process one that never ends.

Chapter Eight
Working Through Toward Integration, Consolidation, and Coherence

How do we help patients create deep and enduring change in their ongoing sense of self, other, and the world? In order to help patients thrive, creating lives of fulfillment, purpose, and connection, we must go beyond mere symptom relief, and learn the steps reliably associated with transformational change (Abbass, 2015; Ecker, Ticic, & Hulley, 2012; Frederickson, 2013). The cathartic release of emotion may provide temporary relief, but is rarely associated with long-term change. Instead, enduring change often requires a process of working through that involves consolidation of the emotional insights achieved in the process of uncovering. Working through has traditionally been referred to as a time consuming and highly repetitive task (Freud, 1914/1962; Roth, 2000; Wachtel, 1993), taking as long as 8–10 years! Need this be so? Evidence suggests that transformational change, in which deeply ingrained patterns of reactivity and behavior are changed permanently and often rapidly, is possible and even probable, when we understand what is required to produce it (Ecker, 2015; Ecker, Ticic, & Hulley, 2012).

Exactly what needs to change varies from patient to patient. However, Malan (1979) has suggested a rather ambitious goal for all, that each of the patient's symptoms, problems, and pathological defenses be replaced by something healthy. Again, the best clinicians are not content with mere alleviation of symptoms, but attempt to promote the revival of health and vitality, such that each patient is operating at his highest level of capacity (Gawande, 2004; Wampold, 2015). We seek to replace despair with hope, depression with aliveness, anxiety with peace and calm, isolation with engagement, and stagnation with growth. Restoration of the patient's authentic sense of self, along with the freedom to love and connect to others, is the ultimate goal of our work. A process of emotional activation and cognitive understanding and integration seems to be the key to achieving such ends. In the end, one of my patients said it best: "I came here wishing I were dead and wanting to change—to be different—to be anyone but me. Somehow, through this process I have come to love being me. In the end, that's been the biggest surprise and the greatest gift of all—just to be who I really am."

In almost all cases, our patients' suffering is the result of unregulated anxiety and/or excessive reliance on defenses against painful and threatening feelings and emotions. Given this, the effective therapist must become adept at developing and maintaining an emotional focus, while keeping anxiety in the optimal range, and helping the patient abandon defenses that block access to emotional activation. When previously avoided feelings are deeply and viscerally experienced, the unconscious origins of the patient's conflicts come unmistakably into view. Once the previously unconscious, implicit emotional conflicts from the past are activated and in conscious awareness, patient and therapist are in a position to reevaluate them from an adult perspective. The corrective emotional experience inherent in this process is of crucial importance. In other words, this is not simply a means of gaining intellectual insight, but of facing the emotional truths that emerge spontaneously as a consequence of the process of de-repression. Suddenly, confusing problems and symptoms make sense. This sudden clarity and coherence will be demonstrated in each of the cases included in this chapter.

History of the Concept

In the early days of psychoanalysis, Freud thought that overcoming the resistance to remembering, and facilitating the cathartic experience of previously repressed feelings, would be sufficient to facilitate the process of change. However, over time he noticed "the return of the repressed" (Freud, 1915/1933), and came to the conclusion that something else was required for permanent change to take place. He suggested that the patient needed to remember (develop insight), experience warded off feelings, and then work through (change behavior) his previously unconscious conflicts regarding his feelings and wishes. He considered this an "arduous task," but one that created the greatest and most lasting change. He came to recognize that resistance was not simply a matter of obstinance on the patient's part but was, in fact, a manifestation of the core conflict he had come to therapy to address. Since the patient was essentially repeating his conflicts in the transference, rather than remember them as coming from the unresolved past, Freud (1914/1962) urged us to make use of the feelings toward the therapist as the major vehicle for working through toward change. He described this as a repetitive process in which defense and resistance were broken down, with feelings and memories breaking through, allowing for links between the transference, the patient's present and past, to be made. However, little clear or specific guidance for conducting this vital process were provided by Freud.

Memory Reconsolidation

Freud's idea that much of our patient's suffering has its origin in implicit, unconscious emotional conflicts from the past, has gained a good deal of scientific support over the years (Ecker, Ticic, & Hulley, 2012; Fisher & Greenberg, 1977). That these previously unconscious conflicts can be brought to conscious awareness via the application of therapeutic interventions has also been substantiated. Recent research on memory reconsolidation (Ecker, 2015; Ecker, Ticic, & Hulley, 2012) has demonstrated that the brain is actually designed to delete and update old, outdated emotional files. This process includes (1) symptom identification, including what happens and when it happens; (2) retrieval into awareness of the implicit emotional learnings (meanings, models, expectations) underlying the symptom viscerally experienced; and (3) disconfirmation of old expectations while feelings and memories are in an activated state. While this research has important implications for clinical work, the major proponents of an approach based on this research (referred to as Coherence Therapy) outline a general process, "without referring to any specific techniques for bringing about therapeutic results" (Ecker, Ticic, & Hulley, 2012, p. 27). While our profession is moving toward agreement about *what* is required to promote healing, a lack of specificity and technical precision about *how* to facilitate such a process leaves therapists in the lurch. This is one of the primary problems reported by experienced therapists (Orlinsky & Ronnestad, 2005), and contributes to poor clinical outcomes and a lack of mastery experienced by most therapists. Filling in these gaps is a primary goal of the present volume.

Emotional Activation

As demonstrated in the preceding chapters, the visceral experience of anxiety-provoking feelings and impulses has proven to be a reliable method of activating the unconscious memory system, bringing past traumas and conflicts into the present, where they can be experienced, shared, and resolved. Research on state dependent memory helps us make sense of this phenomenon (Eich, 1995; Weingartner, Miller, & Murphy, 1977). When we are in an emotionally activated state, the memories associated with that emotion are reliably triggered. Then, during this window of opportunity, previously unconscious feelings and memories are in a labile state where they can be revised and integrated into a cohesive narrative. Learning how to trigger, track, and transform emotional conflicts, in order to facilitate this process, should greatly improve therapeutic effectiveness.

Research suggests that improved mood alone is not a good predictor of long-term results. Instead, the memories, dreams, and associations de-repressed following a breakthrough of previously avoided feelings must be processed and integrated into a coherent whole to ensure long-term results. Pennebaker's

(1997) research found that those who did the best in the end often felt quite emotionally distressed during the process of uncovering. However, only those patients willing to go through the emotional upheaval involved in the process achieved a new and integrated perspective on their lives and, in so doing, lasting results (Pennebaker, 1997).

The Phenomenon of De-Repression

In this chapter we are focusing on the process of understanding and integrating the material that is de-repressed following emotional activation, so that it can be consolidated and integrated into a new and expanded sense of self and life's possibilities. Use of the two triangles (Malan, 1979) is extremely helpful here. We endeavor to help our patients become aware of their inner conflicts (triangle of conflict) in such a way that helps them discover their source in the past, along with insight into how they have been repeating these conflicts in their current life, including with the therapist (triangle of person). This linking of the two triangles is a repetitive and circular process, in which experience, reflection, and meaning making are intertwined. That said, it need not take a protracted period of time, but can take place within one or more sessions.

Once the patient experiences a breakdown in defenses, with a breakthrough of previously avoided feelings, the insights regarding both the source of his conflict, and the unconscious ways he has been repeating it, are often made by the patient in a spontaneous fashion. It is as if the veil has lifted and they see these connections clearly. Patients say things like, "This makes all the difference," "All the Lego blocks are in order," "The puzzle pieces have come together," or "It's like a play with a beginning, a middle, and an end," speaking of the coherence and clarity obtained during this phase of treatment. Once these connections between past and present are made, clear distinctions between them typically follow. This type of linking and differentiation is a hallmark of the process of integration, reflecting optimal brain functioning (Siegel, 2009b). Such integration enables the patient to experience himself, and others, in a new and more adaptive manner.

This type of working through, with its attendant clarity and sense of a new beginning, is essential for deep and transformational change to endure. Follow-up studies of ISTDP suggest that those who obtain positive results by the end of treatment not only maintain therapeutic gains over time, but continue to get better and better over time, with no additional therapy (Abbass, 2003; Shedler, 2010). This finding suggests that development, which has been hampered by the excessive use of defensive and avoidant strategies, takes off and continues once they are removed. In contrast, when relief or management of symptoms is the focus of intervention, follow-up studies reveal high relapse rates (Klerman, Dimascio, Weissman, Prusoff, & Paykel, 1974; Steinart, Hofmann, Kruse, & Lechsenring, 2014). This high relapse rate suggests that we have either been ineffective in getting to the underlying cause of the patient's suffering, or in consolidating the process of change.

The Importance of Emotional Insight and the Corrective Emotional Experience

As Wachtel has reminded us, "In psychotherapy, as in life, it is usually follow through that makes all the difference" (1993, p. 235). Like Freud, he described the resolution of patients' problems and conflicts as laborious and time consuming, suggesting that, "the blinding insight that changes a person's life is far more common in the movies than the consulting room" (1993, p. 235). For rapid and enduring change to occur, both emotional experience and conscious reflection upon that experience seem to be necessary. Further, this "emotional insight" must be put into action, such that new ways of relating to self and other can be attempted and reinforced. Something powerful needs to happen to counteract the symptom generating conflict. It must be resolved and changed at the root, so it no longer gets activated. When this is accomplished, the need to "manage" symptoms is no longer necessary. The patient has healed and transformed the conflicts responsible for the symptom and is no longer troubled by it. A few deep and profound corrective emotional experiences (sometimes only one!) can, when deeply processed, yield transformational change.

Research findings (Castonguay & Hill, 2012; Diener, Hilsenroth, & Weinberger, 2007; Malan, 1963, 1979) attest to the impact of "emotional insight," gained when previously avoided conflicting emotional states are activated and consciously integrated. Such insights seem to be particular meaningful when obtained via the direct interaction between patient and therapist (Barber, Muran, McCarthy, & Keefe, 2013). This is the essence of the "corrective emotional experience" (Alexander & French, 1946), defined as "re-experiencing the old, unsettled conflict with a new ending" (p. 338). Ecker, Ticic, and Hulley (2012) found that being exposed to an experience that was *contradictory* to one's old, habitual expectation was essential in producing deep, transformational change. While activating the old emotional conflict in the here and now was found to be essential, it was not sufficient to produce change. Something new and contradictory must take place, so that "what went wrong has a chance to go right, again and again" (Malan, personal communication). Then, the "exploration of the *experience* of transformation activates a nonlinear, nonfinite transformational spiral" (Fosha, Siegel, & Solomon, 2009, p. 173) that solidifies the process of change. Feelings of freedom, strength, and pride in having faced and overcome anxiety and avoidance tend to deepen and expand as explored.

Such experiences tended to enhance the patient's sense of agency and mastery, vital to the consolidation of change (Lillengren, 2014). This finding emphasizes the need for therapists to become effective at encouraging patients to become actively involved in the therapeutic process, and to take risks to achieve desired goals. Therapists who are either too passive, or too dominant and aggressive, tend to produce poor outcomes (Lillengren, 2014; Wampold, 2015). In contrast, those who are curious and empathic, but also challenging and ambitious, get far better results.

Need for Competence

In addition to our innate needs/drives for autonomy and attachment, Ryan and Deci (2000; Deci & Ryan, 2012) have suggested a third primary psychological need—competence. This involves our fundamental capacity for interest, curiosity, and exploration—exercising our capacities for the sheer joy of it (rather than an extrinsic reward). Whether we view ourselves as competent and masterful, or ineffective and helpless, has a profound impact on our sense of self (and even our physical health). Those who are connected to their innate interest and curiosity achieve more, are more creative and confident, and have higher rates of physical and emotional well-being than their externally focused counterparts (Ryan & Deci, 2000). Yet many of our patients have lost contact with this innate drive. In order to facilitate active engagement in the therapeutic process and enhance enduring change, we must find ways to activate this dormant drive.

Clinical Implications

What does all this research have to do with working through and the process of change in psychotherapy? A great deal, it seems to me. We must make sure that we provide encouragement for our patients to take risks, with no guarantee of external reward; to learn from mistakes and failures; and to value the opportunity to grow, even through struggle. Since neither the patient nor the therapist can guarantee outcome, a focus on making an effort and facilitating a process of learning and growth, no matter what the outcome, seems well placed. Such a focus is consistent with the development of a growth mindset, associated with creativity, flexibility, and enhanced well-being and confidence (Dweck, 2007).

When therapeutic progress is made, it is essential to explore the patient's understanding of how this progress was made. The patient needs to have a thorough understanding of the factors that contributed to his problems, as well as those responsible for recovery. Without such an understanding, it is unlikely that change will be sustained over time. It is incumbent upon therapists to follow up on the experience of change, and its implications for the patient's experience of self, as an enhanced sense of self-efficacy seems essential for long-term change.

Woman Headed for a Heart Attack

In the case of the "Woman Headed for a Heart Attack," the patient experienced an immediate elimination of anxiety when she allowed herself to connect with the visceral experience of anger. Then, much to her surprise, the previously dreaded experience of anger made her feel "full," rather than chronically empty, and, more importantly, "alive!" She was able to assert herself with her husband and her boss, leading to even more experiences of mastery and competence.

Examining the Process of Change

Patient: I realize if I put in more effort, I can really accomplish something. Last week we had this clinical lunch that's led by the boss. He was wonderful in many, many ways and he's the one in charge—he even owns the building. He runs the group and he has very definite ideas. I started to present a case and immediately he cut me off. It was humiliating and I started to feel incompetent.
Therapist: Wait a minute, what was the feeling toward him?
Patient: Anger.
Therapist: So let's not turn that back on you, with you feeling incompetent. So did you know that you were angry at the time?
Patient: No, well a little bit. However, something I wouldn't have done before—I made an appointment with him for next week. I already decided I was going to talk to him about this, which is something I would never have done. Well, I would have talked to him, but always from the one down position, and this time I don't feel that.
Therapist: More on equal footing.
Patient: I've thought about it and want to keep to "I" statements, letting him know that I didn't appreciate it that he interrupted me and dismissed me, basically. When I present again on Monday, I don't want him to say anything until I'm finished.
Therapist: Great.
Patient: I know. But, knowing him, he'll love that. He will love that that I will finally have the balls to say something.

The patient was beaming as she spoke, clearly proud of herself for initiating a discussion with her boss, designed to assert herself in a direct but respectful manner. It also seems clear from the transcript that she was letting the therapist know she had already taken care of this on her own and didn't need any help—only acknowledgement. Several weeks later, even more change was evident. She entered the session with a spring in her step.

Therapist: So, how are you feeling?
Patient: Good!

Therapist: Great! You look good too. You even have more colors on. How does that feel?

Patient: It feels great—I really feel great. I really have never felt this way in my whole life—I mean I've had patches of it, but not where it's—not a vague—that's not the right word.

Therapist: Permeates?

Patient: Yes, permeate is better.

Therapist: So tell me, from the inside out, how it feels like in your body to feel good?

Patient: I just have more pep and more energy. My thinking is much clearer. I even missed or stopped taking the Concerta three to four days in a row, just to see. It started because I forgot to take it and so, around 4 p.m. I usually get an energy droop but at about 6 o'clock I realized I didn't take my Concerta today and I'm moving, I'm working.

Therapist: Wow!

Patient: I'm going to get off it. Now I realize all that trouble with concentration had a large anxiety component to it.

Tremendous feelings of self-efficacy are evident here. This patient, who had been anxious and depressed most of her life, was feeling better than ever. When she entered treatment she was on a long list of medications. Now she was tapering down and eliminating most of them. Being able to regulate her own anxiety and affect, rather than relying on medication, bolstered her confidence even further.

The upward spiral of positive change noted in this case may also be related to the concept of "broaden and build" developed by Barbara Frederickson (2004). When positive emotions are activated, expansion seems to occur. Negative feelings (grief, guilt, and anger) tend to narrow our focus, while positive emotions (joy, love, and pride) broaden our perspective. By examining and deepening our patients' access to the positive feelings that follow pain, rage, and guilt, the process of healing and change deepens and expands. "Joy widens one's view of the world and expands imaginative thought. It activates" (Redfield Jamison, 2005, p. 7). A Chinese proverb suggests that "one joy scatters a hundred griefs." This phenomenon was also apparent in the following case, of a man who had been stuck in feelings of grief and guilt about a divorce that had taken place seven years prior.

The Man With Pain and Depression

In the first session with this patient, feelings of anger toward the therapist and his wife were acknowledged but barely felt. Instead, he became anxious and declared that even mentioning an impulse to push me filled him with guilt. We worked to help him differentiate feelings from action, as well as turn against the defenses of internalization that had created seven years of depression and physical pain. Subsequently, he was able to experience anger toward his wife for insisting he have a fertility work-up; toward the doctor who "poked and prodded" him; and toward his mother, who was described as pushy and demanding.

Patient: It's sort of calming down. I don't feel like the electrical current, but less tension. Ah, it's better.
Therapist: It looks like really hard work.
Patient: It's exhausting.
Therapist: You are breathing hard, like you ran a marathon.
Patient: It also feels good.
Therapist: To be honest with yourself—to speak the truth.
Patient: If I am going to be honest, I must say I am a bit upset at you for putting me through so much today, but at the same time, it is excellent!

This is the experience of mastery—the particular joy of working hard to face and overcoming obstacles to growth. Such experiences reinforce a sense of self as resourceful, capable, and resilient. There is also an element of the corrective emotional experience here. Rather than communicating my lack of belief in him and his capacity, as his mother and wife had done, my challenge to operate at his highest level of capacity revealed my confidence in his abilities.

Understanding the nature of the triggers to his symptoms and conflicts was also vital to the process of working through toward character change. Just having an emotional experience would be insufficient to promote such change. The following sequence demonstrates the importance of cognitive clarity and coherence.

Integration and Consolidation of Insights

Therapist: Both times, the anger toward me came up in relation to your wife. When we go to face the feelings toward her, a big part of you wants to preserve her—just have good feelings, and idealize her, in a way. You are mad at me for wanting to see her as a human being.
Patient: For destroying this image. Yeah, that's it.
Therapist: Even though it's hurting you, a part of you wants to protect her, and is mad at me. So how did you become aware of that? How did you notice it?
Patient: It's an anxiety and a bit of, not as much as anger, but maybe some form of disgust in a way.
Therapist: Ah huh, like you originally said with your wife—you were disgusted with her. But the trigger is always this pushing. Whoever would push you—your mother, me, the doctor, your wife—pushing you to do something difficult.
Patient: Oh yeah. You are so much right about that.

Therapist: Even though it was your will, a part of you is angry and wants me to leave you alone.

Patient: You are so much right.

Therapist: How does that want to come out at me?

Patient: Now, it doesn't want to come out, now that I have this realization of what you just said. Now I feel calmer and things are in line, and the *Lego blocks are all in the right place.*

Therapist: You also want to make sense of this, so what just came together for you?

Patient: How much I was annoyed with both of them and you, all three of you!

Therapist: And the three of us is your mother, wife, and me—these women who are pushing and demanding.

Patient: Yes, I realize that now. It all makes sense. Whew! These realizations are just unbelievable. How it was with all three of you, and I have, in a way, operated here, and you, with special attention, but the two of them, with their own goals and desires, without them considering any of mine and me not being able to speak up and voice my own feelings and desires (therapist getting distinguished from wife and mother).

Many factors associated with the change process were activated and integrated in this therapeutic interaction. There had been a breakdown of rigid and destructive defenses, followed by the experience of intense mixed emotions toward others. Then, links between past and present were made. Spontaneously, these links were replaced with new distinctions. The patient was able to see that he had originally perceived me, and responded to me, as if I were a demanding wife and mother who could never be satisfied. Then he could see that I had encouraged him to work hard on his own behalf. Having faced what he had previously feared and avoided, a newfound sense of clarity and confidence was experienced.

He began the next session by acknowledging, and then experiencing, a profound rage toward his wife for betraying him, falling in love with another man, and getting pregnant with his child—something he had completely buried prior to our work together. Following the experience of this rage, he revealed something he has kept hidden and never told anyone before—that he had a one-night stand after his wife sent him back home while she stayed in Europe. He had never done anything like this before, and did not understand why he had behaved in such a fashion. Together, we are able to put more "Lego blocks" together.

Developing Coherence

Patient: I was in another city, teaching. We went to the hotel bar and I met this woman from the course and we hit it off.

Therapist: Do you remember what was going on with your wife at the time?

Patient: We were not so much in touch—exchanging emails, like "how are you?" Later on, she told me she was having a hard time, realizing she couldn't even sleep at the apartment and sleeping at work under her desk. This was also when she was trying to have an affair with a colleague.

Therapist: But, no intimacy or sharing—not talking on the phone, as any married couple would do.

Patient: No.

Therapist: So you were really detached from your feelings and from her. Then you acted out with this woman without understanding why.

Patient: Yeah. There were other opportunities before and after that, but I never did it.

Therapist: Do you remember how you felt?

Patient: Horrible, guilt, awful.

Therapist: Right away or . . .?

Patient: Right away and it lingered, and then went away. But I really just buried it and never talked about it. You are the first living person I have talked to about it.

Therapist: So what is it like to talk about it, acknowledge it, and begin to make sense of it?

Patient: I feel better because I understand it, why it happened. It was revenge. I never let myself feel the rage over her affair, but just acted in revenge.

Therapist: You see that now.

Patient: My whole history is now being reconstructed, how I see it. It's a very strange experience.

Therapist: So tell me about it—what's shifting and how are you making sense of things now?

Patient: I am making sense of things. For the first time, I see my relationship with my ex-wife in a completely new light. I have seen how I have, and how she has, broken trust and ended the marriage. And seeing this so clearly has enabled me not to blame myself as much as I used to—tortured myself. How it was essentially not an intent of either one of us, yet our incapability of being adults and dealing with emotions as adults, but looking back at everything I've done and how I acted, it seems completely distant from me. I don't even recognize it. It seems like it was impossible, yet it was—destined to be like that.

This is the essence of transformational change—a deep understanding of self and other, accompanying a profound shift in the patient's experience of self. He was able to see what he couldn't see before—yet from a distance, as if his "old self" had become foreign (or dystonic). He could remember what happened and understand it, but at the same time have a completely new perspective. Neither a cathartic discharge of emotion, nor an intellectual understanding of these dynamics alone, would have been sufficient for transformational change to occur. In fact, he was highly intelligent and had ruminated about this for seven years, only creating more misery for himself over time. He had completely distorted and rewritten history in order to keep his feelings under wraps. Once he was helped to face rather than avoid his feelings, the memories of what had actually happened came into consciousness and could be integrated into a coherent whole. This had a profound impact on him.

Understanding the Process of Change

Therapist: What helped you to get this clarity?

Patient: The hard part for me was my ex-wife, because somehow my mind has rearranged the past and erased all the things that did not align with this reconstructed past. Now, through these three days of discussions with you, I have been able to see and uncover how it actually was, and moments that I had completely pushed aside—I was able to recall in details.

Therapist: But why?

Patient: Maybe it's the emotions that came out that allowed this version of truth to exist.

Therapist: That clarity of memory came after the experience of your feelings, in each case. So, as long as you are repressing feelings, you have to distort reality to keep that going. When you let yourself face the feelings, then suddenly things became clear and started to click into place. What is, as well as your feelings about what is.

Patient: Exactly. I feel I am at great peace and ease because of this. I feel I could fly home on my own (laughs with delight).

Therapist: So you have energy and hope and light, not heavy and burdened. How do you feel about what you have been able to do here in such a short time?

Patient: It feels unbelievable—amazing. I didn't think it was possible. I had not such big expectations. I thought maybe we would get somewhere, but then I'd have to come back again, but I never anticipated this change—this profound change that we have achieved, and I think it was mostly these three instances of rage and that I allowed myself to go through that. I had never gone through an experience like this before.

Mastery and Competence

Therapist: Would you say you feel proud of yourself?

Patient: Yes, definitely.

Therapist: And you got more than you ever expected?
Patient: Never.
Therapist: Does it give you confidence that you can do it in your life?
Patient: Definitely, definitely

This case demonstrates the depth of self-understanding, and altered sense of self, that can be achieved through intense emotional experience and exposure of core conflicts. Doing what he never imagined he could do had a dramatic impact on the patient's sense of self—from feeling stuck, burdened, helpless, depressed, and guilty, to aware, capable, and empowered. His view of others had been altered as well. Just as his view of himself as solely responsible for the demise of the marriage had changed, so had his view of his wife as perfect and above reproach. Similarly, following a phase of working through, the patient was able to view the therapist as helpful, supportive, and understanding, rather than as simply another demanding woman who was impossible to please. We attended to the changes within him, as well as between the two of us; chronic pain disappeared; and he experienced enormous growth. Confusion was replaced by clarity, excessive self-blame was replaced with a balanced and integrated view of shared responsibility, and passivity and compliance were replaced with active engagement and self-assertion.

This Changes Everything—Phoenix Rising

Let us return to the question of whether deep and enduring character change needs to take a great deal of time. The following patient, a woman in her 60s, had been plagued by anxiety, depression, and painfully low self-esteem all her life, despite many years of traditional therapy. During a three-day block therapy, in which we met two hours each morning and afternoon, the patient had an experience that, in her own words, "changes everything." In Chapter 4, some beginning work, designed to acquaint her with the cost of habitual defenses, was illustrated. Subsequently, she experienced a breakthrough of rage toward her husband, followed by immediate behavior change (asserting herself with him). In the following session, to be detailed here, she arrived with memories from the past regarding her father, along with resistance to the experience of her feelings toward him.

Patient: An important memory came back to me about my parents—an incident that happened when my father hit a dog with the car and didn't even stop. He pulled out to pass a slower car and another car was coming head on in the opposite lane, which he hasn't seen. We saw it. I screamed. There was a very near miss. He swerved back, with inches to spare. Then he hit a dog and didn't even stop. No one said a word. This memory came back in response to the fantasy I had yesterday (of her husband being hit by a car when he was on a bicycle). I always felt a tremendous attachment to dogs. I totally identify with that dog. And, the fact that he nearly killed us all hours earlier.

Therapist: How do you feel toward him as you tell me about these two incidents?

Patient: I am angry.

Therapist: How do you feel that anger that he endangered your family, hit this dog, and never apologized?

Patient: The anger is not that vivid right now.

Therapist: So where does it go? This is really crucial that you see this.

Patient: Well, I am especially reluctant to experience the anger toward him because he was my only parent.

Therapist: But you are not seven years old and he is not here, so that's not the explanation.

Patient: It certainly felt like that for many years.

Therapist: But do you see how it doesn't make sense right now? You are detached from yourself, from the experience, and then you detach from others also. So, if you don't let yourself experience those feelings, you shut down and you distance. Then you stay lonely.

Patient: Yeah.

Therapist: So is that what you want—to stay detached, alone, isolated? Sentence yourself to solitary confinement really?

Patient: It's extremely familiar.

Therapist: How is it working for you? It seems like there is some conflict about it. Here, you are being invited to open up and connect, so we can look at this together, but you deprive yourself of that opportunity and keep a distance emotionally. You can talk about memories—things you already know—and I don't think the healthy part of you came here just to talk about what you already know, but to have some kind of new experience, right?

The therapist exerted some pressure on the patient to give up defenses being used as a resistance to intervention. The combination of pressure to engage, and challenge to the defenses, constituted a form of head-on collision with the resistance in the transference. These interventions were required to help the patient turn against syntonic defenses.

Patient: Yes

Therapist: So we really have to look at what you are going to do about the detachment because that is really going to undermine us having that kind of new experience.

Patient: There was . . .

Therapist: Right now, what are we going to do about it, because this tendency just to avoid and roll over and give in to these destructive forces. You say, "I'm used to it."

Patient: I used to swear to myself as a kid that I wouldn't get in the car with him again, because he was a dangerous driver.

Therapist: But what does that have to do with now? What you are going to do about the ways that you too ignore and don't look at and don't pay attention to your own feelings? That is something you do to you. It's like you're still that little girl in the back seat. You tell me what happens but we still don't get to see how you feel about it.

Patient: (Nods.)

Therapist: Is that OK with you—that you continue to remain oblivious, in a sense, to that?

Patient: I'd like to be aware of them, and I can see how, theoretically, it could work, that I could become aware.

Therapist: Who are you protecting here? Me? You? What is so dangerous about you getting in touch with these feelings? Because you really are very protective and in a sense, you are still protecting him, even though he is dead. You continue to protect your father and you take it on the chin. You are suffering as the result of this massive repression, detachment, and turning all this against yourself. And then there is this other passive part of you that says, "Oh well."

Patient: I haven't thought about that car incident in year, but I am thinking now of a more recent incident in which it might be a bit easier for me to get access the anger, even though it is less dramatic.

In this more recent memory, she recalled a newspaper interview with her father, in which he stated that all his children had followed his professional footsteps. This was certainly not the case for my patient, who had forged her own path. In essence, her father had wiped her out in the interview—something she now realized she was extremely angry about.

Patient: Reading that made me angry and I can access that.

Therapist: How do you feel that inside?

Patient: I can feel inner tension in my chest, and a current of electricity going down my arms, into my hands.

Therapist: OK, good. So you can feel that?

Patient: Yes.

Therapist: What comes into your hands? So what is the impulse in your arms and hands? What does that anger want to do?

Patient: Well, when I read the article that was sent to me, I wanted to rip up that article. I would like to—I can picture myself hammering on the chest because I am still shorter than him and saying, "Notice me and value me for who I am."

Therapist: So let's see if you can just declare the anger—what you actually feel about the fact that he didn't recognize you.

Patient: "You are negating my existence."

Therapist: That's still about him. Can you declare, "I am furious about this"?

In order to enhance self-efficacy, the therapist encouraged the patient to focus inward, on her own feelings, instead of keeping her focus external—on her father. This external focus produced a sense of hopelessness and helplessness. Owning her own experience, instead of remaining a victim, was viewed as essential in accomplishing this goal.

Patient: Yes, yes, and there was always, kind of implied, that if I forced myself into the right mold, then I would get the attention that I craved—but it really stuck in my throat to do that.

Therapist: So let's see if we can get that out so you're not stuck with it in YOUR throat—this anger that you feel toward him.

Patient: I was going to say, "You have no idea," but of all the taboos in my family, saying you are angry is the worst offense you can commit.

Therapist: So are you going to continue to obey and side with them, while stuffing and swallowing it, or are you going to stand with yourself, here and now, and be honest about what you are actually feeling toward him?

Patient: I am angry at being negated and disregarded.

Therapist: How much of the rage that you know is there are you actually experiencing right now?

Patient: Probably about 20%. It feels like that is as much as I can access.

We were both working hard to help her access the buried rage toward her father. Not wanting to lose momentum, but sensing she was at the top range of her tolerance, I adopted a technique used by Allan Abbass (2015), in which a third party is brought into the picture to help out. While I suggested the Hulk, she immediately had her own association, which provided the vehicle she needed to get to her feelings. The unconscious alliance came to our aid in a direct and unmistakable fashion.

Therapist: So, I know it sounds weird, but if you could put all that rage into the Hulk or you could hire some hit man to do it for you. You know it is there. Do you have a sense of what that would look like, if you put that anger into some other character?

Patient: What's coming to mind is the movie, "Children of a Lesser God." The deaf actress who starred in that was very expressive of anger. I was a teenager when I first saw that, and it made a big impression on me, possibly because she didn't speak. She could still express it, and the little nuances of her hand and facial gestures really expressed that anger.

Therapist: It was on her face and in her body. So if your anger was in her, what do you see her doing? How do you see that anger getting expressed toward your father—no words, right, but confront him with that newspaper.

Patient: Yeah, I could show him with a facial expression—how utterly enraged and disgusted I am—how contemptuous.

The patient no longer needed to use a third party stand-in, but switched to "I could show him," a crucial shift in owning the anger she had been dropping all her life.

Therapist: Rip that right up in his face, you mean?
Patient: Yes—the fantasy went to shoving it in his mouth, with shreds of the article.
Therapist: So he can have it stuck in his throat and he'd be the one choking on it.
Patient: Yes, because he is putting out this information about me.
Therapist: But the anger is at him, so if the anger came out at him, what would it want to do?
Patient: I could grab his head and force him to look at who I really am, including that I am someone who feels angry, because that was never permitted. This is who I am. I am a human being.
Therapist: Right! You treat me like this and I will get really angry.
Patient: Yes, it could escalate if he still persisted, because I don't think he's capable of responding. I could get enraged enough to hit him.
Therapist: Where do you hit him? Open hand or fist or what?
Patient: It's going to be a fist—I don't think he'd notice otherwise. It will call for the most violent I could possibly be. So I am looking at punching him in the face with a closed fist.
Therapist: What else, if you lost control and all this rage came out at him?
Patient: I would like to knock him off the pedestal he always put himself on and lay him out prostrate. Yes.
Therapist: How do you do that? How do you get him down?
Patient: With a powerful hit—possibly more than one. His knees buckle. I would say, "This is the inevitable outcome of the way you treated me my whole life." There is no other way for a human being to respond.
Therapist: It's as if there was no way to get through to him—what do you have to do to have him wake up and see you? It's absolutely enraging. With that, you are saying, "This is over, I won't protect you and be invisible."

Birth of the True Self

Patient: Yes, yeah. Even if I have to kill you to have a life—to assert my right to have a life.
Therapist: So how do you kill him?
Patient: So, he has hit his head on the floor and it's been a fatal blow—he's dead down there.

Therapist: So what does he look like now? How do you know he's dead?

Patient: The same way I saw with my husband yesterday. I look at his eyes and there is no responsiveness there. He is not looking at anything—he is gone.

Therapist: There is certainly a connection between these two men, huh? They check out and can be self-absorbed and rage that you feel about that and not being seen and loved—it is just enraging.

Patient: Yes. Having my life co-opted.

Therapy: And you are not going to collude with that anymore. You said, "If I have to kill you to live, I'm going to do it." So, once he's down and you see he's gone, what kind of feeling do you have?

Once the previously repressed impulse to kill her father had been experienced, the unconscious alliance took over, promoting deep healing. No longer willing to sacrifice herself to maintain an illusion about her father, she declared her right to live her own life in her own way.

De-Repression of Meaningful Dream

Patient: I remember, after my father died, I had a dream I could fly. I was flying over the landscape. I actually, as I was flying up there, I looked down on him. And then, in the dream, I ejaculate, which I've always wondered what that felt like and, in the dream, I experienced that. It was exhilarating. That's what I felt when he died. I felt guilty afterwards because you are supposed to be full of grief when a parent dies.

Therapist: You had that sense of triumph—that a part of you wanted to slay him—have him go down as you take off.

Patient: Yes!

Therapist: When you say ejaculate, did you have a penis?

Patient: Yes! I mean, I don't know if I had a penis or not, I can just tell you, there was this marvelous, orgasmic moment of power.

Therapist: So it's a tremendous sense of power, pleasure, and release. So let's get acquainted with what this feels like to embody your own power and your own pleasure.

Patient: I never expected that feeling to come back to me in my waking life.

Therapist: What does it feel like?

Patient: It feels really good! Wow—so, do some people go around feeling this all the time?

Therapist: Is that possible?

Patient: It must be. *This definitely changes everything.* (Patient sits up and forward, speaking with authority and making very direct eye contact.)

Therapist: Tell me about it—what it feels like.

Patient: Light—my chest feels light and expansive; at ease.

Therapist: Anxiety is gone?
Patient: There are muscles that have been tense for decades that are letting go.
Therapist: And now you don't seem to have any trouble looking at me.
Patient: Yeah.
Therapist: So you are you and free to connect.
Patient: Yeah.

It is difficult to communicate in words the profound change in the patient's entire presentation. It was as if she had come alive before my eyes—as if the entire "false self" suit of armor had collapsed, and her true self was emerging organically. When she said, "This changes everything," I could both observe, and viscerally experience, that profound change in her. The changes were physical, as well as emotional and interpersonal. Chronic pain simply evaporated. Barriers to connection both within her and between us disappeared.

Therapist: So what is that like? I get chills actually—it is such a shift. What is that like to be authentically connected?
Patient: Thank you for helping me get here.
Therapist: You are so welcome (sitting in joyful connection).
Patient: I knew when I got in touch with you—that, in and of itself, was exerting power. There was some possibility I wanted to grab.
Therapist: So it almost looks like tears of gratitude, for both to that healthy part of you that grabbed this opportunity, and toward me too, and what we did together.
Patient: Yes. Thank you for reaching out to me actively enough to pull me along, because, by myself, I just wasn't getting there.
Therapist: Right, these forces are very powerful and you were not able to fight them. So that part of you knew you needed help and an ally so together we could face these feelings and also the reality they are connected with.
Patient: Yes, right!
Therapist: So, how wonderful to recognize that you still have that in you.
Patient: Yes. Now I'm the only one in my family grounded in reality.
Therapist: Clear sighted—feeling your feelings, which is powerful and freeing—you feel full, energized but relaxed. So, talk about finally differentiating from them, right?
Patient: Yes, because it's always seemed as though my very survival depended on the illusion. I've had a recurrent dream of being in a space ship and causing some offense to the powers that be and I was just extruded into outer space, where it is cold and there is nowhere to breathe. That's what it always felt like.
Therapist: And you got stuck in that. Obviously, it was the reality as a child. You could not exist on your own and find your own galaxy. You had to adapt, but you got stuck and ended up really betraying yourself in order to stay loyal and connected to them. So, now when you

shed that and allow you to be you, what do you imagine, because they come to your mind and you are now differentiated from your mother and sisters and father? What is that like?

Patient: I will find out tonight because I am having dinner with my sister and mother.

While appreciative of the therapist and her contribution to the interaction, the patient was also able to claim a sense of agency and responsibility for getting the help she needed. While patients frequently feel angry with us for challenging their defenses and pressing them to experience anxiety-provoking feelings and impulses, they are also profoundly appreciative of our efforts to work hard in order to make a real connection with them at the same time. When we persist in getting through defenses and resistance in order to make a connection to the real person trapped underneath the façade, the rewards are substantial. Having been able to face her feelings toward her father, she felt empowered and her vision was clear. She could face reality without the need to distort it. In so doing, she became increasingly genuine, as well as differentiated from family members. While she imagined this would somehow create distance between her and her loved ones, the opposite turned out to be the case. She described this level of transformation in the next session. There was an effortless quality to the change—an experience of utter delight in her own authenticity, engagement, and newfound sense of agency.

Changes in Relation to Family Members

Patient: It's been such a short time, but a lot has happened. Starting with the dinner I had with my mother and sister last night. You won't believe this. I actually got a chance to hit my mother. (Said in a thoroughly delighted manner.)

Therapist: In reality? Now is that a good thing? We don't usually advocate acting out!

Patient: It was so amazing, as if the fates cooperated. I was sitting beside her at dinner and she choked on her food. It was obvious that someone needed to thump her on the back and I was the closest one. I looked at both my sister and made eye contact with my brother-in-law to make sure it was all OK. They nodded yes, so I whacked her on the back. It helped a little but not totally, so I had to whack her again.

Therapist: How perfect.

Patient: Not only did I get to channel some aggression, but I saved her life. If that happened, and I weren't present, she would be dead. Or, if I hadn't been freed up to feel this without anxiety, I would have frozen on the spot.

Talk about a corrective emotional experience!

Therapist: I get chills listening to this—it was like yesterday—only once you really own and experience that rage toward your father, did you come to life. Here, by letting yourself have access to that aggression and use it constructively . . .

Patient: Decisively!

Therapist: You actually saved her. That is just wild. I mean, wow. How do you feel as you talk about this?

Patient: Happy!

Therapist: What does it feel like to be happy?

Patient: Weird, but I am getting used to it. It almost feels as if there is laughter ready to bubble up. Very buoyant.

Therapist: I notice your shoulders are down and back and you are sitting straight but relaxed. It even appears that your chest is more open and it feels that way on the inside too?

Patient: For years, probably decades, I have been going to physical therapy because I hunch my shoulders. She tells me every single week that my top ribs are out of place and my skeleton is out of place and I've said to her, "What do I do during the week that has it creep into this bad alignment?" and she says it's tension. Suddenly it is completely gone! This is unprecedented.

The depth and breadth of change was experienced on many layers—physical, emotional, and relational. In many ways, this experience profoundly affected her sense of herself from a helpless, depressed, lost cause, to a powerful, determined woman, capable of authentic self-expression. The level of integration and working through achieved here was significant and multilayered. Her body, heart, and mind had all changed and, in many ways, returned to their natural and authentic state. Being with someone through this transformation is deeply affecting.

When the Unconscious Becomes Conscious

A Wolf in Sheep's Clothing

Excerpts from the first session with this depressed patient were included in Chapter 5. The breakthrough of anxiety-provoking feelings and impulses in the transference created a wide opening into the unconscious, with memories and associations emerging to help us make sense of his emotional conflicts. The initial links were between the transference feelings and those from the past with his mother. Now he spontaneously linked these patterns to what had been going on in his relationship with his infant son. He could see the repetitive pattern and was distressed by it.

Patient: Now I feel anxious, because I also have this toward my own son. It's very difficult. I know I have mixed feelings toward my son (starts to cry). I don't want him to have to grow up with this (cries). I have images of squeezing his neck (big sigh).

Therapist: Was there a recent time?

Patient: It just came now, it hasn't been conscious before. I just saw myself with my hands around his neck. I have actually been withdrawing from him. He is there all the time so there is no time for me—or just me and my wife.

Therapist: This is real and about now, but also tied to unresolved feelings toward your mother. You say the same things. I can't be me—there is no time or space for me.

Patient: You're right. I didn't see that before. But there is anger toward my wife too, who is insisting I be there all the time.

Therapist: And your part is swallowing your own needs and feelings, submitting to the woman, feeling angry and then guilty about that—this you can change.

Patient: Yeah, I can feel this power now. I am clear. I want time for myself and also time when I can be alone with my son, without my wife.

Therapist: So you want some one-on-one without the third party always there.

Patient: I feel sad now. I do want to be primary and not always the loser—the third wheel. I can see it over and over—all the time—at work, at home, in my past.

Therapist: It's the same damn thing over and over. You can really see this dynamic. So how do you feel about all you've been able to do so rapidly this morning and how we have been working together?

Patient: I feel good. It's so totally surprising when these unconscious things come up. This opening I was having I couldn't have made happen—it just came up.

This first session had a profound effect on the patient and created an extremely strong conscious and unconscious alliance. He was able to experience all kinds of previously repressed emotions without undue anxiety. As a result, he could see what was getting repeated in the current relationship with his son, as well how he could put a stop to these patterns of reactivity.

Understanding Suicidal Impulses

Despite several previous treatments, the source of his suicidal impulses had never been uncovered. He opened the second session with information leading us directly to the cause of the problem.

Patient: I felt a little guilty over the break, and could feel myself getting a little depressed and shut down about those feelings toward my son.

Therapist: It's the guilt about this rage, so you shut down, turn it toward yourself and get depressed. We could get back to the feelings about your son, but I keep wondering what happened back at 21 and 22, when you got seriously depressed and suicidal. Any thoughts about that?

Patient: I was—had always wanted to be a healer, a doctor—so I went to medical school and it was then that I got depressed. The first one was after six weeks. I put a lot of pressure on myself—studying anatomy.

Therapist: And how do you do that? Just books, or also a dead body?

Patient: Yeah, yeah. There were several bodies. Sometime we would get an arm or a leg or a full body. And also there was a hallway with body parts and a lot of body parts and dead bodies. I never thought about that.

Therapist: What comes to you now about what that must have been stirring up?

Patient: I never thought about that. It's so strange that you just picked that up. I sense something in my body that says there is something here. I would study and study, but at night when I went to sleep I would see bones.

Therapist: And it was after this first course that you got depressed.

Patient: It was too much for me. I regressed and called my parents and moved home. It was so painful to me, so demoralized. I had suicidal thoughts.

Therapist: What form did they take?

Patient: One night I wanted to steal my Dad's car and go to the forest and gas myself with a tube. That's the one I remember now. What comes to me—I am getting a little dizzy or almost feel doped.

While the patient could sense we were on to something here, he started to become dizzy and disoriented, a signal that anxiety was too high and needed to be down-regulated. A focus on the internal experience of his anxiety was successful in bringing it down to a tolerable level. At this point, he let me know that he was having mixed feelings toward me. In this instance, the link was with his father.

Therapist: Now you are getting in touch with anger toward your father for his passivity.

Patient: Yeah! I wish he could show his own energy and aggression, so I don't have to be so scared about it.

Therapist: You want to be two powerful men—not one up and one down.

Patient: Yeah—that's right. He has my mother and I have my woman now.

Therapist: What's coming up?

222 • Integration, Consolidation, Coherence

Patient: It's weird, I have this impulse to kick him in the balls. I don't know why. I want to kick him and he bends over but I want him to stand up.

Therapist: You are angry because he goes limp.

Patient: I want to take him and put him down. I put my foot on his chest, "Come on—show up." Be a man. In a way, when I put him up against the wall, I wanted to see him fight back, not just get scared.

Therapist: What did you want?

Patient: "Don't do that." Deal with me, man to man. It's like in a movie and we are in a saloon and have a real fight. I kick him and he comes back at me and we really fight and are really rolling on the floor. I take a bottle and break it. Then I see this throat. Oh, now this isn't funny. He's choking and bleeding from his neck.

Therapist: What do you feel now?

Patient: He's dying. There is silence. It's like a bad dream. That's why I'm so scared of my power (deeply felt insight). It's really tensing up in my shoulder right now. I become stiff. The body is stopping me.

Therapist: Who would be stiffening up? This comes up after you killed your father and slitting his throat. You do to yourself what you did to him—go dead, frozen, stiff.

Patient: It's still there. It's really intense and it's been like that for years, but it's intensified. I want to get rid of him, so part of me feels good about it. I thought I should be sad when he was lying there, but I actually feel OK. This is strange. I must be closing down because if that really happened I wouldn't be OK.

Therapist: But if you see your father's body dead.

Patient: (Starts crying.) That wouldn't good. I love him and want to comfort him, but he is so weak I get angry and don't want that. Now the anger comes up again. This is a wave of power. This is really strong. This is the energy I want to hold onto to. Totally enraged—then I shut down.

Therapist: It's toward him and this weakness in him.

Patient: Ah! Ah! I am scared because it's really strong.

Therapist: Can you contain it?

Patient: I can get scared you can't handle it.

Therapist: Does it look that way?

Patient: NO! (Starts to weep; huge sigh.) It's really strong. It comes in waves and then comes guilt.

Therapist: All these feelings come so close together. You love him and are enraged with him.

Patient: Ah! Kicking and biting and tearing him apart. I get this picture of taking his arms and legs off and his dick off and his head. Ah! Impulses to punch on his chest. Ah! This . . . ah! I have this impulse to scream and bite.

Therapist: Bite where?
Patient: On his throat. Like a wild animal. Bite him in the throat. Growl. A dog biting and shaking his head. Tear his throat out, and his head off. Punching and stabbing with a knife in his chest, in the heart and slashing—flay him. I want to squeeze his balls—destroy them. Knee him. Damn. I am just angry!
Therapist: Indeed.
Patient: Primitive rage! This energy is new to me. Ah! I almost can't contain it. I want to stand up and kick and punch. And squeezing his throat and slapping him—wake up! It seems almost endless.
Therapist: He's dismembered—arms and legs—you bit his throat, slit him down the middle. What is the scene here?
Patient: Like pieces of meat.
Therapist: And body parts.
Patient: Like—like at medical school. Now I really see it—those arms and legs and bodies and torsos, heads. Now it makes sense (big sighs).

Now the patient has achieved a deeply felt emotional insight into the link between his suicidal impulses and unconscious guilt over murderous impulses toward his father. It was no coincidence that he wanted to kill himself in his father's car! His tendency to do to himself what he wished to do to his father was crystal clear in this sequence. This served the dual purpose of protecting his beloved father from his rage and punishing himself for his wish to be rid of him. In his previous therapies, he was never helped to understand why he became acutely suicidal after being exposed to dead bodies and severed body parts during anatomy lab. This insight must be deepened and clarified in order to facilitate integration and prevent future relapse (Town, Hardy, McCullough, & Stride, 2012). It should also be noted that the patient does nearly all the work at this point, and little is required from the therapist other than presence and support.

Therapist: How does it come together?
Patient: (Head in hands and sighing heavily.) It makes sense that I got depressed when I saw those body parts. You just saw it. Now it is very clear to me—arms and legs.
Therapist: So unconsciously . . .
Patient: It was my Dad. That's why I wanted to gas myself—you know how, when you have an operation, you have to be knocked out. Then I can protect him. Even when I get dizzy, it weakens me so I can't hurt him.
Therapist: Not just to punish yourself but to protect others from this violent, destructive rage. You could feel how intense that rage was—that you could kill with your hands and teeth, so you anesthetize yourself.
Patient: Anesthetize—that's it.
Therapist: To protect others out of love, as if you are dangerous.

Patient: This is what I came for. This is it. Thank you (starts to sob, deep waves, over and over). It's strange, it's like this crying is from another time. It's even stronger with my father than my mother. I have been angry with my mother all my life. I am more angry with my Dad, but I could never get to it. Now I see how I wanted to be rid of him to just have my mother. My mother isn't perfect but she's really engaged.

Therapist: It was when you said, "This is what I wanted. Thank you," that the damn broke and this deep grief came through.

Patient: Because I just knew, in some way, that I needed to feel this anger toward my Dad before I could deeply connect to my son. When my heart opens, this rage comes up. Like it was with you before. It happens with the one I'm with. When someone wants to be open and close to me, the anger comes up. So, it's like a curse. When something good happens, the anger comes up, I suppress it, and then it destroys it. No more! This is really what I was coming for—what I was hoping for and I am full of gratitude.

Therapist: We have been there together.

Patient: For the first time, I could really feel this rage. I wasn't pretending—it was really there.

As in so many of the cases presented here, words simply pale in comparison to the felt experience of healing and transformation in the session with the patient. This man was coming alive, creating coherence, and transforming in front of my eyes. It was a profoundly moving experience, with the ring of emotional truth, a sense of something almost sacred being shared and witnessed. He understood himself deeply and could clearly see what had been driving him to behave in a destructive manner.

This is why we do what we do (or at least why I do what I do)—the reward for the hard work required to get to the unconscious source of the patient's suffering. When we can facilitate this kind of profound experience, we are changed as well. While many writers (Cabaniss, Cherry, Douglas, & Schwartz, 2011; Wachtel, 1993) have asserted that these kinds of rapid and dramatic results only happen in the movies, and not in our consulting rooms, it is not so. We can help our patients in rapid order, when we understand the steps required to facilitate the therapeutic process.

Man Who Couldn't Get Divorced

As in the previous cases, we are able to see that the experience of previously avoided feelings serves as a trigger unlocking the unconscious and reviving memories of the original traumas associated with the patient's conflicts. In the following case, a middle-aged man had been unable to "pull the trigger" and get divorced, despite having been separated for three years. In this session, we discover the unconscious source of his need to stay tied to a woman he doesn't love. Following a passage of murderous rage toward his wife, the following material emerged spontaneously.

Patient: You know, I think the guilt goes back to a previous relationship. The first woman I ever slept with in my 20s, and had been dating since high school. At one point, I didn't want to be with her anymore. There was a neighborhood woman who caught my eye and I had sex with her. The whole neighborhood found out. It was about the time I wanted to be done with that relationship anyway, but instead of being upright and forthright and honorable, I did this lousy thing.

Therapist: It hurt her and made you look like a louse. I'm gathering from what you are saying—rather than acknowledge what you had done and apologize—it went into a pattern of self-punishment?

Patient: Yeah. The woman I really want to apologize to is Joan. I wish I hadn't behaved the way I had—wish I had a greater level of maturity.

Therapist: But you did, so what would you like to say? To acknowledge what you did and the impact . . .

Patient: What was your question?

Therapist: Where are you going? (I could see that the patient was having new memories surface—a clear indication of the opening of the unconscious.)

Patient: I was just thinking about the circumstances and how it all played out. Scenes of that neighborhood are playing through my mind.

Therapist: What do you see?

Patient: I am very sorry for what I did. I know it was hurtful. I am also thinking that, at the time, even then, I had kind of cut myself off from my feelings.

Therapist: You were already doing that—cut off your feelings and be a tough guy. Now you realize, not in the way of an excuse, but that you were already cut off. When did that happen, that you cut off from your feelings and distancing? This is a major mechanism also cutting off from love and connection.

Patient: Yeah, it's a repeated pattern. I don't know that I ever let myself go completely to connect with her.

Therapist: Have you ever?

Patient: No, I haven't.

Therapist: You've been on your guard. The best defense is a good offense—never let anyone too close to hurt you. Who had already hurt you by then?

Patient: My parents.

Therapist: What comes to your mind?

Patient: Just a sense—a feeling I have of, ultimately, always being alone. Feeling like I was the only one in this world that I could depend on.

Therapist: Desolate. What is the picture you get of that time? You just felt alone or you were left alone?

Childhood Memories of Abuse

Patient: There was another seminal event in my life, when I was in junior high. A couple of friends and I were exploring our sexuality. A couple of guys and this one guy—he and I used to give each other oral sex behind this bush—the perfect place to go hide. At one point he turned on me and started telling other friends that I was sucking his cock, and so I put up with it and ignored it for a while, but he got more public and insistent. At one point he was taunting me with friends in tow. I said to him, "Well if I sucked your cock, then you sucked my cock." I turned and kept walking. The friends said, "Is that true?" He got all pissed off. Not too long after that I was accosted by a group of people, beaten, kicked, and basically forced me to suck this guy's penis. I was sexually assaulted.

Therapist: They beat you, kicked you, forced you to submit and service this guy? That is humiliating as well.

Patient: And, that was the point where I really felt that there was just me and me alone.

Therapist: Can you let yourself feel those feelings—how awful—not just to be treated in such a brutal fashion, but beaten and betrayed, with no one to turn to. At that point you decided to shut down—shut off your own feelings and never let anyone do that to you again. Do you feel that sadness?

Patient: Huge sadness and feeling welling up. Also, a bit of shame—a lot of shame.

Therapist: What are you ashamed of?

Patient: That I didn't fight back more during the sexual assault. When I faced the penis.

Therapist: What did you really want to do?

Patient: Turn away and run.

Therapist: Or what else?

Patient: Bite it! But I didn't. I submitted.

Therapist: Actually, there is a part of you turning against that passivity now— what you had learned early, to submit to cruelty. You're beginning to get in touch with the part that wants to fight for you.

Patient: Yeah, I do. You know, I've always kept this a secret—felt so bad about it—that it meant there was something wrong with me and I don't deserve to be loved. Now I can see that acting as I did with Joan, and then marrying my wife—a safe bet, but someone I never really loved—was all part of this. I just want to love and be loved before I die. Enough of this suffering and staying tied to this woman in such a crazy way. It's no good for her either. Now I feel like I genuinely want to apologize to her. How awful to marry someone you don't really love. It wasn't fair to her. I can say that without needing to beat myself up. It's all very sad but true. Strangely, though, I feel lighter and optimistic somehow. It's like we can both be free to be happy now.

Alexander and French (1946) asserted that "experiencing the old unsettled conflict with a new ending" was the secret to every penetrating therapeutic result. In this case, profound and transformational change was possible when defenses were abandoned, warded off feelings were faced, and traumatic memories were brought to consciousness, where they were experienced and processed in new and healthy ways. This man had suppressed his feelings of pain, rage, and guilt regarding parental neglect and sexual abuse for most of his life. Despite this, these feelings were driving a good deal of his behavior, albeit outside of conscious awareness.

Following initial waves of guilt, he experienced a deep sense of understanding and compassion for himself, and the women in his life, including his wife. Prior to this, he only had hostile feelings toward her. Now he felt tenderness and guilt about his cold and uncaring attitude toward her. This allowed him to apologize in a heartfelt manner, to release them from one another, and to find genuine love.

Summary

It seems fitting to end this chapter, and this volume, with a quote from Rilke: "For one person to be able to advise or even help another, a lot must happen, a lot must go well, a whole constellation of things must come right in order once to succeed."

The integration of multiple factors within the context of a trusting relationship has been shown to reliably facilitate the process of deep and lasting change. As Edna St. Vincent Millay put it, "In life, it's not one damn thing after the other, it's the same damn thing over and over again." In other words, we tend to repeat core conflicts and habitual patterns of behavior over time and across varying situations. By implementing specific methods designed to access and resolve the patient's core conflicts, change is likely to be both rapid and pervasive. In other words, a change in one sector of the patient's life, or in one relationship, can and often does have significant ripple effects in other areas. Instead of having to go over all the important relationships in the patient's life, a thorough examination of one that illustrated the pattern is often enough to produce change deep and lasting change (Alexander & French, 1946; Ecker, Ticic, & Hulley, 2012).

More recent research (Abbass, 2006, 2015; Abbass, Town, & Driessen, 2012) provides additional support for the cost and clinical effectiveness of this type of dynamic, emotion-focused work. ISTDP appears to be effective across a very wide spectrum of patients, as well as across settings. Follow-up data suggest that the effects of this type of treatment are long lasting and even increase over time (Shedler, 2010).

The ways in which therapeutic results are reliably and consistently accomplished have been elucidated here. The ability to heal is innate (Coughlin, 2009). However, the capacity to heal is often blocked by defensive processes. When defenses are disrupted, and true feelings break through the repressive barrier, healing takes place quite naturally. This is a humbling and profoundly moving experience for therapists. Because the patient is, in fact, doing much of the work himself at this point in the process, his sense of mastery, confidence, and competence is profoundly enhanced in the process. Development that had been stalled resumes and the patient becomes increasingly authentic and available for connection with others.

Bibliography

Abbass, A. (2003). The cost effectiveness of short-term dynamic psychotherapy. *Journal of Pharmacoeconomics Outcome Research, 3,* 535–539.

Abbass, A. (2004). Small group videotape training for psychotherapy skills development. *Academic Psychiatry, 28,* 151–155.

Abbass, A. (2015). *Reaching through the Resistance.* Kansas City, MO: Seven Leaves Press.

Abbass, A., Campbell, S., Magee, K., Lenzer, I., Hann, G. & Tarzwell, R. (2010). Cost savings of treatment of medically unexplained symptoms using intensive short-term dynamic psychotherapy (ISTDP) by a hospital emergency department. *Archives of Medical Psychology, 2,* 34–44.

Abbass, A., Campbell, S. & Tarzwell, R. (2009). Intensive short-term dynamic psychotherapy to reduce rates of emergency department return visits for patients with medically unexplained symptoms: Preliminary evidence from a pre-post intervention. *Canadian Journal of Emergency Medicine, 11,* 529–534.

Abbass, A., Hancock, J.T., Henderson, J. & Kisely, S. (2006). Short-term psychodynamic psychotherapies for common mental disorders. *Cochrane Database Systematic Review, 4,* CD004687.

Abbass, A., Joffres, M.R. & Ogrodniczuk, J.S. (2008). A naturalistic study of intensive short term dynamic psychotherapy trial therapy. *Brief Treatment and Crisis Intervention, 8*(2), 164–170.

Abbass, A., Kisely, S. & Kroenke, K. (2009). Short term psychodynamic psychotherapy for somatic symptom disorders: A systematic review and meta-analysis. *Psychotherapy and Psychosomatics, 78,* 265–274.

Abbass, A., Lovas, D. & Purdy, A. (2008). Direct diagnosis and management of emotional factors in the chronic headache patient. *Cerphalalgia, 28,* 1305–1314.

Abbass, A., Rabung, S., Leichsenring, F., Refseth, J. & Midgley, N. (2013). Psychodynamic psychotherapy for children and adolescents: A meta-analysis of short-term psychodynamic models. *Journal of American Academy of Child and Adolescent Psychiatry, 52,* 863–875.

Abbass, A., Tarzwell, R., Hann, S.G., Lenzer, I., Campbell, S. & Maxwell, D. (2010). Implementing an emotion focused consultation service to examine medically unexplained symptoms in the emergency department. *Archives of Medical Psychology, 1,* 44–51.

Abbass, A. & Town, J.M. (2013). Key clinical processes in Intensive short-term dynamic psychotherapy. *Psychotherapy, 50,* 433–437.

Abbass, A., Town, J.M. & Driessen, E. (2012). ISTDP: A systematic review and meta-analysis of outcome research. *Harvard Review of Psychiatry, 20*(2), 97–108.

Ackerman, S.J. & Hilsenroth, M.J. (2001). A review of therapists characteristics and techniques negatively impacting the therapeutic alliance. *Psychotherapy: Theory, Research, Practice and Training, 38,* 171–185.

Alexander, F. & French, T.M. (1946). *Psychoanalytic Therapy, Principles, and Application.* Lincoln, NE: University of Nebraska Press.

Anderson, T., Ogles, B., Patterson, C., Lambert, M. & Vermeersch, D. (2009). Therapist effects: Facilitative interpersonal skills as a predictor of therapist success. *Journal of Clinical Psychology, 65,* 755–768.

Angell, M. (2011, June 23). The epidemic of mental illness: Why? *New York Review of Books,* retrieved from http://www.nybooks.com/articles/2011/06/23/epidemic-mental-illness-why/.

Ankarberg, P. & Falkenstrom, F. (2008). Treatment of depression with anti-depressants is primarily a psychological treatment. *Psychotherapy: Research, Practice and Training, 45,* 329–339.

Ardito, R.B. & Rabellino, D. (2011). Therapeutic alliance and outcome of psychotherapy: Historical excursus, measurements, and prospects for research. *Frontiers in Psychology, 2*, 270–285.

Atkinson, B. (2004). Altered states: Why insight itself is not enough for lasting change. *Psychotherapy Networker, 28*, 43–45, 67.

Balint, M. (1995). *The Doctor, His Patient and the Illness*. London: Churchill Livingston.

Banders, J.L. & Betan, E.J. (2013). *Core Competencies in Brief Dynamic Psychotherapy*. New York: Routledge.

Barber, J.P., Connolly, M.B., Crits-Christoph, P., Gladis, L. & Sinqueland, L. (2000). Alliance predicts patients' outcome beyond in-treatment change in symptoms. *Journal of Consulting and Clinical Psychology, 68*, 1027–1032.

Barber, J.P., Muran, C.J., McCarthy, K.S. & Keefe, J.R. (2013). Research on dynamic therapies. In M.J. Lambert (Ed.) *Bergin and Garfield's Handbook of Psychotherapy and Behavior Change* (6th ed., pp. 443–495). Hoboken, NJ: John Wiley & Sons.

Barlow, D.H. (2000). Unraveling the mysteries of anxiety and its disorders from the perspective of emotion theory. *American Psychologist, 55*, 1247–1263.

Barlow, D.H. (2004). Psychological treatments. *American Psychologist, 59*, 869–878.

Barlow, D.H. (2010). Negative effects from psychological treatments. *American Psychologist, 65*, 13–20.

Barlow, D.H., Allen, L.B. & Choate, M.L. (2004). Toward a unified theory of emotional disorders. *Behavior Therapy, 35*, 205–230.

Barlow, D.H., Ellard, K.K., Fairholme, C.P., Farchione, T.J., Boisseau, C.L., May, J.T.E. & Allen, L.B. (2011). *Unified Protocol for Transdiagnostic Treatment of Emotional Disorders*. New York: Oxford University Press.

Bergin, A.E. (1966). Some implications of psychotherapy research for therapeutic practice. *Journal of Abnormal Psychology, 71*, 235–246.

Bergin, A.E. & Strupp, H.H. (1972). *Changing Frontiers in the Science of Psychotherapy*. Chicago: Aldine-Atherton.

Beutler, L.E., Mlerio, C.M. & Talebi, H. (2002). Resistance. In J.C. Norcross (Ed.) *Psychotherapy Relationships that Work* (pp. 129–143). New York: Oxford University Press.

Binder, J.L. & Betan, E.J. (2013). *Core Competencies in Brief Dynamic Psychotherapy*. New York: Routledge.

Blatt, S.J. (2004). *Experiences of Depression: Theoretical, Clinical and Research Perspectives*. Washington, DC: American Psychological Association.

Blatt, S.J. & Fonagy, P. (2008). *Polarities of Experience*. Washington, DC: American Psychological Association.

Blatt, S.J. & Ford, R.Q. (1994). *Therapeutic Change: An Object Relations Perspective*. New York: Springer.

Blatt, S.J., Sanislow, C.A., Zuroff, D.C. & Pilkonis, P.A. (1996). Characteristics of effective therapists: Further analyses of data from the National Institute of Mental Health Treatment of Depression Collaborative Research Project. *Journal of Consulting and Clinical Psychology, 64*, 1276–1284.

Bonanno, G. (2007). What predicts resilience after disaster? The role of demographics, resources, and life stress. *Journal of Consulting and Clinical Psychology, 75*, 671–682.

Bond, M. & Perry, C. (2005). Long term changes in defensive styles with psychodynamic psychotherapy for depressive, anxiety and personality disorders. *Focus, 3*, 429–437.

Bond, M.P. & Vaillant, J.S. (1986). An empirical study of the relationship between diagnosis and defense style. *Archives of General Psychiatry, 43*, 285–288.

Bordin, E.S. (1979). The generalizability of the psychoanalytic concept of the working alliance. *Psychotherapy: Theory, Research and Practice, 16*(3), 252–260.

Bordin, E.S. (1994). Theory and research on the therapeutic working alliance: New directions. In A.O. Horvath & L.S. Greenberg (Eds.) *The Working Alliance: Theory Research and Practice* (pp. 13–37). New York: Wiley.

Bowlby, J. (1969). *Attachment and Loss, Volume One*. London: Tavistock.

Brenner, C. (1976). *Psychoanalytic Technique and Psychic Conflict*. New York: International Universities Press.

Brown, G., Lambert, J., Jones, E.R. & Minami, T. (2005). Identifying highly effective psychotherapists in managed care environment. *The American Journal of Managed Care, 11*, 513–520.

Buckley, P., Karasu, T.B. & Charles, E. (1981). Psychotherapists view their personal therapy. *Psychotherapy: Theory, Research, Practice, 18*, 299–305.

Burgoon, J.K., Guerrero, L.K. & Floyd, K. (2009). *Nonverbal Communication*. Boston, MA: Allyn & Bacon.

Butler, S.F. & Strupp, H.H. (1986). Specific and nonspecific factors in psychotherapy: A problematic paradigm for psychotherapy research. *Psychotherapy, 23*, 30–40.

Cabaniss, D.L., Cherry, S., Douglas, C.J. & Schwartz, A.R. (2011). *Psychodynamic Psychotherapy: A Clinical Manual.* New York: Wiley-Blackwell.

Carryers, J.R. & Greenberg, L.S. (2010). Optimal levels of emotional arousal in experiential therapy of depression. *Journal of Consulting and Clinical Psychology, 78*, 190–199.

Carveth, D. (2006). Self punishment as guilt evasion. *Canadian Journal of Psychoanalysis, 14*, 177–198.

Castonguay, L.G., Constantino, M.J. & Holtforth, M. (2006). The working alliance: Where are we and where should we go? *Psychotherapy: Theory, Research, Practice and Training, 43*, 271–279.

Castonguay, L.G., Goldfried, M.R., Wiser, S., Raue, P.H., & Hayes, A.M. (1996). Predicting the effect of cognitive therapy for depression: A study of unique and common factors. *Journal of Consulting and Clinical Psychology, 64*, 497–504.

Castonguay, L.G. & Hill, C.E. (Eds.) (2012). *Transformation in Psychotherapy: Corrective Emotional Across Cognitive Behavioral Humanistic and Psychodynamic Approaches.* Washington, DC: American Psychological Association Press.

Coughlin, P.A. (2009). Facilitating emotional health and well being. In D. Monit & B.D. Beitman (Eds.) *Integrative Psychiatry* (pp. 383–407). New York: Oxford University Press.

Coughlin Della Selva, P. (1992). Achieving character change in ISTDP: How the experience of affect leads to a consolidation of the self. *International Journal of Short Term Psychotherapy, 7*, 73–87.

Coughlin Della Selva, P. (1996/2004). *Intensive Short Term Dynamic Psychotherapy: Theory and Technique.* New York: Wiley/London: Karnac.

Cozolino, L. (2010). *The Neuroscience of Psychotherapy.* New York: Norton.

Craddock, N. & Owen, M.J. (2010). The Kraepelinian dichotomy—going, going . . . but still not gone. *British Journal of Psychiatry, 196*, 92–95.

Cramer, P. (1999). Personality, personality disorders and defenses mechanisms. *Journal of Personality, 67*, 535–554.

Cramer, P (2000). Defense mechanisms today: Further processes for adaptation. *American Psychologist, 55*, 637–646.

Cramer, P. (2002). Defense mechanisms, behavior, and affect in young adulthood. *Journal of Personality, 70*, 103–126.

Cramer, P. (2003). Defense mechanisms and psychological adjustment in childhood. *Journal of Nervous and Mental Disorders, 191*, 487–495.

Cramer, P. (2006). *Protecting the Self: Defense Mechanisms in Action.* New York: Guilford Press.

Craske, M.F. & Barlow, D.H. (2008). Panic disorder and agoraphobia. In D.H. Barlow (Ed.) *Clinical Handbook of Psychological Disorders* (4th ed., pp. 1–64). New York: Guilford Press.

Crits-Christoph, P. & Mintz, J. (1991). Implications of therapist effects for the design and analysis of comparative studies of psychotherapy. *Journal of Consulting and Clinical Psychology, 59*, 20–26.

Damasio, A.R. (1994). *Descartes Error.* New York: Putnam.

Damasio, A.R. (2000). *The Feeling of What Happens.* Orlando, FL: Harcourt.

Darwin, C. (1872). *Expression of Emotions in Man and Animals* (3rd ed.). New York: Appleton.

Davanloo, H. (Ed.) (1978). *Basic Principles and Techniques in Short-Term Dynamic Psychotherapy.* Woodstock, GA: Spectrum Publishers.

Davanloo, H. (Ed.) (1980). *Short-Term Dynamic Psychotherapy.* New Jersey: Aronson.

Davanloo, H. (1990). *Unlocking the Unconscious.* New York: Wiley.

Davanloo, H. (1995). The technique of unlocking the unconscious in patients suffering from functional disorders: Part 1: Restructuring the ego's defenses. In H. Davanloo (Ed.) *Unlocking the Unconscious* (pp. 283–306). New York: Wiley.

Davanloo, H. (2000). *Intensive Short Term Dynamic Psychotherapy.* New York: Wiley.

Deci, E.L. & Ryan, R.M. (2012). Motivation, personality and development within embedded social contexts: An overview of self-determination theory. In R.M. Ryan (Ed.) *Oxford Handbook of Human Motivation* (pp. 85–107). Oxford: Oxford University Press.

Del Re, A.C., Fluckinger, C., Horvath, A.O., Symonds, D. & Wampold, B.E. (2012). Therapists effects in the therapeutic alliance-outcome relationship: A restricted-maximum likelihood meta-analysis. *Clinical Psychology Review, 32*, 642–649.

Della Selva, P.C. (1993). The significance of attachment theory for the practice of intensive short term dynamic psychotherapy. *International Journal of Short Term Psychotherapy, 8*, 189–206.

Della Selva, P.C. & Dusek, J.B. (1984). Sex role orientation and resolution of Eriksonian crises during the late adolescent years. *Journal of Personality and Social Psychology, 47*, 204–212.

Della Selva, P.C. & Dusek, J.B. (1986). The relationship between identity development and self-esteem during the late adolescent years: Sex differences. *Journal of Adolescent Research, 1,* 251–265.

Diamond, D.M., Campbell, A.M., Park, C.R., Halonen, J. & Zoladz, P.R. (2007). The Temporal Dynamics Model of emotional memory processing: A synthesis of on the neurobiological basis of stress induced amnesia, flashbulb and traumatic memoires and the Yerkes-Dodson Law. *Neural Plasticity,* retrieved from http://downloads.hindawi.com/journals/npi/2007/060803.pdf.

Diener, M.J., Hilsenroth, M.J. & Weinberger, J. (2007). Therapist affect focus and patient outcome in psychodynamic psychotherapy: A meta-analysis. *American Journal of Psychiatry, 164,* 936–941.

Doidge, N. (2007). *The Brain that Changed Itself.* New York: Penguin.

Driessen, E., Cuijpers, P., de Matt, S., Abbass, A., deJonge, F. & Dekker, J. (2010). The efficacy of short-term psychodynamic psychotherapy for depression: A meta-analysis. *Clinical Psychology Review, 30,* 25–36.

Duncan, B. (2010). *On Becoming a Better Therapist.* Washington, DC: APA Press.

Dunning, D. & Kruger, J. (1999). Unskilled and unaware: How difficulties in recognizing one's own incompetence lead to inflated self assessments. *Journal of Personality and Social Psychology, 77,* 1121–1134.

Dweck, C. (2007). *Mindset: The New Psychology of Success.* New York: Ballentine.

Ecker, B. (2015). Psychotherapy's mysterious efficacy ceiling: Is memory re-consolidation the breakthrough? *The Neuropsychotherapist, 16,* 7–26.

Ecker, B., Ticic, R. & Hulley, L. (2012). *Unlocking the Emotional Brain: Eliminating Symptoms at Their Roots Using Memory Reconsolidation.* New York: Routledge.

Edwards, V.J., Holden, G.W., Felitti, V.J. & Andra, R.F. (2003). Relationship between multiple forms of childhood maltreatment and adult mental health in community respondents. *American Journal of Psychiatry, 160,* 1453–1460.

Eich, E. (1995). Searching for mood dependent memory. *Psychological Science, 6,* 67–75.

Ekman, P. (1999). Basic emotions. In T. Dalgleish & M. Power (Eds.) *Handbook of Cognition and Emotion* (pp. 301–320). Sussex, UK: Wiley & Sons.

Ekman, P. (2007). *Emotions Revealed* (2nd ed.). New York: Holt Paperback.

Ekman, P. & Davidson, R.J. (1994). *The Nature of Emotion: Fundamental Questions.* New York: Oxford University Press.

Ekman, P. & Friesen, W.V. (1975). *Unmasking the Face.* New Jersey: Prentice-Hall.

Elkin, I. (1995). Further differentiation of common factors. *Clinical Psychology: Science and Practice, V2N1,* 75–78.

Elkin, I. (1999). A major dilemma in psychotherapy outcome research: Disentangling therapists from therapies. *Clinical Psychology: Science and Practice, 6,* 10–31.

Falkenstrom, R., Granstrom, F. & Homquist, R. (2013). Therapeutic alliance predicts symptomatic improvement session by session. *Journal of Counseling Psychology, 60,* 317–328.

Farber, E.W. (2009). Prioritizing case formulation in psychotherapy training. *The Psychotherapy Bulletin, 44,* 21–24.

Farchione, T.J., Fairholme, C.P., Ellard, K.K., Boisseau, C.L., & Barlow, D.H. (2012). Unified protocol for transdiagnostic treatment of emotional disorders: A randomized clinical trial. *Behavior Therapy, 43,* 666–678.

Felitti, V.J., Anda, R.T., Williamson, D.F., Nordenberg, D., Edwards, V., Spitz, N.D., Koss, M.P. & Marks, J.P. (1998). Relationship of childhood abuse and household dysfunction and many of the leading causes of death in adults. *American Journal of Preventive Medicine, 14,* 245–258.

Ferenzi, S. & Rank, O. (1925). *The Development of Psychoanalysis.* Washington, DC: Nervous and Mental Disease Publishing.

Firestone, R.W. & Catlett, J. (1999). *Fear of Intimacy.* Washington, DC: American Psychological Association.

Fisher, S. & Greenberg, R.P. (1977). *The Scientific Credibility of Freud's Theory and Therapy.* New York: Basic Books.

Flannery, R.B. & Perry, J.C. (1990). Self-rated defense style, life stress, and healthy status. *Psychosomatics, 31,* 313–320.

Foley, G.N. & Gentile, J.G. (2010). Nonverbal communication in psychotherapy. *Psychiatry, 7,* 38–44.

Fonagy, P., Gergely, G., Jurist, E. & Target, M. (2005). *Affect Regulation, Mentalization and the Development of Self.* New York: Other Press.

Foreman, S.A. & Marmar, C.R. (1985). Therapist actions that address initially poor therapeutic alliances in psychotherapy. *American Journal of Psychiatry, 142(8),* 922–926.

Fosha, D. (2000). *The Transforming Power of Affect.* New York: Basic Books.

Fosha, D. (2002). Trauma reveals the roots of resilience. *Constructivism in the Human Sciences, 6,* 7–15.

Fosha, D. (2007). Transformance, recognition of self by self, and effective action. In K.L. Schneider (Ed.) *Existential-Integrative Psychotherapy: Guideposts to the Core of Practice* (pp. 290–320). New York: Routledge.

Fosha, D., Siegel, D.J. & Solomon, M.F. (Eds.) (2009). *The Healing Power of Emotions: Affective Neuroscience, Development and Clinical Practice.* New York: Norton.

Frederickson, B. (2001). The role of positive emotions in positive psychology: The broaden-and-build theory of positive emotion. *American Psychologist, 56,* 218–226.

Frederickson, J. (2013). *Co-Creating Change.* Kansas City, MO: Seven Leaves Press.

Freemont, S.K. & Anderson, W. (1988). Investigation of factors involved in therapists' annoyance with clients. *Professional Psychology: Research and Practice, 19,* 330–335.

Freud, A. (1979). *The Ego and the Mechanisms of Defense.* (Revised ed.) New York: International Universities Press.

Freud, S. (1894/1962). The neuro-psychoses of defense. *The Complete Psychological Works of Sigmund Freud* (Vol. 3, pp. 43–61). London: Hogarth Press. (Original work published 1894).

Freud, S. (1914/1962). Remembering, repeating and working through. *The Complete Psychological Works of Sigmund Freud* (Vol. 12, pp. 145–157). London: Hogarth Press. (Original work published 1914).

Freud, S. (1915/1933). *Introductory Lectures.* New York: Norton.

Freud, S. (1926/1959). *Inhibitions, Symptoms and Anxiety.* New York: Norton.

Fromm-Reichman, F. (1950). *Principles of Intensive Psychotherapy.* Chicago, IL: University of Chicago Press.

Garfield, S.L. (1997). The therapist as a neglected variable in psychotherapy research. *Clinical Psychology: Science & Practice, 4,* 40–43.

Gawande, A. (2004, December 6). The bell curve. *The New Yorker,* pp. 82–91.

Gawande, A. (2011, October 3). Personal best. *The New Yorker,* pp. 44–53.

Goldfried, M.R., Raue, P.H. & Castonguay, L.G. (1998). The therapeutic focus in significant sessions of master therapists. *Journal of Consulting and Clinical Psychology, 66,* 803–810.

Goleman, D. (1995). *Emotional Intelligence.* New York: Bantam.

Goleman, D. (2007). *Social Intelligence: The New Science of Human Behavior.* New York: Bantam.

Grawe, K. (2007). *Neuropsychotheapy.* New York: Taylor & Francis Group.

Greenberg, L.S. (2002). *Emotion-Focused Therapy: Coaching Clients to Work through Their Feelings.* Washington, DC: American Psychological Association.

Greenberg, L.S. (2008). Emotion and cognition in psychotherapy: The transforming power of affect. *Canadian Psychology, 49,* 49–59.

Greenson, R. (1967). *The Technique and Practice of Psychoanalysis.* New York: International University Press.

Gross, J.J. (1998). The emerging field of emotional regulation: An integrative view. *Review of General Psychology, 2,* 271–299.

Haggerty, G. & Hilsenroth, M. (2011). The use of video in psychotherapy supervision. *British Journal of Psychotherapy, 27,* 193–210.

Harnett, P., O'Donovan, A. & Lambert, M. (2010). The dose response relationship in psychotherapy: Implications for social policy. *Clinical Psychologist, 14,* 39–44.

Hartman, K. & Levenson, H. (1995, June). Case Formulation in TLDP. *Presentation at the Annual Meeting of the Society for Psychotherapy Research.* Vancouver, Canada.

Hersoug, A.G., Sexton, H.C. & Hoglend, P. (2002). Contribution of defense functioning to the quality of the working alliance and psychotherapy outcome. *American Journal of Psychotherapy, 56,* 539–554.

Hess, S.A., Knox, S., Schultz, J.M., Hill, C.E., Sloan, L., Brandt, S., Kelly, F. & Hoffman, M.A. (2008). Pre-doctoral interns' non-disclosure in supervision. *Psychotherapy Research, 18,* 400–411.

Hibbard, S. & Porcerelli, J. (1998). Further validation for the Cramer Defense Mechanism Manual. *Journal of Personality Assessment, 70,* 460–483.

Hill, C.E. (2004). Immediacy. In C.E. Hill (Ed.) *Helping Skills: Facilitating Exploration, Insight and Action* (2nd ed., p. 285). Washington, DC: American Psychological Association.

Hill, C.E., Wonjin, S., Spangler, P., Stahl, J. & Sullivan, C. (2008). Therapist immediacy in brief psychotherapy. *Psychotherapy: Theory, Research, Practice, Training, 45,* 298–315.

Hillsenroth, M. & Cromer, T. (2007). Clinical intervention related to alliance during the initial intervention and psychological assessment. *Psychotherapy, 44,* 205–218.

Ho, B., Andreasen, N.C. & Magnotta, V. (2012). Long-term antipsychotic treatment and brain volumes. *Archives of General Psychiatry, 68,* 128–137.

Hockenbury, D.H. & Hockenbury, S.E. (2007). *Discovering Psychology*. New York: Worth.

Hofmann, S. & Weinberger, J. (2006). *Art and Science of Psychotherapy*. New York: Routledge.

Hogelend, P., Arnlo, S., Marble, A., Bogwalkd, K., Sorbye, O., Sjaastad, M.D. & Heyerdah, I. (2006). Analysis of patient therapist relationship in dynamic psychotherapy: An exploratory study of transference interpretations. *American Journal of Psychiatry, 163*, 1739–1746.

Hoglend, P. (1999). New findings and implications for training and practice. *Journal of Psychotherapy: Practice and Research, 8*, 257–263.

Hollon, S.D., DeRubeis, R.J. & Evans, M.D. (1992). Cognitive therapy and pharmacotherapy for depression: Singly and in combination. *Archives of General Psychiatry, 49*, 774–781.

Hollon, S.D., DeRubeis, R.J., Fawcett, J., Amsterdam, J.D., Shelton, R.C., Zajecks, J., Young, P.R. & Gallop, R. (2014). Effect of cognitive therapy with antidepressant medications vs antidepressants alone on the rate of recovery in major depressive disorder: A randomized clinical trial. *JAMA Psychiatry, 71*, 1157–1164.

Holmquist, R., Strom, P. & Foldemo, A. (2014). The effects of psychological treatment in primary care in Sweden. *Nordic Journal of Psychiatry, 68*, 204–212.

Horvath, A.O., Del Re, A.C., Fluckiger, C. & Symmonds, D. (2011). The alliance in adult psychotherapy. In J.C. Norcross (Ed.) *Psychotherapy Relationships that Work* (2nd ed., pp. 25–69). New York: Oxford University Press.

Horvath, A.O. & Greenberg, L.S. (1994). *The Working Alliance*. New York: Wiley.

Horvath, A.O. & Symonds, B.D. (1991). Relationship between working alliance and outcome in psychotherapy. *Journal of Counseling Psychology, 38*, 139–149.

Hsu, M.C., Schubiner, H., Lumley, M.A., Stracks, J.S., Clauw, D.J. & Williams, D.A. (2010). Sustained pain reduction through affective self-awareness in fibromyalgia: A randomized controlled trial. *Journal of General Internal Medicine, 25*, 1064–1070.

Hubble, M.A., Duncan, B.L. & Miller, S.D. (1999). *The Heart and Soul of Change*. Washington, DC: American Psychological Association.

Imel, Z.Z.E. (2007). Untangling the alliance-outcome relationship. *Journal of Consulting and Clinical Psychology, 75*, 842–852.

Insel, T. (2013, April 29). Director's Blog: Transforming Diagnosis. National Institute of Mental Health. http://nimh.nih.gov/about/director/2013/trasnforming-diagnosis.shtml.

Ivey, G. (2006). A method of teaching psychodynamic case formulation. *Psychotherapy, 43*, 322–336.

Josephs, L., Sanders, A. & Gorman, B.S. (2014). Therapeutic interaction with an older personality disordered patient. *Psychodynamic Psychotherapy, 42*, 151–172.

Kalpin, A. (1994). Effective use of Davanloo's "head on collision". *International Journal of Short-Term Dynamic Psychotherapy, 9*, 19–36.

Karlsson, H. (2011, August 11). How psychotherapy changes the brain. *Psychiatric Times, 28*(8), retrieved from http://nwmedicalhypnosis.com/documents/How%20Psychotherapy%20Changes%20the%20Brain.

Karlsson, H., Hirvonen, J., Kajander, J., Markkula, J., Rasi-Hakala, H., Salminen, J.K., Nagre, K., Aalto, S. & Hietala, J. (2010). Research letter: Psychotherapy increases brain serotonin S-HTIA receptors in patients with major depressive disorder. *Psychological Medicine, 40*, 523–528.

Kasper, L.B., Hill, E.C. & Klvlighan, D. (2008). Therapist immediacy in brief psychotherapy: Case study 1. *Psychotherapy: Theory, Research, Practice and Training, 45*, 281–297.

Katzman, J. & Coughlin, P. (2013). The role of therapist activity in psychodynamic psychotherapy. *Psychodynamic Psychiatry, 41*, 75–90.

Kendjelic, E.M. & Eells, T.D. (2007). Generic psychotherapy case formulation improves formulations and reality. *Psychotherapy: Practice, Theory and Research, 44*, 66–77.

Kennedy-Moore, E. & Watson, J.C. (1999). *Expressing Emotion: Myths, Realities and Therapeutic Strategies*. New York: Guilford Press.

Kernberg, O., Brunstein, E.D., Coyne, L., Appelbaum, A., Horowitz, L. & Voth, H. (1972). *Psychotherapy and Psychoanalysis*. Topeka, KS: Menninger Foundation.

Kirsch, I. (2008). Challenging received wisdom: Antidepressants and the Placebo effect. *McGill Journal of Medicine, 11*, 219–222.

Kirsch, I. & Sapirstein, G. (1998, June 26). Listening to Prozac but hearing placebo: A meta-analysis of antidepressant medication. *Prevention and Treatment*, Article 002a.

Kirtner, W. & Cartwright, D. (1958). Success and failure in client-centered therapy as a function of initial in-therapy behavior. *Journal of Consulting Psychology, 22*, 329–333.

Klein, C, Milrod, B.L., Busch, F.N., Levy, K.N. & Shapiro, T. (2003). A preliminary study of clinical process in relation to outcome in psychodynamic psychotherapy for panic disorder. *Psychoanalytic Inquiry, 23*, 308–331.

Klein, D.N., Schwartz, J.E., Santiago, N.J., Vivian, D., Vocisano, C., Castonguay, L.G., Arnow, B., Blalock, J.A., Manber, R., Markowitz, J.C., Riso, L.P., Rothbaum, B., McCullough, J.P., Thase, M.E., Borian, F.E., Miller, I.W. & Keller, M.B. (2003). Therapeutic alliance in depression treatment: Controlling for prior change and patient characteristics. *Journal of Consulting and Clinical Psychology*, *71*, 997–1006.

Klerman, G.L., Dimascio, A., Weissman, M., Prusoff, B. & Paykel, E.S. (1974). Treatment of depression by drugs and psychotherapy. *American Journal of Psychiatry*, *131*, 186–191.

Koelen, J.A., Houtveen, J.H., Abbass, A., Luyten, P., Eurelings-Bontekoe, E.H., Van Broeckhuysen-Kloth, S.A., Buhring, M.E. & Geenen, R. (2014). Effectiveness of psychotherapy for severe somatoform disorder: Meta-analysis. *British Journal of Psychiatry*, *204*, 12–19.

Kring, A.M. & Sloan, D.M. (2010). *Emotion Regulation and Psychopathology*. New York: Guilford Press.

Kwon, P. (2000). Hope and dysphoria: The moderating role of defense mechanisms. *Journal of Personality*, *68*, 199–223.

Kwon, P. (2002). Hope, defense mechanisms and adjustment: Implications for false hope and defensive happiness. *Journal of Personality*, *70*, 207–231.

Laaksonen, M.A., Sirkia, C., Knekt, P. & Lindfors, O. (2014). Self reported immature defensive style as a predictor of outcome in short-term and long term psychotherapy. *Brain and Behavior*, *4*, 495–503.

Ladany, N. & Bradley, L.T. (Eds.) (2010) *Counselor Supervision* (4th ed.). New York: Routledge.

Lam, D.C.K., Salkovskis, P.M. & Hogg, L.I. (2015). 'Judging a book by its cover': An experimental study of the negative impact of a diagnosis of borderline personality disorder on clinician's judgment of uncomplicated panic disorder. *British Journal of Clinical Psychology*, published online July 25. DOI: 10.1111/bjc 12093.

Lambert, M.J. & Ogles, B.M. (2004). The efficacy and effectiveness of psychotherapy. In M.J. Lambert (Ed.) *Bergin and Garfield's Handbook of Psychotherapy and Behavior Change* (5th ed., pp. 139–153). New York: Wiley.

Langer, E. (2014). *Mindfulness: 25th Anniversary Edition*. Mahwah, NJ: Merloyd Lawrence Books.

Le Doux, J. (1998). *The Emotional Brain: The Mysterious Underpinnings of Emotional Life*. New York: Simon and Schuster.

Lehto, S.M., Tolmunen, T. & Joesnsuu, M. (2008). Changes in midbrain serotonin transporter availability in atypical depressed patients after one year of psychotherapy. *Progressive Neuropsychopharmalogical Biological Psychiatry*, *32*, 229–237.

Lillengren, P. (2014). *Exploring Therapist Action In Psychoanalytic Psychotherapy: Attachment to Therapist and Change*. Stockholm, Sweden: Stockholm University.

Lindemann, E. (1979). *Beyond Grief*. Northvale, NJ: Aronson.

Llewelyn, S.P. (1988). Psychological therapy as viewed by clients and therapists. *British Journal of Clinical Psychology*, *27*, 223–227.

Lowenstein, G. & Lerner, J.S. (2003). The role of affect in decision making. In R.J. Davidson & H.H. Goldsmith (Eds.) *Handbook of Affective Sciences* (pp. 619–642). New York: Oxford University Press.

Luborsky, L., McLellan, A.T., Diguer, L., Woody, G. & Seligman, D.A. (1997). The psychotherapist matters: Comparison of outcomes across twenty-two therapists and seven patient samples. *Clinical Psychology: Science and Practice*, *4*, 53–65.

Luborsky, L., McLellan, A.T., Woody, G.E., O'Brien, C.P. & Auerbach, A. (1985). Therapist success and its determinants. *Archives of General Psychiatry*, *42*, 602–611.

Lupien, S.J., Maheu, F., Tu, M., Fiocco, A.l. & Schranck, T.E. (2007). The effects of stress and stress hormones on human cognition: Implications for the field of brain and cognition. *Brain and Cognition*, *65*, 209–237.

Main, M. (1995). Attachment: Overview with implications for clinical work. In S. Goldberg, R. Muir & J. Kerr (Eds.) *Attachment Theory* (pp. 407–474). Hillsdale, NJ: Analytic Press.

Malan, D. (1963). *A Study of Brief Psychotherapy*. London: Tavistock Publications.

Malan, D. (1976). *The Frontiers of Brief Psychotherapy*. New York: Springer.

Malan, D. (1979). *Individual Psychotherapy and the Science of Psychodynamics*. London: Butterworth.

Malan, D. (1980). The most important development since the discovery of the unconscious. In H. Davanloo (Ed.) *Short Term Dynamic Psychotherapy* (pp. 13–24). Northvale, NJ: Aronson.

Malan, D. & Coughlin Della Selva, P. (2007). *Lives Transformed*. London: Karnac.

Malarkey, W.R. (2001). Behavior: The endocrine-immune interface and health outcomes. In T. Treorell (Ed.) *Everyday Biological Stress Mechanisms, Vol. 22* (pp. 104–115). Basel: Karger.

Markowitz, J.C. & Milrod, B. (2011). The importance of responding to negative affect in psychotherapies. *American Journal of Psychiatry*, *168*, 124–128.

Marks, I., Boulougouris, J. & Marset, P. (1971). Flooding versus desensitization in the treatment of phobic patients: A cross over study. *British Journal of Psychiatry*, 119, 353–375.

Martin, D.J., Garske, J.P. & Davis, K. (2000). Relation of the therapeutic alliance with outcome and other variables. A meta-analysis and review. *Journal of Consulting and Clinical Psychology*, 68, 438–450.

Mate, G. (2003). *When the Body Says No*. Hoboken, NJ: John Wiley & Sons.

Mayer, J.D. & Salovey, P. (1995). Emotional intelligence and the construction and regulation of feelings. *Applied and Preventive Psychology*, 4, 197–208.

McCarthy, K.S., Keefe, J.R. & Barber, J.P. (2015). Goldilocks on the couch: Moderate levels of psychodynamic and process-experiential technique predicts outcome in psychodynamic psychotherapy. *Psychotherapy Research*, 3, 1–11.

McConkie Erickson, D. (2013). Scheduled Healing: The Relationship between Session Frequency with Psychotherapy Outcome in a Naturalistic Setting. Scholarshiparchives@byu.edu.

McCullough Vaillant, L. (1997). *Changing Character*. New York: Basic Books.

McKay, K.M., Imel, Z.G. & Wampold, B.E. (2006). Psychiatrist effects in the psychopharmalogical treatment of depression. *Journal of Affective Disorders*, 92, 287–290.

McWilliams, N. (2004). *Psychoanalytic Psychotherapy: A Practitioners Guide*. New York: Guilford Press.

McWilliams, N. (2011). *Psychoanalytic Diagnosis: Understanding Personality Structure in the Clinical Process* (2nd ed.). New York: Guilford.

Meisser, W.W. (2006). The therapeutic alliance: A proteus in disguise. *Psychotherapy*, 43, 264–270.

Menninger, K.A. (1958). *Theory of Psychoanalytic Technique*. New York: Basic Books.

Miller, S.D. & Hubble, M. (2011). The road to mastery. *Psychotherapy Networker*, 32, 22–60.

Miller, S.D., Hubble, M. & Duncan, B.L. (2007). Supershrinks. *Psychotherapy Networker*, 31, 26–35.

Miller, S.D., Wampold, B.E., Hubble, M.A. & Duncan, B.L. (2010). *The Heart and Soul of Change* (2nd ed.). Washington, DC: American Psychological Association.

Mohr, D.C. (1995). Negative outcome in psychotherapy: A critical review. *Clinical Psychology*, 2, 1–27.

Moran, T.P., Taylor, D., & Moser, J.S. (2012). Sex moderates relationship between worry and performance monitoring brain activity in undergraduates. *International Journal of Psychophysiology*, 85, 188–194.

Mosher, J.S., Baker, M.W. & Moran, T.P. (2012). Enhanced attentional capture in trait anxiety. *Emotion*, 12, 213–216.

Muris, P. & Merckelbach, H. (1996). The short version of the defense style questionnaire: Factor structure and psychopathological correlates. *Personality and Individual Differences*, 20, 123–126.

Nadar, K. (2003). Memory traces abound. *Trends in Neuroscience*, 26, 65–72.

Nadar, K. & Einarsson, E.O. (2010). Memory reconsolidation: An update. *Annals of the New York Academy of Science*, 1191, 27–41.

Neisser, J.M. (2006). Unconscious subjectivity. *Psyche*, 12(3), retrieved from http://psyche.cs.monash.edu.au/.

Nezu, A.M. & Nezu, C.M. (2005). Comments on "evidence-based behavior medicine: What is it and how do we achieve it?" The interventionist does not equal the intervention—the role of therapist competence. *Annals of Behavior Medicine*, 29, 80.

Norcross, J.C. (2002). *Psychotherapy Relationship that Work: Therapist Contributions and Responsiveness to Patients*. New York: Oxford Universities Press.

Norcross, J.C. & Orlinksy, D.E. (Eds.) (2005). *The Psychotherapist's Own Psychotherapy: Patient and Clinician Perspectives*. New York: Oxford University Press.

Nummenmaa, L., Glerean, E., Hari, R. & Hietanen, J.K. (2013). Bodily maps of emotions. *Proceedings of the National Academy of Science*, 111, 646–651.

Nyman, S.J., Nafzinger, M.A. & Smith, T.B. (2011). Client outcomes across counselor training level with a multi-tiered supervision model. *Journal of Counseling and Development*, 88, 204–209.

Ogden, P., Pain, C., Minton, K. & Fisher, J. (2005). Including the body in mainstream psychotherapy for the traumatized individual. *Psychologist-Psychoanalyst*, XXV(4), 19–24.

Orlinsky, D.E. & Ronnestad, M.H. (2005). *How Psychotherapists Develop*. Washington, DC: American Psychological Association.

Patten, S.B. (2004). The impact of antidepressant treatment on population healthy: Synthesis of data from 2 national data sources in Canada. *Population Health Metrics*, 2(9). DOI: 10.1186/1478-7954-2-9.

Pebbles-Kleiger, M.J. (2002). *Beginnings: The Art and Science of Planning Psychotherapy*. Hillsdale, NJ: Analytic Press.

Pennebaker, J. (1990). *Opening Up: The Healing Power of Confiding in Others.* New York: William Morrow & Co.

Pennebaker, J. (1997). *Opening Up: The Healing Power of Expressing Emotions.* New York: Guilford Press.

Peterson, C. (2006). *A Primer of Positive Psychology.* New York: Oxford University Press.

Pink, D.H. (2009). *Drive: The Surprising Truth about What Motivates Us.* New York: Riverhead Press.

Piper, W.E., Ogrodniczuk, J.S., Joyce, A.S., McCallum, M., Rosie, J.S., O'Kelly, J.G. & Steinberg, P.I. (1999). Prediction of dropping out in time-limited interpretive individual psychotherapy. *Psychotherapy, 36,* 114–122.

Pitman, S., Slavin-Mulford, J. & Hilsenroth, M. (2014). Psychodynamic techniques related to outcome for anxiety disorder patients at different points in the therapy. *Journal of Nervous and Mental Disorders, 202,* 391–396.

Polaschek, D.L. & Ross, E.C. (2010). Do early therapeutic alliance, motivation, and stages of change predict therapy change for high risk, psychopathic violent prisoners? *Criminal Behavior and Mental Health, 20,* 100–111.

Porras, J., Emery, S. & Thompson, M. (2007). *Success Built to Last: Creating a Life That Matters.* Upper Saddle River, NJ: Wharton School Publishing.

Przybyslawski, J. & Sara, S.J. (1997). Reconsolidation of memory after it's re-activation. *Behavior and Brain Research, 84,* 241–246.

Raio, C., Oredery, T.A., Palazzolo, L., Schurick, A.A. & Phelps, E.A. (2013, August 26). Cognitive emotional regulation fails the stress test. *Proceeding of the National Academy of Sciences, 110,* 15139–15144.

Reandeau, S.G. & Wampold, B.E. (1991). Relationship of power and involvement to working alliance: A multiple case sequential analysis of brief therapy. *Journal of Counseling Psychology, 38,* 107–114.

Redfield Jamison, K. (2005). *Exuberance: The Passion for Life.* New York: Vintage.

Reich, W. (1972). *Character Analysis.* New York: Farrar, Straus & Giroux.

Reich, W. (1980). *Character Analysis.* (3rd ed.). New York: Farrar, Straus & Giroux.

Rendon, J. (2015). *Upside: The New Science of Post-Traumatic Growth.* New York: Touchstone/ Simon & Schuster.

Ricks, D.F. (1974). Supershrinks: Methods of a therapists judged successful on the basis of adult outcomes of adolescent patients. In D.F. Ricks, M. Roff & A. Thomas (Eds.) *Life History Research in Psychopathology* (pp. 288–308). Minneapolis, MN: University of Minnesota Press.

Rosenthal, R. (1990). How are we doing in soft psychology? *American Psychologist, 45,* 775–777.

Roth, S. (2000). *Psychotherapy: The Art of Wooing Nature.* Northvale, NJ: Aronson.

Ryan, R.M. (2007). Motivation and emotion: A new look and approach for two re-emerging fields. *Motivation and Emotion, 31,* 1–3.

Ryan, R.M. & Deci, E.L. (2000). Self determination theory and the facilitation of intrinsic motivation, social development and well being. *American Psychologist, 55,* 68–78.

Sachs, J.S. (1983). Negative factors in brief psychotherapy: An empirical assessment. *Journal of Consulting and Clinical Psychology, 51,* 557–564.

Sapyta, J., Riener, M. & Bickman, L. (2005). Feedback to clinicians: Theory, research and practice. *Journal of Clinical Psychology: In Session, 61,* 145–153.

Sarno, J.E. (1999). *Mind Over Back Pain.* New York: Penguin Putnam.

Sarno, J.E. (2006). *The Divided Mind: The Epidemic of Mind-Body Disorders.* New York: HarperCollins.

Saxon, D. & Barkham, M. (2012). Patterns of therapist variability: Therapist effects and the contribution of patient severity and risk. *Journal of Consulting and Clinical Psychology, 80,* 535–546.

Schiller, D., Monfils, M.R., Raio, C.M., Johnson, D.C., Ledoux, J.E., Phelps, E.A. (2010). Preventing the return of fear in humans using reconsolidation update mechanisms. *Nature, 463,* 49–53.

Schimel, J., Greenberg, J. & Martens, A. (2003). Evidence that projection of a feared trait can serve a defensive function. *Personality and Social Psychology Bulletin, 29,* 969–979.

Schnarch, D. (2009). *Intimacy and Desire.* New York: Beaufort Books.

Schore, A.N. (2001). The effects of early relational trauma on right brain development, affect regulation, and infant mental health. *Infant Mental Health Journal, 22,* 201–269.

Schore, A.N. (2003). *Affect Regulation and Repair of the Self.* New York: Norton.

Schore, A.N. (2012). *The Science of the Art of Psychotherapy.* New York: Norton.

Schubiner, H. (2011). *Unlearn Your Pain.* Pleasant Ridge, MI: Mind Body Publishing.

Schubiner, H. & Betzhold, M. (2012). *Unlearn Your Pain.* Pleasant Ridge, MI: Mind Body Publishing.

Sennett, R. (2008). *Craftsman*. New Haven, CT: Yale University Press.

Sexton, H., Littauer, H., Sexton, A. & Tommeras, E. (2005). Building the alliance: Early therapeutic process and the client-therapist connection. *Psychotherapy Research, 5*, 103–116.

Seyle, H. (1978). *The Stress of Life* (revised ed.). New York: McGraw-Hill.

Shedler, J. (2010). The efficacy of psychodynamic psychotherapy. *American Psychologist, 65*, 98–109.

Shedler, J. (2014). A D/R conversation with Jonathan Shedler. *Division Review: A Quarterly Psycho-analytic Forum, 10*, 30–33.

Shedler, J., Karliner, R. & Katz, E. (2003). Cloning the clinician: A method for assessing illusory mental health. *Journal of Clinical Psychology, 59*, 635–650.

Shedler, J., Magman, M. & Manis, M. (1993). The illusion of mental health. *American Psychologist, 48*, 1117–1131.

Sherer, R. & Rogers, R.W. (1980). Effects of therapists nonverbal communication on rated skill and effectiveness. *Journal of Clinical Psychology, 36*, 696–700.

Shore, A. (2007). Psychoanalytic research: Progress and process: Developmental affective neurosci-ence and clinical practice. *Psychologist and Psychoanalyst, 27*(3), 6–15.

Siegel, D.J. (2001). *The Developing Mind: How Relationships and the Brain Interact to Shape Who We Are*. New York: Guilford Press.

Siegel, D.J. (2009a). Emotion as integration. In D. Fosha, D.J. Siegel & M.F. Solomon (Eds.) *The Healing Power of Emotion* (pp. 145–171). New York: Norton.

Siegel, D.J. (2009b). Right brain affect regulation. In D. Fosha, D.J. Siegel & M.F. Solomon (Eds.) *The Healing Power of Emotion* (pp. 112–144). New York: Norton.

Siegel, D.J. (2010). *The Mindful Therapist*. New York: Norton.

Silberschatz, G. & Curtis, J.T. (1993). Measuring the therapist's impact on the patient's therapeutic process. *Journal of Consulting and Clinical Psychology, 61*, 403–411.

Sinek, S. (2011). *Start with Why*. New York: Portfolio/Penguin.

Smith, M.L., Glass, G.V. & Miller, T.I. (1980). *The Benefits of Psychotherapy*. Baltimore, MD: The Johns Hopkins University Press.

Snowe, O. (2013). *Fighting for Common Ground*. New York: Weinstein Books.

Solbaken, O.A. & Abbass, A. (2013). Effective care of treatment resistant patients in an ISTDP-Based in-patient treatment program. *Psychiatric Annals, 43*, 516–522.

Soldz, S. & McCullough, L. (Eds.) (2000). *Reconciling Empirical Knowledge and Clinical Experience: The Art and Science of Psychotherapy*. Washington, DC: American Psychological Association.

Steinart, C., Hofmann, M., Kruse, J. & Lechsenring, F. (2014). Relapse rates after psychotherapy for depression: Stable long-term effects? A meta-analysis. *Journal of Affective Disorders, 168*, 107–118.

Strauss, J.S. & Harden, D.W. (1981). The Case Record Rating Scale: A method for rating symptom and social function data from case records. *Psychiatric Research, 4*, 333–345.

Strunk, D.R., Brotman, M.A. & DeRubeis, R.J. (2010). The process of change in CBT for depression: Predictors of early inter-session symptom gains. *Behavior Research and Therapy, 48*, 599–606.

Strupp, H.H. (1995). The psychotherapist's skill revisited. *Clinical Psychology: Science and Practice, V2N1*, 70–74.

Strupp, H.H. & Binder, J. (1984). *Psychotherapy in a New Key*. New York: Basic Books.

Summer, F. (2013). Psychoanalysis in the Age of Nikeism. *Presented Address: Spring Meeting of Divi-sion of Psychoanalysis*, April 13, Boston, MA.

Sutie, I.D. (1999). *Origins of Love and Hate*. New York: Routledge.

Svartsberg, M. & Stiles, T.C. (1991). Comparative effects of short term dynamic psychotherapy: A meta-analysis. *Journal of Consulting and Clinical Psychology, 59*, 704–714.

Svartsberg, M., Stiles, T.C. & Seltzer, M.H. (2004). Randomized, controlled trial of the effectiveness of short-term psychodynamic psychotherapy and cognitive therapy for cluster C personality disorders. *American Journal of Psychiatry, 161*, 810–817.

Tang, P. (2002). *The Effect of Exposure to Erotic Images on Defense Mechanisms*. Unpublished Doc-toral Dissertation, Pacific Graduate School of Psychology, Palo Alto, CA.

Tang, T.Z. & DeRubeis, R.J. (1999). Sudden gains and critical sessions in cognitive-behavioral ther-apy for depression. *Journal of Consulting and Clinical Psychology, 67*, 894–904.

Tatkin, S. (2012). *Wired for Love*. Oakland, CA: New Harbinger Publishing, Inc.

ten Have-de Labije, J. & Neborsky, R.J. (2012). *Mastering Intensive Short Term Dynamic Psycho-therapy: A Roadmap to the Unconscious*. London: Karnac.

Thomas, S.P., Groer, M., David, M., Droppleman, P., Mozingo, J. & Pierce, M. (2000). Anger and cancer: An analysis of the linkages. *Cancer Nursing, 23*(5), 344–349.

Timulack, L. (2010). Significant events in psychotherapy: An update on research findings. *Psychol-ogy and Psychotherapy: Theory, Research and Practice, 83*, 421–447.

Town, J.M., Abbass, A.A. & Hardy, G. (2011). Short-term psychodynamic psychotherapy for personality disorders: A critical review of randomized controlled trials. *Journal of Personality Disorders, 25*, 723–740.

Town, J.M., Hardy, G.E., McCullough, L. & Stride, C. (2012). Patient affect experiencing following therapist interventions in short-term dynamic psychotherapy. *Psychotherapy Research, 22*(2), 208–219.

Tracey, T.J.G., Wampold, B.E., Lichtenberg, J.W. & Goodyear, R.K. (2014). Expertise in psychotherapy: An elusive goal? *American Psychologist, 69*, 218–229.

Tyron, G.S. & Winograd, G. (2011). Goal consensus and collaboration. *Psychotherapy: Theory, Research, Practice, Training, 48*, 50–57.

Vacisano, C., Klein, D.N., Arno, R.T., Ivara, C., Blalok, J.A., Rothbain, B., Vivian, D., Markowitz, J.C., Kocsis, J.H., Manber, R., Catonguay, L., Rush, A., Borian, R.D., McCullough, J.P., Kornstein, S.G., Riso, L.P. & Thase, M.P. (2004). Therapist variables that predict symptom change in psychotherapy with chronically depressed outpatients. *Psychotherapy: Theory, Research, Practice and Training, 41*(3), 255–265.

Vaillant, G. (1993). *The Wisdom of the Ego*. Cambridge, MA: Harvard University Press.

Vaillant, G. (1998). *Adaptation to Life*. Cambridge, MA: Harvard University Press.

Vaillant, G. (2015). *Triumphs of Experience*. New York: Belknap Press.

Wachtel, P.L. (1993). *Therapeutic Communication: What to Say When*. New York: Guilford Press.

Wachtel, P.L. (1997). *Psychoanalysis, Behavior Therapy and the Relational World*. Washington, DC: American Psychological Association.

Wampold, B.E. (2001). *The Great Psychotherapy Debate*. Mahwah, NJ: Lawrence Erlbaum Associates.

Wampold, B.E. (2007). *Qualities and Actions of Effective Therapists*. Systems of Psychotherapy Video Series #43108888. American Psychological Association: Continuing Education/Education Directorate.

Wampold, B.E. (2010). Introduction. In M.A. Hubble, B.L. Duncan, S.D. Miller & B.E. Wampold. *The Heart and Soul of Change: Delivering What Works in Therapy* (2nd ed.) (pp. 23–46). Washington, DC: American Psychological Association.

Wampold, B.E. (2011). *Qualities and Actions of Effective Psychotherapists*. Video Series I. Systems of Psychotherapy. Washington, DC: American Psychological Associates.

Wampold, B.E. (2013). *The Great Psychotherapy Debate* (revised ed.). New York: Routledge.

Wampold, B.E. (2015). How important are the common factors in psychotherapy: An update. *World Psychiatry, 14*, 27–77.

Wampold, B.E. & Brown, G.S. (2005). Estimating variability in outcomes attributable to therapists: A naturalistic study of outcomes in managed care. *Journal of Consulting and Clinical Psychology, 73*, 914–923.

Wampold, B.E. & Budge, S.L. (2012). The 2011 Leona Tyler Award address: The relationship—and it's relationship the common and specific factors of psychotherapy. *The Counseling Psychologist, 40*, 601–623.

Wang, P.S., Lane, M., Olfson, M., Pincus, H.A., Wells, K.B. & Kessler, R. (2005). Twelve month use of mental health services in the US: Results from the national comorbidity survey replication. *Archives of General Psychiatry, 62*, 629–648.

Webb, C.A., DeRubeis, R.J. & Barber, J.P. (2010). Therapist adherence, competence, and treatment outcome: A meta-analytic review. *Journal of Consulting and Clinical Psychology, 78*, 200–211.

Weinberger, J. (1995). Common factors are not so common: The common factors dilemma. *Clinical Psychology, 1*, 45–60.

Weingartner, H., Miller, H. & Murphy, D.L. (1977). Mood-state-dependent retrieval of verbal associations. *Journal of Abnormal Psychology, 86*, 276–284.

Weinstein, J., Tosteson, T.D., Lurie, J.D., Tosteson, A.N., Hanscom, B., Skinner, J.S., Abdu, W.A., Hillbrand, A.S., Boden, S.D. & Deyo, R.A. (2006). Surgical vs non-operative treatment for lumbar disk herniation: The Spine Patient Outcomes Research Trial (SPORT): A randomized trial. *Journal of the American Medical Association, 296*, 2441–2450.

Werner, E.E. & Smith, S. (1982). *Vulnerable but Invincible: A Longitudinal Study of Resilient Children and Youth*. New York: McGraw-Hill.

Wexler, B.E. & Cicchetti, D.V. (1992). The outpatient treatment of depression: Implications of outcome research for clinical practice. *The Journal of Nervous and Mental Disease, 180*, 277–286.

Whelton, W.J. (2004). Emotional processes in psychotherapy: Evidence across therapeutic modalities. *Clinical Psychology and Psychotherapy, 11*, 58–71.

Whitaker, R. (2010). *Mad in America* (2nd ed.). New York: Basic Books.

Wiborg, I.M. & Dahl, A.A. (1996). Does brief dynamic psychotherapy reduce relapse rate of panic disorder? *Archives of General Psychiatry, 53*, 689–694.

Wierzbicki, M. & Pekarik, G. (1993). A meta-analysis of psychotherapy drop out. *Professional Psychology: Research and Practice, 24*, 190–195.

Wilson, T.D. (2002). *Strangers to Ourselves: Discovering the Adaptive Unconscious.* Cambridge, MA: The Belknap Press of Harvard University Press.

Winkielman, P., Berridge, K.C. & Wilbarger, J.L. (2005). Unconscious affective reactions to masked happy versus angry faces influences consumption behavior and judgment of values. *Personality and Social Psychology, 31*, 122–135.

Winnicott, D.W. (1963). The development of the capacity for concern. *Bulletin of the Menninger Clinic, 27* (July), 167–176.

Winston, A., Laikin, M., Pollack, J., Samstag, L.W., McCullough, L. & Muran, J.C. (1994). Short-term psychotherapy of personality disorders. *American Journal of Psychiatry, 151*, 190–194.

Wyatt, J. (1995). Early intervention in schizophrenia: Can the course of the illness be altered? *Biological Psychiatry, 38*, 1–3.

Yerkes, R.M. & Dodson, J.D. (1908). The relation of strength of stimulus to rapidity of habit formation. *Journal of Comparative Neurology and Psychology, 18*, 459–482.

Zajonc, R.B. (2000). Feeling and thinking: Closing the debate over the independence of affect. In J.P. Forgas (Ed.) *Feeling and Thinking: The Role of Affect Tin Social Cognition* (pp. 131–158). Cambridge, UK: Cambridge University Press.

Zicha-Mano, S., Dinger, U., McCarthy, K.S. & Barber, J.P. (2014). Does alliance predict symptoms throughout treatment or is it the other way around? *Journal of Consulting and Clinical Psychology, 82*, 931–935.

Zolli, A. & Healy, A.M. (2013). *Resilience: Why Things Bounce Back.* New York: Simon & Schuster.

Index

Note: Italicized page numbers indicate a figure on the corresponding page.